APOSTLES
of the
SELF-MADE MAN

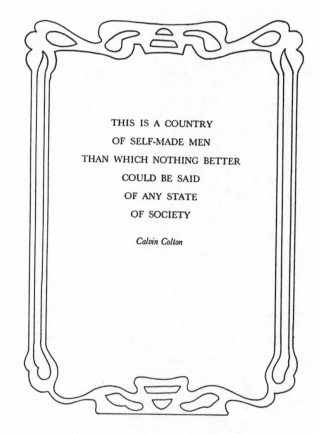

THIS IS A COUNTRY
OF SELF-MADE MEN
THAN WHICH NOTHING BETTER
COULD BE SAID
OF ANY STATE
OF SOCIETY

Calvin Colton

APOSTLES
of the
SELF-MADE MAN

By

JOHN G. CAWELTI

———

THE UNIVERSITY OF CHICAGO PRESS
Chicago and London

The University of Chicago Press, Chicago 60637
The University of Chicago Press, Ltd., London

ISBN 0-226-09870-2
LCN 65-25123

TO JON, BRENT, AND ANDREA,

WHO,

IN SPITE OF THE EFFORTS

OF THEIR FATHER,

DOUBTLESS WILL TURN OUT TO BE SELF-MADE

AFTER ALL

FOREWORD

When I embarked upon the research which led to this book, it was my hope to produce a thorough and systematic history of changing conceptions of success. Three things made me modify my goal. First, I soon discovered that to produce a work of the scope originally intended would have required more than a lifetime of research. In America almost everyone —politicians, businessmen, clergymen, writers, and the ordinary citizen— has had something to say about the self-made man. Second, other historians had made thorough examinations of the theme of success in certain areas, and it seemed more profitable to use their work as a basis for further, more intensive, explorations of the subject than to go over the same ground again. Finally, I decided that I could make a more useful contribution to the study of American attitudes toward success by a more complex treatment of selected sources than by an attempt to survey extensively the vast range of materials in which the theme of self-improvement was a significant element. Thus, I have concentrated my attention on three main sources: individual figures like Franklin, Jefferson, Emerson, and Horatio Alger who had a major role in the formulation of the ideal of success or who were particularly associated with that ideal in the public eye; the success manuals and guides of different periods; and novels for adults and stories for children in which the self-made man was a central figure. In each case, I have attempted to define the characteristic complex of ideas about the self-made man which each individual or group expressed and to indicate the major differences between them. Finally, without insisting that the reader accompany me through a simplified and schematic account of American social history, I have suggested what seem to be the connections between changing social patterns and differing ideals of success.

This cannot pretend to be a definitive study of the vast topic of American ideas about success. Some readers may not agree with my selections and emphases, but I hope that I have assembled enough material to show that attitudes toward success have not been as unchanging and monolithic as has generally been assumed; on the contrary, the ideal of self-improvement has had a rich and varied history.

Literature as a Source of Social History

Since the use of works of fiction as a historical source has many difficulties, I would like to say a few words in explanation and justification of the methods I have employed. The advantages of fictional materials in the study of social attitudes are twofold: because the novelist must create a world in which to set his characters and actions, the novel enables us to see how the writer places character types like the self-made man and themes like success in a context of political and philosophical belief. In addition, the novel is a work of fantasy and imagination as well as an imitation of reality; its patterns of action often reveal covert attitudes or judgments which significantly qualify the explicit positions taken by the writer. For example, the self-made hero in the sentimental novel of the nineteenth century invariably succeeds by marrying the boss's daughter, an action at variance with the explicit belief that industry, frugality, and piety are the only keys to success. Ambiguities of this sort are far less apparent in success manuals or political tracts where the element of imagination plays a minor role.

Novels, on the other hand, are problematic as a source of popular attitudes because there is no way of knowing just how representative they are and because they require a special kind of analysis. The first problem comes up in any use of literary sources or in any study of attitudes. The writer is an individual. How can we infer with any certainty that his views reflect those of a larger social group?

Some students of popular attitudes have dealt with this problem by concentrating their attention on best-sellers. They assume that, because a book is widely read, it must reflect the accepted beliefs of its readers. This is probably a safer assumption in the case of non-fiction than of fiction. Novels may be best-sellers because readers find the story or the characters interesting irrespective of the attitudes expressed by the author. *Uncle Tom's Cabin* is a case in point. Although Mrs. Stowe wrote the book as an attack on slavery, one cannot be certain that the majority of those who read the book shared her views. *Uncle Tom's Cabin* continued to be popular as novel and play long after slavery had been abolished, which suggests that many readers, perhaps the majority, were less interested in Mrs. Stowe's social attitudes than in such exciting and dramatic episodes as Eliza's flight across the ice, the underground railroad in operation, and the death of Little Eva. While best-sellers presumably do not express attitudes completely abhorrent to the majority of their readers, it is not safe to conclude that a novel is popular because it accurately reflects the attitudes of its readers.

In making this study, I have tried to overcome this difficulty by taking as wide a sample as possible. Rather than using best-sellers alone, I tried to identify as many novels of the self-made man as I could through such catalogues as Lyle Wright's bibliography of American fiction. Then I read and studied these novels until I had defined to my own satisfaction the major kinds and their dominant themes. My analyses of the novels of success are based on this method. To avoid overloading the text with notes, I have not cited all the evidence for each generalization; readers interested in my sources are invited to consult the bibliographical notes at the end of this volume.

The second difficulty in the use of fictional sources arises from the fact that novels are primarily stories rather than explicit expositions of a point of view. The presence of a narrative as the organizing principle means that a novel cannot be analyzed in the same terms as a work of non-fiction. Instead, the historian must adopt the literary critic's approach and infer attitudes from what the characters say and do, and from the kind of world which the novelist has created for them to move in. I have attempted to develop an analytical technique for this purpose. The reader will discover that my generalizations about attitudes are usually supported and developed by careful analyses of characteristic plots from the novels under consideration.

This study was begun as a doctoral dissertation under Alexander C. Kern of the University of Iowa and was completed under the direction of John C. Gerber. To both I would like to offer my thanks for their unfailing help and good counsel. Both as teacher and adviser, and later as critic, Samuel P. Hays, now of the University of Pittsburgh, helped give this book what intelligibility of structure and significance of theme it may have. He cannot be held responsible for my failings in American history, but certainly he is responsible for my interest in the subject. Charles T. Miller of the University of Iowa was an influential guide through nineteenth-century American literature. Theodore Waldman was also an important influence in the early stages of this book, and many of its ideas are the result of conversations with him.

Several of my colleagues at the University of Chicago have advised and encouraged me. Robert Streeter and Robert Albrecht have read much of the manuscript, and their comments have been of help to me in seeing what I was attempting to do. Perrin Lowrey, Marvin Meyers, and Alan Simpson also read sections of the manuscript, to my benefit.

The libraries of the University of Chicago and of the University of Iowa provided most of the materials for this study, and I would like to thank their staffs for unfailingly courteous service. In particular, my friend Robert Rosenthal, curator of Special Collections, the University of Chicago Library, was a great help to me.

A Howard Willett fellowship from the College of the University of Chicago enabled me to complete work on this study.

Finally, to my wife Betty, who put up with the self-made man these many years, I can only say what goes beyond words.

CONTENTS

INTRODUCTION: The Meaning of the
Self-made Man   1

I NATURAL ARISTOCRACY AND
THE NEW REPUBLIC: The Idea of
Mobility in the Thought of Franklin
and Jefferson   9

II THE AGE OF THE SELF-MADE MAN   39

III SELF-IMPROVEMENT AND SELF-
CULTURE: Ralph Waldo Emerson   77

IV FROM RAGS TO RESPECTABILITY:
Horatio Alger   101

V THE SELF-MADE MAN AND
INDUSTRIAL AMERICA: The Por-
trayal of Mobility in the Nineteenth-
Century Novel   125

Contents

VI   PHILOSOPHERS OF SUCCESS   167

VII DREAM OR RAT RACE: Success in the
     Twentieth Century   201

VIII INDIVIDUAL SUCCESS AND
     THE COMMUNITY: John Dewey's
     Philosophy of Success   239

     NOTES   249

     BIBLIOGRAPHICAL NOTES   259

     INDEX   273

INTRODUCTION: The Meaning of the Self-made Man

Americans have always been the world's most enthusiastic proponents of the self-made man. Many still believe that he is not only an American invention but a unique national product. This is, of course, a myth. The worthy type who rises from poverty and obscurity to fame and fortune is as old as history and as widespread as human society. He has appeared most notably in times of rapid change and transition. Fifth- and sixth-century Greece, the later Roman Empire, and the Renaissance saw self-made men in profusion, and it would be difficult to imagine a static society in which an ambitious man could not rise from the ranks.

In modern times, industrial economies with their built-in dynamic of change have encouraged a high degree of "vertical mobility"—the sociologist's tag for the process by which men rise and fall in wealth and status. Those who have undertaken the difficult task of measuring and comparing mobility in different countries have concluded that in recent years America and most of the western European countries have had a similarly high percentage of changing wealth and position from generation to generation. Current estimates place European and American mobility rates at around 30 per cent. Most students of the subject believe that a high rate of social mobility will accompany the world-wide spread of industrial economies.

But statistics only tell part of the story. Although mobility rates in different countries seem to be similar, cultural attitudes toward the self-made man vary greatly. If you tell an American that he has no more chance to get ahead than a Frenchman, he will probably not believe you, for Americans are fiercely proud of the opportunities which they believe their uniquely open society offers the average man. Every American boy has the chance to become President of the United States, or at least a wealthy businessman. This theme is, or at least used to be, a commonplace in newspaper, sermon, political speech, and fiction. When he becomes successful, the American self-made man likes to boast of his achievement, to exaggerate the obscurity of his origin, and to point out the "Horatio Alger" quality of his career. In Europe, where class traditions are stronger, the successful man often prefers to forget his origins if they are in a lower class. Even the words which different countries have created to describe the "mobile man" indicate significant differences in attitude. Americans coined the term "self-made man." The French expressions *parvenu* and *nouveau riche* point to the newness of the individual's rise and not to the fact that he has succeeded by his own exertions; in addition they carry a tone of condescension which is absent from the American term.

Many social and geographical circumstances shaped

American enthusiasm for the self-made man. The manifest opportunities of a large and relatively empty continent and the openness of a rapidly growing and changing society impressed the idea of self-improvement on the public imagination. Immigration, too, helped make America a country of devotees of success by sending to her shores men who believed in their right and their need to better their condition. The ideal of rising in society was never subjected to the continual and devastating criticism of exponents of a traditional ideal of culture as it was in England, where, in spite of influential propagandists like Samuel Smiles, the self-made man was one of the prime targets of such big guns as Carlyle, Ruskin, and Arnold. The contrast between nineteenth-century English and American attitudes toward self-improvement appeared often in the comments of English travelers in America. Mrs. Trollope, who visited America in the 1830's, was stupefied by the pride that leading Americans took in the fact that they were self-taught and self-made, which, as she acidly remarked, meant to her only that they were badly taught and badly made.

In spite of their persistent devotion to the idea of success, Americans have differed greatly in the way they defined it. That is the subject of this book. My major concern has not been with the nature and extent of mobility, for that inquiry is a quantitative one which can best be tackled with the statistical tools of the sociologist. Nor have I been primarily concerned with the continuity and persistence of the myth of success. Years ago, A. Whitney Griswold pointed out the basic continuity between the Puritan ethic of the seventeenth century and the philosophy of success of the early twentieth century. More recently, Irvin G. Wyllie, in *The Self-Made Man in America,* made a concise analysis of the basic pattern of ideas reflected in the success manuals of the nineteenth century. Many other scholars have studied the idea of success in one or another of its manifestations, but most of these studies are concerned with the persistence rather than the variety of ideas of success.

This book seeks to describe basic changes in the ideal of the self-made man. That men as different as Franklin, Emerson, and Horatio Alger were, in their way, apostles of the self-made man suggested to me that important differences in emphasis and interpretation must have been given to the ideal of success by its various exponents. This, then, is an examination of different interpretations of the ideal of the self-made man, and a study of the way in which these interpretations have changed over the course of the past one hundred and fifty years of American history.

The Meaning of the Self-made Man

My investigation has indicated that the self-made man meant many things to many people. It seems reasonable to conclude that he persisted as a popular hero and as a central symbol of American society because Americans were able to synthesize, under his aegis, many conflicting strands of belief and aspiration. Out of the variety of competing versions of the ideal of success, three main strands of thought and feeling emerge. The first was the conservative tradition of the middle-class Protestant ethic which stressed the values of piety, frugality, and diligence in one's worldly calling. This tradition of thought assumed a static, hierarchical social order within which success was the attainment of a respectable competence in this world and eternal salvation in the world to come. Exponents of this tradition had profound reservations concerning the idea of free mobility in a competitive, open society and were suspicious of most of the major social developments of the nineteenth century. This was also the oldest tradition. Brought to America in the seventeenth and eighteenth centuries, it became the basis of most of the self-help literature of the late eighteenth and early nineteenth centuries. Reasserted by Horatio Alger and others in the children's books of the second half of the nineteenth century, it gradually declined before the impact of industrialism and an increasingly secular, scientific frame of mind. In the twentieth century, certain success writers, like Norman Vincent Peale, have attempted to re-establish a religious base for the ideal of success, but in other respects they have departed greatly from the conservative-Protestant tradition.

The second tradition of thought about the self-made man placed its major emphasis on the individual's getting ahead. Its definition of success was largely economic. Its proponents suggested a great variety of ways to wealth, for this tradition was often mixed with elements of the Protestant ethic. However, where the religious tradition stressed industry, frugality, honesty, and piety—the self-disciplinary and religious virtues— the second strand indorsed such secular qualities as initiative, aggressiveness, competitiveness, and forcefulness. Moreover, where the Protestant tradition assumed a stable social order, proponents of the second version of success were sympathetic to social change and enthusiastic about the progress of industrialism. First appearing in the early nineteenth century, the second tradition of success became dominant in the literature of self-help toward the end of the nineteenth century. Although shaken by the impact of depression, it has persisted to the present day.

The third strand was more complex and rarely appeared in popular self-help literature. Its definition of success was tied to individual fulfilment and social progress rather than to wealth or status. This tradition

5

also showed a greater concern for the social implications of individual mobility than the other two strands of thought. It received its first major formulation in Franklin and Jefferson's concept of a natural elite of talent and virtue and was further developed in Emerson's philosophy of self-culture and self-reliance. Under the impact of twentieth-century social change and the influence of contemporary sociological and psychological thought this tradition has become an increasingly important element of American thought.

It is with the initial formulation of the third strand of the American ideal of the self-made man that my inquiry will begin.

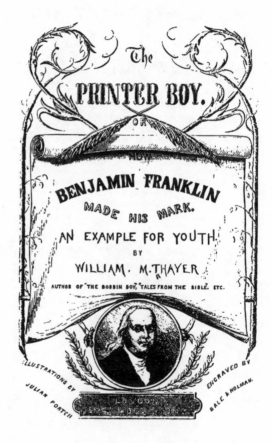

The

PRINTER BOY.

OF

HOW

BENJAMIN FRANKLIN

MADE HIS MARK.

AN EXAMPLE FOR YOUTH.

BY

WILLIAM. M. THAYER

AUTHOR OF "THE BOBBIN BOY," "TALES FROM THE BIBLE," ETC.

ILLUSTRATIONS BY
JULIAN PORTCH

ENGRAVED BY
BALE & HOLMAN.

LONDON
JAMES HOGG & SON.

CHAPTER I

NATURAL ARISTOCRACY AND THE NEW REPUBLIC: The Idea of Mobility in the Thought of Franklin and Jefferson

> It would have been inconsistent in creation to have formed man for the social state, and not to have provided virtue and wisdom enough to manage the concerns of the society. May we not even say, that that form of government is the best, which provides the most effectually for a pure selection of these natural aristoi into the offices of government?
>
> Thomas Jefferson, Letter to John Adams, October 28, 1813

Benjamin Franklin was not the first self-made man, but certainly he was the archetypal self-made man for Americans. In the European tradition, the folk hero who came from obscurity to win the beautiful princess preceded Franklin. So did historical figures like the Greek leader Themistocles and a number of medieval barons and Renaissance *condottieri*. But in America Franklin became the model for the tradition of the self-made man. More than any other individual, he exemplified in his own person and articulated in his writings a new hero, different in character from traditional military, religious, and aristocratic conceptions of human excellence and virtue.

The Self-made Hero

Compared to that other great figure of his time, George Washington, the hero created by Franklin had

9

several new elements. Washington was a great leader in the traditional mold. His virtues were those of a Roman senator set down in the eighteenth century, a point often made by his admirers. As a leader, and the founder of a nation, Washington was revered for his unique moral excellence and his power of command over men, and not primarily for intellectual, artistic, or economic accomplishments. His unique excellence was a birthright rather than a quality developed by years of arduous self-improvement. The later legends which grew up about his childhood, although they softened and sentimentalized the austere figure of the father of his country, stressed this point. Parson Weems's famous cherry tree story, for example, demonstrated how even as a young child Washington had been uniquely honest and courageous. Washington was an Olympian, an image of excellence to be revered and admired, but beyond the ordinary man's powers of comprehension or imitation.

In actuality, Franklin was as remarkable as Washington. His scientific genius, his literary skill, his ability as publicist and practical politician were qualities at least as unique and individual as those of Washington. Yet the public figure which Franklin created and the picture of himself which he presented in his *Memoirs* were of a totally different order. We can see how contemporaries responded to this image by comparing typical early nineteenth-century portraits of Washington and Franklin. Where Washington was stern and aloof, dressed in aristocratic wig and elegant clothes, and rather idealized in features, the typical portrait of Benjamin Franklin presented a wise and benevolent older man dressed in simple middle-class garb. His face was treated realistically. With heavy wrinkles, double chin, and spectacles, there was nothing elegant or distinguished about him. Instead of the Olympian figure we

10

find a rather ordinary looking old man whose squat and dumpy figure suggests his relationship to common life and humanity.

This pictorial image reflected the public figure which Franklin assiduously cultivated in his later years. When, in 1776, he went to France as the agent of the revolutionary government, Franklin created a sensation by appearing in court and salon in plain middle-class dress instead of the usual aristocratic costume. With the current intellectual fashion for noble savages, the French were prepared to be enthusiastic about a frontier philosopher, and Franklin shrewdly exploited this fashion to gain sympathy for the American cause. But, as his presentation of his career in his *Memoirs* shows, this gesture had a deeper meaning as well. Aristocratic dress was the outer symbol of a whole attitude toward man and society. It proclaimed that the individual belonged to a fixed social station or rank, with its appropriate qualities, duties, sphere of action, and deportment. Within this system a few individuals might change their station from time to time, but in doing so they took on a new way of life. For example, the successful English merchant of the eighteenth century often moved into the lesser aristocracy by retiring from business, purchasing a country estate, and marrying into the gentry. Franklin himself almost followed this pattern in his early career. Carl Van Doren reports that among Franklin's first purchases when he arrived in London in the late 1750's were wigs, swords, a sword knot, "two pairs of silver shoe and knee buckles, two razors and a case, and copies of the *Gentleman's Magazine*," [1] all articles necessary to the complete aristocrat. But his experience with the British aristocracy as colonial agent, his changing political views, and, finally, his involvement in the American revolution led Franklin to

11

reject the aristocratic ideal. The public figure of his later years and of his *Memoirs* represented the emergence of a new ideal of human excellence and virtue and a correspondingly new conception of the social order.

The essence of this conception was the belief that the individual's place in society should be defined by his ability to perform useful actions and not by his rank in a traditional hierarchy. By wearing the dress of an ordinary man, Franklin implied that he was to be judged solely on the basis of his achievements, his ability, and his individual character. This was a significant gesture. Even in the eighteenth century, the idea of established social ranks was intrenched in men's minds. Although the philosophers who wrote of natural rights asserted man's right to revolt against a government which ignored the general welfare, they did not question the desirability of a stable, hereditary social order. Franklin's new-style public figure implied just that, and reflected a profound shift in human attitudes. It meant that men were beginning to think of themselves not as members of a traditionally defined group with an established social role but as individuals with the capacity to choose between social roles, or to create new ones; it meant the emergence of the dream that individuals could aspire to any social position that their energies and abilities could gain for them; it meant a shift from the traditional conception of an ordered social hierarchy, with each rank having its particular duties and privileges, to the modern idea of social class as an aggregate of individuals loosely differentiated by function, wealth, influence, and prestige; finally, it meant that the individual was no longer given an identity by birth, but that he had to create one for himself. Through Franklin's example, the eighteenth-century *parvenu,* the *nouveau riche,* was on his way to becoming, in the guise of the self-made man, an archetype of American society.

Franklin and the Idea of Self-Improvement

The idea of self-improvement which Franklin expressed in his *Memoirs* was a broad, humane, and responsible idea of human development. Franklin synthesized creatively the Puritanism of his early environment with his own experience and his reading in classical and eighteenth-century philosophy. As a young man he wrote a number of short speculations and satires in a manner typical of the eighteenth century. His sketch of "Cato," in the *Busy-Body No. 3* (1728), is particularly interesting as a corrective to the common interpretation of Franklin as a narrow advocate of economic success. Cato was a man "whom fortune has placed in the most obscure part of the country" and whose "circumstances are such as only put him above necessity." [2] Yet, as presented by Franklin, Cato was a man of pre-eminent merit. In essence, the lesson of Cato's character was that no matter how humble his circumstances, a man could be supremely virtuous. Indeed, the sketch was redolent of the eighteenth-century concept of natural goodness, the belief that a person who lived "far from the madding crowd's ignoble strife" was more likely to be just, temperate, and wise than one who stood in danger of being corrupted by the artificialities of society. Franklin was too much of an activist to hold such a view for long. And yet the ideal of excellence which he developed in his sketch of Cato was the image of a benevolent man free from the petty interests of society, and it remained an important element of Franklin's thought. Even when he became more directly involved in problems of social policy, he still believed that the inadequacy of governments could be attributed largely to the vices of individuals.

As he grew older, Franklin became an inveterate

13

promoter of devices for bringing men of virtue into positions of social authority. He also wrote popular ethical tracts which he hoped would stimulate the mass of men to control their passions and to develop prudence in the conduct of their lives. Early in his career, Franklin concluded from his reading of history

that few in Public Affairs act from a meer View of the Good of their Country, whatever they may pretend; and tho' their Actings bring real Good to their Country, yet men primarily consider'd that their own and their Country's Interest was united, and did not act from a Principle of Benevolence.[3]

There is certainly nothing remarkable in this conclusion, but in his proposal for remedying the situation we see the authentic Franklin. Franklin determined to form a voluntary association of men of virtue:

There seems to me at present to be great Occasion for raising an united Party for Virtue, by forming the Virtuous and good Men of all Nations into a regular Body, to be govern'd by suitable good and wise Rules, which good and wise Men may probably be more unanimous in their Obedience to, than common People are to common Laws.[4]

Naïve as it may seem, this notion bore fruit in the important voluntary associations—subscription libraries, fire companies, philosophical associations—which Franklin later founded. This idea also reflected a weakness in Franklin's social thinking: his failure to recognize the importance of established social institutions. It is surprising that a man of Franklin's practical political experience would have neglected the importance of institutions, but without this oversight he might never have arrived at his conception of the self-made man. For Franklin's conception of self-improvement was closely related to his belief in the necessity of a self-selecting and self-disciplining elite, men of virtue voluntarily assuming the leadership of society. Although he never succeeded in establishing his "United Party for Virtue," Franklin was still, in 1788, "of Opinion that it was a practicable scheme." [5]

Human happiness and social welfare were, in Franklin's view, dependent on two things: teaching prudence and self-restraint to the mass of men and encouraging the development of a new self-made leadership composed of men of practical ability and disinterested benevolence. That these conditions could be fulfilled in the Old World, Franklin doubted. There a corrupt and self-interested aristocracy and a degraded working class were incapable of rising above passion, vice, and self-interest. But in America the circumstances of society were different. As early as 1751, Franklin observed the rapid growth of the colonies. He attributed it to high wages resulting from the presence of cheap land for farmers and plentiful customers for artisans. In such a situation, he felt that any man willing to work could, with prudence and industry, become an independent and responsible citizen. Furthermore, since an industrious man was using his mind and body productively and disciplining his natural tendency to inertia and surrender to the passions, Franklin believed that the habit of industry and prudence, together with the geographic advantages of America and the "safety-valve" of cheap land, would create a happy and virtuous people. How better stimulate men to the practice of this habit than by showing that wealth and comfort could be achieved by this means? This was the role of Poor Richard. In the *Memoirs* Franklin clearly stated the ethical purpose of his almanac:

Observing that it was generally read, scarce any Neighbourhood in the Province being without it, I consider'd it as a proper Vehicle for conveying Instruction among the common People, who bought scarce any other Books. I therefore filled all the little Spaces that occurr'd between the Remarkable Days in the Calen-

15

dar, with Proverbial Sentences, chiefly such as inculcated Industry and Frugality, as the Means of procuring Wealth and thereby securing Virtue, it being more difficult for a Man in Want to act always honestly, as (to use here one of those Proverbs) *it is hard for an empty sack to stand upright.*[6]

In 1757, while he was on his way to England to assume his duties as colonial agent, Franklin prepared a preface to the 1758 edition of *Poor Richard* in which he summed up his many maxims on industry and frugality through the device of a speech given by a sage old countryman, Father Abraham. This preface, soon reprinted as "The Way to Wealth," was undoubtedly the single most popular and influential work written by Franklin. The popularity and simplicity of "The Way to Wealth" has had an unfortunate effect on the interpretation of Franklin's *Memoirs,* which too often has been read as an extended commentary on the simple philosophy of work, save, and grow wealthy which the former expressed. On the contrary, although written in a lucid and simple style and full of vivid and dramatic incident, the *Memoirs* presented a broad and humane ideal of self-improvement. Where "The Way to Wealth" stressed industry, thrift, and attention to business, the *Memoirs* continually emphasized the development of the mind, the achievement of self-discipline and wisdom, and the assumption of responsibility toward one's fellow man. The theme of public responsibility was important from the beginning; witness Franklin's account of his ancestry. Uncle Thomas Franklin, whose character bore such a remarkable resemblance to Benajmin's own, was "chief Mover of all publick-spirited Undertakings for the County or Town of Northampton, & his own Village." [7] On his mother's side, grandfather Peter Folger took a public part in agitation for freedom of conscience in seventeenth-century New England. Franklin's own father had the same public spirit. Franklin's father resembled "Cato" in the early sketch mentioned above:

His great Excellence lay in a sound Understanding, and solid Judgment in prudential Matters, both in private & publick Affairs. In the latter indeed he was never employed, the numerous Family he had to educate & the straitness of his Circumstances, keeping him close to his Trade, but I remember well his being frequently visited by leading People, who consulted him for his Opinion in Affairs of the Town or of the Church he belong'd to & show'd a good deal of Respect for his Judgment and Advice. He was also much consulted by private Persons about their Affairs when any Difficulty occur'd, & frequently chosen an Arbitrator between contending Parties.[8]

Coming from a line of men who concerned themselves with the affairs of their neighbors, it is not surprising that the subject of the *Memoirs* displayed a precocious talent for useful enterprises. Referring to the time when he and his youthful companions built a wharf in a salt marsh with stone "borrowed" from a nearby construction, Franklin remarked: "I was generally a Leader among the Boys, and sometimes led them into Scrapes, of wch I will mention one Instance, as it shows an early projecting public Spirit, tho' not then justly conducted." [9]

As the *Memoirs* proceed, we see how the young Franklin continually sought ways of improving whatever group he joined by making the conditions of its existence happier and more virtuous. As a youngster in Boston, he soon became known as a "young Genius that had a Turn for Libelling & Satyr." [10] The young journeyman in Philadelphia and London undertook the reformation of his fellow workers; as a young businessman in Philadelphia he founded the Junto to propose and sponsor public improvements. Later, he entered politics, and became a leader in the colony.

This series of incidents illustrates the young Franklin's progressively growing understanding of the public good and of the methods most appropriate to furthering it. Early disposed to the performance of good actions by the example of his father and by the moral discourses of the family dining table, Franklin first developed a rather pugnacious and disputatious conception of virtue. He became satirical, argumentative, and an adherent of fads and radical movements like Deism and vegetarianism. Each of these fashions became valuable only when he learned moderation. The great lesson of this period was that persuasion and co-operative action were far more effective means of doing good than personal criticism and dogmatism.

I wish wellmeaning sensible Men would not lessen their Power of doing Good by a Positive assuming Manner that seldom fails to disgust, tends to create Opposition, and to defeat every one of those Purposes for which Speech was given us.[11]

An early incident brought out this crucial point in the education of a man of virtue. Franklin's self-assertiveness and dogmatism led him into conflict with his brother and caused him to break with him. This, Franklin remarks, was one the first *errata* of his life. Clearly, Franklin means a moral rather than a strategic error. His personal success was actually hastened by breaking with his brother and emigrating to rapidly growing Philadelphia. The break lost Franklin both the friendship of his brother and his place in a social group. His opportunity to associate with others in the performance of useful and benevolent activities was cut off until he had re-established himself among those who shared his views.

The next stage of Franklin's development took place in Philadelphia, where he had two particularly important experiences, one with his friend Collins and another with Governor Keith. His friendship with Collins demonstrated to the young Franklin that he could not help others by encouraging them to indulge their passions. Franklin learned from Governor Keith to take the promises of important men with a grain of salt—and the value of consulting the experience and knowledge of his fellow man.

Had it been known that I depended on the Governor, probably some Friend that knew him better would have advis'd me not to rely on him, as I afterwards heard it as his known Character to be liberal of Promises which he never meant to keep.[12]

The final insight which Franklin gained from his difficulties with the governor was in some respects like those he learned from his mistakes with Collins. It is dangerously foolish for a man, especially a public man, to try to please everyone.

In the *Memoirs,* Franklin discussed at length the assumption of social responsibility, beginning with his attempts to reform the London printing shop in which he worked, continuing through his early public projects in Philadelphia, the Junto, the library, the fire company, and his complete immersion in public affairs. The great majority of his experiences had a direct bearing on the growth of his insight and skill in the initiation and accomplishment of public-spirited undertakings. Gradually, through failures and partial successes, he learned what kind of activities and projects were truly useful and the best means of enlisting others in their accomplishment.

On the other hand, he paid surprisingly little attention to his business and money-making activities—only the most important facts of his rise in business: his first partnership, the establishment of his own business, his store, the most important of his publications, and government printing jobs. The other passages about business activities dealt largely with matters of personal discipline and habits of industry.

The second major theme of the *Memoirs* was Franklin's self-education, his intellectual and moral growth. After his early reading in his father's books and the casuistry to which he was exposed at the family dinner table, Franklin became skeptical of traditional beliefs, and went through a phase of using his intellectual gifts for their own sake and not for moral purposes. He was easily dissuaded from becoming a poor poet, but his delight in argument for argument's sake was much harder to shake. During a fling with Deism, in London, he wrote a philosophical dissertation to exhibit his skill at argument, another *erratum*. But soon his contact with brilliant, if erratic, men like James Ralph made him realize that he had to use his intellectual powers for rational and beneficial purposes if he wished to become a useful citizen.

"The Art of Virtue" section was in many ways the climax of the *Memoirs,* for it brought together lessons learned through early experience and presented a method of self-improvement which the aspirant to virtue could follow, the famous system of moral book-keeping. Franklin developed this system because, in spite of his desire to perfect himself, he found that without a definite plan for self-improvement his efforts were of no avail. He concluded that a more consistent and demanding scheme was in order so that habits not conducive to virtue might be broken and good habits established. Without this, wrote Franklin, we cannot "have any Dependance on a steady uniform Rectitude of Conduct." [13]

To achieve this end, Franklin prepared a little book listing thirteen virtues: Temperance, Silence, Order, Resolution, Frugality, Industry, Sincerity, Justice, Moderation, Cleanliness, Tranquillity, Chastity, and Humility. Attached to each of these virtues was a precept which "express'd the extent I gave to its meaning." As Franklin himself reminds us, any list of virtues is susceptible to a variety of interpretations which can narrow their application to trivialities. It is true that in striving for simplicity and clarity, he invited this sort of interpretation, but it must be recalled that he prepared his precepts in the light of his own particular character-istics and did not intend these particular precepts to have universal applicability. If he had prepared the full-scale "Art of Virtue" which he contemplated, the vir-tues would have been more fully treated, and he might well have prepared different precepts for men of differ-ing characteristics.

Even with these reservations, the "Art of Virtue" is no narrow course for the aspirant to financial success, although it was often read in this fashion in the nine-teenth century. It is, indeed, utilitarian, but not because Franklin considered virtue as a means to some further end. On the contrary, the virtues described in the "Art of Virtue" are clearly presented as techniques for the development of self-discipline, without which the true moral and intellectual virtues—doing good to others and leading a rational, orderly, and harmonious life—are impossible.

This point becomes clear when we examine a few of the central virtues and their precepts. The precept which accompanies the virtue of temperance, "eat not to dullness; drink not to elevation," might seem at first glance an invitation to what Weber calls "worldly as-ceticism." It does not imply, of course, either total ab-stinence or the avoidance of good food and drink. It is "dullness" and "elevation" which are to be avoided, not eating and drinking, and the reason is obvious: either state is inconsistent with the life of reason, for the ra-tional faculty does not operate well if the body is over-loaded with food or intoxicated with drink.

As in "The Way to Wealth," frugality was a prime virtue in the "Art of Virtue." In "The Way to Wealth" the emphasis was on saving, because "a fat kitchen makes a lean will"; "if you would be wealthy think of saving as well as of getting"; and "many a little makes a mickle." In the "Art of Virtue" the principle is quite different. Here we are advised: "make no expense but to do good to others; i.e., waste nothing." The contrast is between an employment of money which is economically useful and one which is morally useful. In one instance we are enjoined to be generally frugal in order to be financially secure, in the other to avoid a use of money which produces no benefit to anyone.

We have already examined what industry meant to Franklin. Similar observations can be made in the case of each of the virtues listed. This was not the "barbed-wire morality" D. H. Lawrence thought it to be. It was a strenuous creed, but not a narrow and ascetic one. The results which Franklin ascribed to his practice of the "Art of Virtue" should not be ignored:

To *Temperance* he ascribes his long-continu'd Health, & what is still left to him of a good Constitution. To *Industry* and *Frugality,* the early Easiness of his Circumstances, & Acquisition of his Fortune, with all that Knowledge which enabled him to be an useful Citizen, and obtain'd for him some Degree of Reputation among the Learned. To *Sincerity* & *Justice* the Confidence of his Country, and the honourable Employs it conferr'd upon him. And to the joint Influence of the whole Mass of the Virtues, even in the imperfect State he was able to acquire them, all that Evenness of Temper, & that Cheerfulness in Conversation which makes his Company still sought for, & agreeable even to his younger Acquaintance.[14]

Health of mind and body, material prosperity, wisdom, honor, usefulness, and with it all, good temper and cheerfulness—these are the ends which Franklin's *Memoirs* sets forth, together with the means for attaining them. The "Art of Virtue" completed the lessons learned from earlier experiences and presented a ra-

tional plan for the attainment of the end toward which
the young Franklin was disposed : the assumption of his
duties as a useful citizen and the attainment of moral
and intellectual virtue.

Franklin's *Memoirs* presented a broad ideal of indi-
vidual self-improvement based on the industrious pur-
suit of a profession, the cultivation of the moral and in-
tellectual virtues, and the assumption of a responsible
role in the general progress of society. Franklin be-
lieved that society could be radically improved by bring-
ing this new type of individual into power, and by rais-
ing the level of reason and virtue among the mass of
men with a meaningful promise of economic security
and material comfort. This implied a mobile, expanding
society dedicated to economic progress and technologi-
cal change, and, with his pragmatic, experimental bent,
Franklin was hospitable to change. His own inventions
and scientific investigations were important technologi-
cal innovations. Yet Franklin's very openness to the
new made him indifferent to the value of tradition and
its function in the preservation and transmission of
ideals. Although he formulated a broad ideal of *individ-
ual* self-improvement, he gave little attention to the em-
bodiment of this ideal in social institutions. Franklin's
failure to concern himself with the social process by
which the new self-made hero was to be selected and en-
couraged reflected a fundamental ambiguity in the ideal
of success which was never entirely resolved. Should the
new self-made elite be those who had fought their way to
the top of the social and economic ladder, or should so-
ciety try to select and foster those who, regardless of
birth, had the virtues and talents appropriate to intelli-
gent and responsible leadership? Franklin's solution
seemed to be that the new democratic elite should select
itself, but he attempted to inspire his countrymen with
an ideal of disinterested public responsibility. Later

philosophers of success followed Franklin in the assumption that the new elite would select itself, but they narrowed Franklin's ideal of intellectual, moral, and economic improvement to a conception of individual economic achievement. There were others, however, who believed that social institutions should play a central part in the development of a new kind of "natural aristocracy" suitable to the needs of republican government. The most important of these was Thomas Jefferson.

Natural Aristocracy

Thomas Jefferson had a profound sense of the influence of the social order on the conditions of individual life. He saw individual success in relation to the whole structure of the democratic community. Since he looked upon society as a political community, the question of individual mobility was, for him, a problem of criteria and processes for the selection of political leaders. Like Franklin, Jefferson believed that bringing men of talent and disinterested virtue into power was a primary concern of social policy. But, unlike Franklin, he was unwilling to look to the voluntary exertions of a "United Party of Virtue." Jefferson realized that society could not depend on the benevolence of individuals to maintain and develop standards of reason and responsibility. Americans had to create a social organization which would insure that the most able individuals would rise to positions of leadership. "May we not even say," he asserted in a letter to John Adams, "that that form of government is the best, which provides the most effectually for a pure selection of [men of pre-eminent talent and virtue] into the offices of government." [15] Jefferson shared Franklin's belief that aristocratic social orders with their emphasis on hereditary status had failed to accomplish this end. Against Adams' insistence that "mankind have not yet discovered any remedy against irresistible corruption in elections to offices of great power and profit, but making them hereditary," Jefferson produced his well-known distinction between natural and artificial aristocracy. Nature makes some men superior to others in talent and virtue, but it does so without regard to *artificial* distinctions of rank or class. This natural elite is "the most precious gift of nature, for the instruction, the trusts, and government of society." [16] The artificial aristocracy which results from the acceptance of false criteria like birth or wealth "is a mischievous ingredient in government, and provision should be made to prevent its ascendency." [17]

Jefferson's conception of natural aristocracy can be read as the belief that those few members of the lower classes who have the personal qualities and talents which would make them effective and useful members of the existing ruling class should be advanced despite their humble origins.

This was not Jefferson's idea, however. Jefferson's *aristoi,* like Franklin's "United Party of Virtue," were not to be selected in terms of their usefulness to the status quo. Quite the contrary, they were supposed to be free from the interests and irrationalities of existing social factions or classes, and therefore capable of helping society formulate and achieve new values. Jefferson's program for America implied, as a first step, the elimination of institutions which perpetuated arbitrary and artificial distinctions among men. But it also involved the establishment of a new institutional framework within which the process of mobility would be channeled and shaped.

The success of Jefferson and his followers in eliminating aristocratic vestiges like primogeniture, entail, and the established church, together with the adoption of the principle of democratic election has overshadowed, to a certain extent, this additional aspect of Jefferson's program, which was largely a failure. For all his faith in democratic elections, Jefferson was fully aware that, in an open society, established social institutions would have a strong influence on the process of mobility. The last, and crucial, step of his program was the creation of new institutions which would support the rise of the natural aristocracy by giving all men the experience and discipline of self-government, together with the education necessary to understand and further their common purpose.

Jefferson did not succeed in persuading his countrymen to establish the educational system he had envisioned or to adopt the principle of universal public education. But perhaps even more important was the failure of Jefferson's main hope, the growth of strong, relatively self-sufficient and autonomous local communities. He explained the importance of this element of the republican program in a letter to Samuel Kercheval:

Divide the counties into wards of such size as that every person can attend, when called on, and act in person. Ascribe to them the government of their wards in all things relating to themselves exclusively. . . . [This] will relieve the county administration of nearly all its business, will have it better done, and by making every citizen an acting member of the government, and in the offices nearest and most interesting to him, will attach him by his strongest feelings to the independence of his country, and its republican Constitution. . . . These wards, called townships in New England, are the vital principle of their governments, and have proved themselves the wisest invention ever devised by the wit of man for the perfect exercise of self-government, and for its preservation . . . the whole is cemented by giving to every citizen, personally, a part in the administration of the public affairs.[18]

The development of truly self-governing communities of men, with each individual given the maximum responsibility in the achievement of the common purpose, was the essence of the Jeffersonian program. A common purpose and experience in the responsibilities it entailed would instil in the average citizen both the desire and the judgment to select those natural leaders whose abilities would be most instrumental in furthering the public good. To this natural aristocracy the responsibility for broader social policy would be intrusted, subject to the check of regular and frequent elections. Such was Jefferson's conception of the open society.

If Jefferson's program had been adopted, it might have changed the course of American life by tying the idea of mobility through a coherent institutional structure to the development of a democratic community. In such a society, much of the irresponsible individualism and social dislocation of the nineteenth and twentieth centuries might have been averted. Doubtless some aspects of Jefferson's vision were too sanguine and did not sufficiently take into account human inertia and irrationality, but, on the whole, the Jeffersonian vision remains one of the most practical and realistic versions of the good society ever devised by man. The reasons for its failure lay not in its utopianism, but in the inability or unwillingness of later generations to implement the positive aspects of Jefferson's program and to extend and re-evaluate Jefferson's principles in the light of changing experience.

Two elements of Jefferson's own thinking contributed to this failure. Like most Americans of his time, Jefferson did not foresee the development of industrialism. He assumed that the small farm would remain the primary basis of the American economy for an indefinite period. If this had been the case, Jefferson's strong, self-governing political institutions based on locality might well have developed. But, as the economy turned decisively toward industrialism, each section of the country became dependent on all the rest. This interdependence demanded increased co-ordination and planning, and the erection of elaborate networks of transportation, communication, and distribution of goods. Local institutions and even state governments proved unable to carry out the necessary planning for these developments. Increasingly the crucial political and economic decisions were taken out of the hands of local institutions. Jefferson's followers did not respond to this necessity by a re-examination of their principles. Almost by default, economic co-ordination became the prerogative of private corporations. However well-disposed these corporations were toward the public interest, they were not democratic institutions of the sort Jefferson had envisioned. Yet, in a sense, they came to fill the function in American society that Jefferson had imagined for local government by creating a level of decision between the individual and the state.

Instead of shaping the development of industrialism in America, the Jeffersonian ideal gradually became a fixed ideology of anti-industrialism, and ultimately an ideological weapon in the South's struggle to maintain a social system which was a travesty of the Jeffersonian program. Only at the beginning of the twentieth century, when Americans began to think seriously about the need for the general government to take an active part in creating the conditions in which equality of opportunity might flourish, did the Jeffersonian tradition undergo a renaissance.

Jefferson himself was incurably suspicious of the power of the federal government. Erected into a fixed theory by his followers, this was the second element of his thinking which helped to prevent the development of the Jeffersonian program. As a practical politician, Jefferson often made imaginative use of the national government to advance his conception of democracy. In his plan for the Northwest Territory, he was fully prepared to use the power of Congress to encourage the establishment of strong local government. By insisting that the territories organize their own state and local governments and be admitted to equal partnership in the union at the earliest possible moment, he sought to prevent any of the original colonies from becoming too large for democratic institutions, and to encourage the political decentralization he believed to be essential to the growth of a democratic social order. But, in theory, his conception of the federal government remained negative, and he helped to fix this conception with such eloquent statements as that of the First Inaugural Address:

a wise and frugal government, which shall restrain men from injuring one another, which shall leave them otherwise free to regulate their own pursuits of industry and improvement, and shall not take from the mouth of labor the bread it has earned. This is the sum of good government, and this is necessary to close the circle of our felicities.[19]

It was all too easy to overlook the injunction to "regulate their own pursuits of industry and improvement," a role which Jefferson had marked out for local government. In the expansion and change of the nineteenth century, Jefferson's followers were very slow to take up the possibility that, with the atrophy of local institutions, the national government might have to play a creative role in the development of patterns of mobility.

The Farmer's Friend; or, No Irish Need Apply

Two works of imaginative literature written at the end of the eighteenth century show how some of Franklin and Jefferson's contemporaries responded to their ideas. Both were by men who considered themselves sympathetic admirers of Franklin and Jefferson. One of them was a Jeffersonian politician. Yet neither grasped the full significance of Franklin's ideal of the self-improving individual or of Jefferson's conception of the natural aristocracy with its supporting social institutions.

The Farmer's Friend, or The History of Mr. Charles Worthy, Who, from being a poor Orphan, Rose, through various Scenes of Distress and Misfortune, to Wealth and Eminence, by Industry, Economy, and Good Conduct, deserves commemoration as the first Horatio Alger story published in America. It is the strenuously didactic story of a young self-made farmer, dedicated appropriately to the farmers of the United States, and published in 1793 by the Rev. Enos Hitchcock, D.D. Its title is, in good eighteenth-century fashion, a sufficient summary of its plot. Like its innumerable nineteenth-century progeny, and the seventeenth and eighteenth-century English didactic tales from which it springs, the novel shows how a poor young man who diligently pursues his calling, and the virtues of frugality, honesty, and piety, rises to comfort and respectability in his station. The chief difference between *The Farmer's Friend* and its English predecessors is a somewhat greater emphasis on the dignity of labor and the moral equality of the diligent farmer with the well-to-do man of fashion. Although one of his mouthpieces professes to believe that "labor is the first and most indispensable duty of man, from which no one can have a right to withdraw himself," and that "if . . . there is any difference between one human being and another, that part of them must be the most valuable who cultivate the ground, and provide necessaries for all the rest," [20] it should be noted that Hitchcock places this bit of wisdom in the mouth of a member of the upper classes. Imaginatively, Hitchcock is still clearly bound by the traditional Protestant ethic and by the image of a fixed,

hierarchical society. It is quite evident from his treat-
ment of characters and his explicit statements that even
in the new American republic he does not envision any
change in this traditional order. His hero, Charles
Worthy, though he becomes a freeholding farmer,

never betrayed the least disposition to quit the business he had
been so far brought up in, that of farming . . . . His views were
not elevated above his employment, which proved a great ad-
vantage to him afterwards. He never felt so happy as when con-
scious of industriously following his occupation, and faithfully
discharging the trust committed to him.[21]

His general advice to ambitious young men similarly be-
trays Hitchcock's fundamental commitment to the tra-
ditional social hierarchy. The young man's duty is not
to improve himself so that he can play a role in the gen-
eral improvement of society. Instead, he must learn to
be diligent in the station to which God has called him.

In order to merit the esteem of others, we must become acquainted
with the duties of our particular professions, occupations or sta-
tions in life, and discharge the duties of them in the most useful
and agreeable manner.[22]

Although he cites approvingly the examples and ideas
of Jefferson and Franklin, Enos Hitchcock's conception
of the new republican society remains in the traditional
mold. He does not imagine that the democratic ideas of
equal rights and opportunities are inconsistent in the
least degree with the traditional idea of a hierarchical
social order. For him, rising in society means essentially
rising within the rank to which one has been born. Self-
improvement means learning to perform the duties and
obligations of that station cheerfully and industriously.
All Hitchcock's instincts are against those who try to
rise from one class to another. Ironically, this first
American creator of a self-made fictional hero has the
gravest doubts about the open society. His novel, to a

considerable degree, is an attempt to persuade young men to eschew the promise of fame and fortune and to content themselves with the achievement of industry, self-discipline, and piety in the rank to which they were born.

H. H. Brackenridge's *Modern Chivalry,* the first part of which was published in 1792, not only has far greater literary merit than Hitchcock's moralistic tract but is more vigorously democratic in spirit. Although Brackenridge was sometimes reviled as a reactionary, he was in fact a Jeffersonian politician, participated in the 1800 campaign, and received an appointment to the Pennsylvania Supreme Court from a Jeffersonian governor. Brackenridge's major satirical target was not democracy. Rather, he attacked the upstarts who tried to rise to positions of honor and power without the requisite talent and virtue, and the gullibility of the mass of citizens which permitted them to do so.

Modern Chivalry is a long picaresque novel in the tradition of *Don Quixote.* Its hero, Captain Farrago, is a middle-aged country gentlemen who resembles Franklin's "Cato." Its Sancho Panza is the captain's servant, Teague O'Regan, an immigrant Irish "bog-trotter." The narrative centers around Teague's various attempts to rise in society. Cervantes' Sancho Panza is the embodiment of everyday common sense and complacency, but Teague is a distillation of the self-made upstart and go-getter. Seen to be fundamentally stupid and boorish, Teague is also shrewd, unscrupulous, and enterprising, with a plentiful admixture of blarney and nerve, and able to persuade men to give him the power and status his talents do not warrant. Typical of the incidents described in the book is a village election, in progress when Captain Farrago and Teague arrive, with an ignorant weaver as the leading candidate. Remonstrating with the people against the candidacy of a man so unsuited for statesmanship, a "man of education" makes the following speech, clearly echoing the sentiments of the author.

"Fellow citizens . . . I pretend not to any great abilities; but am conscious to myself that I have the best good will to serve you. But it is very astonishing to me, that this man should conceive himself qualified for the trust. For though my acquirements are not great, yet his are still less. The business which he pursues, must necessarily take up so much of his time, that he cannot apply himself to political studies. I should therefore think it would be more answerable to your dignity, and conducive to your interest, to be represented by a man at least of some letters, than by an illiterate man like this. It will be more honourable for himself, to remain at his loom and knot threads, than to come forward in a legislative capacity; because in the one case, he is in the sphere suited to his education; in the other, he is like a fish out of water; and must struggle for breath in a new element. It is not because he is a weaver that I object to him, but because he is nothing but a weaver, and entirely destitute of the qualifications necessary to fill the office to which he aspires. The occupation a man pursues for a livelihood is but a secondary consideration, if any consideration at all. Warriors and statesmen, and sages, may be found at the plough and the work bench, but this man has not the slightest pretensions beyond the mysteries of his trade." [23]

To these remarks Captain Farrago adds a few of his own, emphasizing the Jeffersonian insistence on education and natural aristocracy.

"To rise from the cellar to the senate house, would be an unnatural hoist for one whose mind has not been prepared for it by a previous course of study or training, either self-instructed, and gifted with superior intellect or having the good fortune to have received an education, with also the advantage of actual experience in public affairs. To come from counting threads, and adjusting them to the splits of a reed, to regulate the finances of a government, would be preposterous; *there being no congruity in the case.*" [24]

The last sentence is particularly revealing of the Jeffersonian failure to foresee the growing importance of business pursuits in America.

While the captain tries to persuade the villagers of the necessity of electing a man of demonstrable ability and training to office, Teague is busy on his own. By the time the Captain finishes expostulating with the weaver, the irrepressible bog-trotter Teague has the election in his pocket. To the captain's shocked remonstrance, the voice of democracy in full swing replies:

"It is a very strange thing . . . that after having conquered Burgoyne and Cornwallis, and got a government of our own, we cannot put in whom we please. This young man may be your servant, or another man's servant; but if we choose to make him a delegate, what is that to you? he may not yet be skilled in the matter, but there is a good day coming. We will empower him; and it is better to trust a plain man like him, than one of your high-flyers, that will make laws to suit their own purposes.[25]

Teague is all ready to assume his new dignity, but the captain is able to dissuade him by stressing the rigor and hardships of a political life. The episode ends with the election of the weaver.

Brackenridge's experience of the rough-and-tumble politics of the new West suggests that democratic elections will not guarantee the advancement of the truly wise and good, the natural *aristoi*. This insight might have led to a recognition of the importance of Jefferson's positive proposals: general experience of self-government, universal education, the recognition of a common purpose. But, fundamentally sympathetic to Jeffersonian ideas, Brackenridge's imagination does not extend to the point of seeing the need for new social institutions. Although he accepts the principle of natural aristocracy, his conception of the new democratic elite is largely bounded by the eighteenth-century ideal of the cultivated gentleman of leisure. The self-made man might be accepted into this elite only if he could meet its standards of refinement and education. In essence, Brackenridge still believes that the fundamental values of society reside in a particular social class, and he is prepared to accept the parvenu only if he has assimilated the attitudes, habits, and methods of that class. He is not prepared to come to terms with a rising level of aspiration and rapidly changing social patterns. It is significant that his comic villain is an early version of the stereotype Irish immigrant. Like many early nineteenth-century Americans, Brackenridge responds to the aspirations of new groups with amusement, disbelief, and ultimate refusal. Instead of encouraging and shaping the average man's desire to better his condition, Brackenridge views this ambition as a prime danger to the republic. In the end, his advice to his fellow citizens is hardly different from Enos Hitchcock's. Brackenridge puts it more eloquently, but the same counsel of contentment with one's station is there:

I shall have accomplished something by this book, if it shall keep some honest man from lessening his respectability by pushing himself into public trusts for which he is not qualified; or, when pushed forward into public station, if it shall contribute to keep him honest by teaching him the folly of ambition, and further advancement; when in fact, the shade is more to be coveted, and the mind, on reflection will be better satisfied with itself, for having chosen it. This is in great part, the moral of this book.[26]

Three Conceptions of the Self-made Man

Since the decline of the aristocratic ideals associated with Federalism, most Americans have spoken the language of opportunity, self-improvement, and mobility. But they do not mean the same thing. Franklin and Jefferson were hopeful that, in the new American republic, men might achieve a new ideal of human devel-

35

opment and a new kind of social order. Others like Enos Hitchcock and Henry Brackenridge were more concerned with the perpetuation in the new world of traditional religious and social patterns. For them, and for those who shared their concern for the preservation of gentility and piety, the ideal of self-improvement became a means for encouraging young Americans to follow in the secure and respectable paths of the established social and religious tradition rather than an invitation to enterprise and innovation. Yet, more often than not, the young American of the nineteenth century listened with respect to the advice of these advocates of tradition and then went on to mark out his own conception of the self-made man as an aggressive, go-getting, and rapidly moving entrepreneur. The interplay of these three different versions of the self-made man shaped the development of the ideal of self-improvement in the nineteenth century.

CHAPTER II

THE AGE OF THE SELF-MADE MAN

> Ours is a country, where men start from an humble origin . . . and where they can attain to the most elevated positions, or acquire a large amount of wealth, according to the pursuits they elect for themselves. No exclusive privileges of birth, no entailment of estates, no civil or political disqualifications, stand in their path; but one has as good a chance as another, according to his talents, prudence, and personal exertions. This is a country of self-made men, than which nothing better could be said of any state of society.
>
> Calvin Colton, *Junius Tracts* (1844)

The main theme of Thomas Jefferson's First Inaugural Address was the consensus Americans had forged in the controversies of the early years of the new republic. "We are all republicans—we are all federalists," he proclaimed, soothing political antagonism. A kind Providence had given Americans "a chosen country, with room enough for our descendants to the hundredth and thousandth generation," and had separated them by a wide ocean from the havoc and degradation of the rest of the world. Americans were agreed on the principles of "equal right to the use of our own faculties, to the acquisitions of our industry, to honor and confidence from our fellow citizens, resulting not from birth but from our actions and their sense of them." Finally, the whole was capped by a benign religion "practised in various forms, yet all of them including honesty, truth, temperance, gratitude, and the love of man."

39

For Jefferson, these principles implied a complex political and social program. Consensus on the anti-aristocratic aspects of this program was enthusiastic enough. Though old-line Federalists grumbled and thundered at the rising hordes of democracy, Americans were busy sweeping away the vestiges of institutionalized aristocratic privilege. Entail and primogeniture, the established church, limitations on the franchise, and distinctions in dress and manners were rapidly eliminated. By the second quarter of the nineteenth century, both political parties had adopted the rhetoric and symbols of the open society. Democrats and Whigs vied with each other in proclaiming their devotion to the interests of the self-made man, and, to prove it, brought to the forefront of their campaigns the log cabins which supposedly existed in the background of their candidates. The lesson of Old Hickory's broad popular appeal was not lost on the Whigs. The dashing, aristocratic Henry Clay became "the mill boy of the slashes." Daniel Webster carefully tempered the patrician eloquence of his rhetoric with memories of his happy youth in a humble cabin in the hills of New Hampshire. General William Henry Harrison, scion of one of the first families of Virginia, turned out to be a simple frontier farmer. The log cabin which was fortunately still part of his Ohio mansion was a feature of the "hard cider" campaign of 1840. Nor, somewhat later, did the new Republican party fail to realize the importance of these earlier examples. In the dramatic story of Abraham Lincoln's rise from railsplitter to President, from poverty and obscurity to savior of the union, the ideal of the self-made man found its greatest epic.

Enthusiasm for the self-made man spilled into other areas of American life. In the 1850's, T. S. Arthur complained that "American biography has confined itself too closely to men who have won political or literary

distinction." Arthur wanted "the histories of our self-
made men spread out before us, that we may know the
ways by which they came up from the ranks of the peo-
ple." [1] John Frost, in *Self-Made Men of America*
(1848), had already attempted this job, and his example
was followed by such inspirational biographies of suc-
cessful men as Charles Seymour's *Self-Made Men*
(1858) and James McCabe's *Great Fortunes and How
They Were Made; or, The Struggles and Triumphs of
Our Self-Made Men* (1871). Nor were self-made politi-
cians and businessmen the only heroes of self-improve-
ment. In the age of Jackson and Lincoln, the self-taught
artist and the self-educated intellectual also had their
place in the popular esteem. Elihu Burritt, the black-
smith-philosopher, who, despite his extraordinary self-
acquired scholarship and increasing prominence as a
lyceum speaker, continued to ply his trade, was consid-
ered a true embodiment of American ideals. Chester
Harding, a self-taught portrait painter, had such a vogue
in the early 1820's that, for a time, he had more com-
missions than the famous Gilbert Stuart. In the eyes of
his admirers, Harding was living proof of the virtues of
self-improvement. Miss Louisa J. Park of Boston eulo-
gized her hero in terms similar to those George Ban-
croft employed to apotheosize Andrew Jackson:

> Most wondrous gift, from nature's self derived
> His genius of all foreign aid deprived,
> Sprung up and bloomed amid our wilds obscure
> And won its self-taught way to glory sure.[2]

Truly, this was "a country of self-made men."

Self-Improvement and Economic Opportunity

Eliminating traditional aristocratic institutions and
manifesting enthusiasm for self-made politicians, busi-

nessmen, and artists was not the same thing as the implementation of Jefferson's positive program for the republican community. In 1838, *The Youth's Friend,* a magazine devoted to the moral instruction of the young, conveyed to its readers an interpretation of success which was both simpler and narrower than anything Jefferson had in mind.

If he has good health and is industrious, even the poorest boy in our country has something to trade upon; and if he be besides well educated, and have skill in any kind of work, and add to this moral habits and religious principles, so that his employers may trust him, and place confidence in him, he may then be said to set out in life with a handsome capital, and certainly he has a good chance of becoming independent and respectable, and perhaps rich, as any man in the country.[3]

The Jeffersonian conception of mobility was a political one, focused on the need of the republican community for able leadership in the achievement of its common purposes. *The Youth's Friend,* on the other hand, put chief emphasis on individual social and economic advancement. Of course, Jefferson had nothing against individual success, but he did not confuse it with the political goals of democracy: the common welfare and the preservation of individual rights. In the early nineteenth century, however, under the impact of a rapidly growing economy and the expansive mood of manifest destiny, with the prospect of a vast supply of cheap land, rapidly expanding markets, an increasingly more efficient transportation system, and high wages continuing into the indefinite future, it was easy to believe that if individuals were sufficiently enterprising and society put no artificial barriers in their way, the general welfare would take care of itself. As the predominantly agricultural economy of the early nineteenth century rapidly evolved into the emergent industrialism of the

1870's, even the small farmer, although he persisted in thinking of himself as the self-sufficient Jeffersonian yeoman, actually became an entrepreneur producing goods for a distant market. The theory of natural aristocracy was overshadowed by a philosophy of individual success and the concept of the republican community gave way to the image of a loose association of individuals, each making his own way in the world.

The emergence of the expression "self-made man" as the most popular designation of the mobile individual was itself a sign of changing attitudes toward mobility. In the United States Senate in February, 1832, Henry Clay rose to answer the attacks which had mounted against his "American System" of internal improvements, a protective tariff, and a central bank. Replying to the charge that tariff walls would create a privileged aristocracy of manufacturing corporations, Clay defended business enterprise in terms that have become classic. The joint-stock corporation, he argued, could not possibly endanger democracy because it was nothing more than a voluntary association "by means of which the small earnings of many are brought into a common stock, and the associates, obtaining corporate privileges, are enabled to prosecute, under one superintending head, their business to better advantage. Nothing could be more essentially democratic or better devised to counterpoise the influence of individual wealth." As to the charge that the directors of such corporations constituted a privileged aristocracy, anyone who looked around him could see that this was not the case. The manufacturers of America had not inherited their positions, they had earned them. "In Kentucky, almost every manufactory known to me is in the hands of enterprising and self-made men, who have acquired whatever wealth they possess by patient and diligent labor." [4]

Clay's use of "self-made man" differentiated his conception of mobility from those of Franklin and Jefferson. First, there was the implication in the term itself that mobility was completely dependent on the will and actions of the individual, that a man could make of himself what he would, and that the individual who failed had only himself to blame. Neither Franklin nor Jefferson would have accepted these propositions. As they understood it, the process of mobility was a complex transaction between inborn qualities, intellectual and moral cultivation, and the needs and values of society. Even the less astute Enos Hitchcock laid emphasis on the fact that worthy men often failed to get ahead through no fault of their own. Clay, however, reflected the optative mood of the early nineteenth century. Americans had freed themselves from the artificial social restrictions of the aristocratic past. A virgin continent, immeasurably rich in land and resources, sang its song of infinite promise. How could a man fail in such an environment, except through laziness or vice? Those who carried this view to the extreme of insisting that the poor and unfortunate deserved their sufferings were probably few, but faith in America made it a commonplace that a man could become rich if he worked at it.

Another attitude was implicit in Clay's use of the term "self-made man": the belief that democracy had nothing to fear from concentrations of economic power, so long as they were not hereditary. Nothing is more striking about nineteenth-century American culture than its general failure to recognize the political import of economic power. Americans tended to make a basic distinction between political and economic power; to fear and restrict political power, to regard economic power as essentially benevolent. Between the Jacksonian war on the bank in the 1830's and the Populist-Progressive agitation of the 1880's and 1890's, few political leaders or movements questioned the concentration of private economic power. Marvin Meyers has argued that even the Jacksonian attack on the bank was not a clear attack on economic power, but an emotional crusade generated by the diverse anxieties growing out of rapid social change. According to Meyers, Americans "found in the anti-bank crusade, and in the Jacksonian appeal generally, a way to damn the unfamiliar, threatening, sometimes punishing elements in the changing order by fixing guilt upon a single protean agent." [5] In *The Age of Reform,* Richard Hofstadter makes a similar point about the emotional tone of the Populist movement. Unwilling to give up the dream of free opportunity and unlimited abundance, Americans sought out a particular villain to account for the dislocations, inequalities, and anxieties they could not ignore. If only the duplicity and corruption of the bank, the eastern monopolists, or the grasping railroads could be stopped, everything would be all right.

Finally, in speaking of the manufacturers of Kentucky, Clay identified the self-made man with the activities and pursuits of business enterprise. We can probably discount the frequent criticism that nineteenth-century Americans were selfish, materialistic worshippers of the almighty dollar. There were, of course, some unscrupulous individuals who pursued wealth and power as ends in themselves, but they were not admired by the majority of Americans, unless, like Jim Fisk, they were great rascals whose careers had the quality of legend. Rarely, in the voluminous self-help literature of the nineteenth century, was there an assertion that wealth was a sufficient end in itself. In part, we can doubtless attribute this to an unwillingness to avow materialistic motives where public profession of religious piety and democratic principles was a *sine qua non,* but there is no reason to doubt that the majority of Americans sincerely believed what they publicly professed:

that individual economic advancement and productivity was the best way of assuring both the individual and the general welfare. The argument ran like this: America is the land of opportunity; any individual willing to work hard can tap these opportunities; continuous growth and economic expansion are the best way of creating more opportunities; therefore, the pursuit of economic advancement is not only to the individual's advantage, but the best way to help others. Under the stimulus of economic opportunity, the methods of enterprise and the figure of the successful businessman gradually eclipsed the Jeffersonian image of the democratic community with its natural aristocracy, and the ideal of the mobile society was dominated by the apolitical ethos of individual economic advancement.

The Gospel of Self-Improvement

Mid-nineteenth-century Americans eagerly embraced the economic opportunities which opened before them. They swarmed across the continent; they speculated on the rapid growth of towns and cities; they hastily constructed roads, canals, and railroads to unite the country into a single thriving market; they rushed into all kinds of business enterprise. But the surge of expansion and change inevitably produced anxiety and insecurity. However eagerly they may free themselves from it, men do not throw over a traditional way of life with ease. At many points the pursuit of individual success came into conflict with traditional social and religious ideals. The result was often an uncertainty about the ends of life and the moral duties of the individual. In a mobile, individualistic society, man's responsibilities to his fellow men and to God were no longer clearly defined by the traditional duties of his station or by the authority of a religious establishment. Without the psychological security of a clearly defined social role, the pursuit of happiness through individual economic advancement had many ambiguities. Contemporary observers noted the restlessness of American life. At times the search for happiness seemed to be a futile, unceasing quest. De Tocqueville observed:

In the United States a man builds a house in which to spend his old age, and he sells it before the roof is on; he plants a garden and lets it just as the trees are coming into bearing; he brings a field into tillage and leaves other men to gather the crops; he embraces a profession and gives it up; he settles in a place, which he soon afterwards leaves to carry his changeable longings elsewhere. If his private affairs leave him any leisure, he instantly plunges into the vortex of politics; and if at the end of a year of unremitting labor he finds he has a few days vacation, his eager curiosity whirls him over the vast extent of the United States, and he will travel fifteen hundred miles in a few days to shake off his happiness. Death at length overtakes him, but it is before he is weary of his bootless chase of that complete felicity which forever escapes him.[6]

The mixed attitude with which Americans embarked upon the creation of an industrial society was apparent in the popular literature which grew up around the pursuit of individual success. Far from being enthusiastic advocates of the pursuit of wealth, the popular exponents of self-improvement in the age of Jackson and Lincoln sought above all to strike a balance between traditional social and religious ideals and the spirit of individual economic enterprise. To judge from the rather great discrepancy between the recommendations of the most popular self-help books and the behavior of Americans as described in the testimony of observers, the primary function of the self-improvement handbook was not so much to guide behavior as to explain the dynamic changes of American life in terms of badly shaken traditional verities. Thus, as its advocates pre-

47

sented it, self-improvement was a moral and religious as well as a worldly struggle. The path to success was hedged about with the lures of Satan, and only the highest moral and religious motives could prevent the aspirant to fame and fortune from falling into his clutches.

From this view every young man can see how great is the responsibility resting upon him as an individual. If he commence with right principles as his guide,—that is, if in every action he have regard to the good of the whole, as well as to his own good,—he will not only secure his own well-being, but aid in the general advancement toward a state of order. But if he . . . follow only the impulses of his appetites and passions, he will retard the general return to true order, and secure for himself that unhappiness in the future which is the invariable consequence of all violations of natural or divine laws.[7]

The result of this attempt to synthesize the Christian vision of man's final regeneration with social progress and individual success was a general failure to deal with the problems of the present. Instead of grappling imaginatively with the realities of a democratic society, the preachers of self-help fell back upon the ethical injunctions which had been commonplaces since the seventeenth century. In an era of unprecedented movement from place to place and from occupation to occupation, the guidebooks urged Americans to work diligently in the calling to which God had appointed them. In his earnestly didactic novel *Richard Edney and the Governor's Family* (1850), Sylvester Judd sums up his message with the hope that his book will

speak to our Young Men, and tell them not to be so anxious to exchange the sure results of labor for the shifting promise of calculation,—tell them that the hoe is better than the yardstick. Instruct them that the farmer's frock and the mechanic's apron are as honorable as the merchant's and clerk's paletot or the student's cap. Show them how to rise *in* their calling, not out of it; and that intelligence, industry and virtue, are the only decent way to honor and emolument.[8]

In the age of Jackson, speculation, particularly in land, often reached the frenzied zeal which Harriet Martineau describes:

I never saw a busier place than Chicago was at the time of our arrival. The streets were crowded with land speculators, hurrying from one sale to another. A negro, dressed up in scarlet, bearing a scarlet flag, and riding a white horse with housings of scarlet, announced the times of sale. At every street-corner where he stopped, the crowd flocked round him; and it seemed as if some prevalent mania infected the whole people. The rage of speculation might fairly be so regarded.[9]

Yet, the preachers of self-help repeat over and over again the traditional Christian prohibition against speculation, dismissing it as a peculiarly desperate and depraved form of gambling. Mrs. H. F. Lee, in *The Log Cabin* (1844), tearfully criticizes the practice:

It is a great mistake, endeavoring to own a very large farm; the landholders are inclined to run into this error, and often purchase more than they can fence in, or cultivate. Their idea is to cultivate and sell out. A farmer who gets upon this speculating plan seldom grows rich or lives comfortably. Home happiness hardly comes into his account. His house, his stock, even his plunder are mere articles of trade. One woman told me with tears in her eyes, that her old man (he was about thirty-two) had sold out three times. . . . Thus does this destructive habit of speculation intrude itself into the most remote situations, and whether in polite, or less cultivated life, saps the foundations of domestic happiness.[10]

Rejecting speculation and emigration, the self-improvers emphasize faith in God and the traditional self-disciplinary virtues as keys to success. Furthermore, they offer little in the way of practical business advice, for, according to them, success grows out of a man's moral character rather than his practical actions or skills. As Freeman Hunt puts it, "the steps from the foot to the summit are not many, but each has a name which must be distinctly known by all who would seek to climb. The first step is faith, and without this, none can safely rise; the second, industry; the third, perseverance; the fourth, temperance; the fifth, probity; and the sixth, independence." [11] This list of virtues was, of course, the traditional middle-class Protestant calendar, which can be found in almost the same form in Franklin's "The Way to Wealth" or as far back as the beginning of the eighteenth century in Cotton Mather's *Essays to do Good*. Occasionally one of the more adventurous writers suggested that personal qualities useful to winning friends and making sales might well be cultivated. Hunt advised his readers that "a merchant ought to acquire and maintain an easiness of manner, a suavity of address, and a gentlemanly deportment without which the finest talents and the most valuable mental acquirements are often incapable of realizing the brilliant expectations which they induce their possessor to form." [12] On the whole, however, the apostles of self-improvement had little to add to the tradition of piety, industry, frugality, honesty, and perseverance.

Along with their concern for stringent self-discipline, the popular self-help writers dwell at great length on the temptations and dangers facing the ambitious young man. Indeed, the self-help literature of the age of Jackson and Lincoln is almost obsessively minatory. Henry Ward Beecher and T. S. Arthur revel in the dangers of extravagance, drink, and "strange women." In somber but glowing, almost loving, detail they set forth the awful degradation which awaits the young man who unwarily sets his feet on the primrose path. Nor is the corruption of personal vices the only source of danger. The temptation of "making haste to be rich" by false and immoral methods can also lead to ruin. Asa Greene, in *The Perils of Pearl Street* (1834), anathematizes corrupt business practices like "drumming," "shinning," "flying the kite," and speculation. Greene assures young men that only "a patient and steady perseverance, a fair and honorable course of dealing will ultimately produce the best results," [13] while speculation, sharp practices, and extravagant expectations inevitably lead to bankruptcy and moral corruption "The young merchant is no sooner started in business, than he fancies himself making money; and relying on this fancy, he is apt to launch into a sea of extravagance, which would swallow up a much larger income than his; and the inevitable consequence is that he is soon involved in ruin." [14]

This obsession with the dangers facing the rising young man and the need for rigid personal discipline seems curiously disparate with the optimism of the assumption that, in America, every young man has a real opportunity to improve himself. In part, this fascination with sin can be understood as a reflection of the traditional Calvinist view of man's basic depravity. But it also suggests that the apostles of self-improvement were uneasy about the emergent business society. The growing industrial cities of the 1840's and 1850's held out the promise of wealth and abundance, but they were also breaking up traditional ways of life and generating new social patterns and values. Enthusiasm for the new industrial system mixed with an anxious apprehension of urban life is a common element of both self-improvement handbooks and didactic fiction. Richard Edney's first view of the factories of Woodylin (Lowell), Massachusetts, is sheer enchantment:

Of a sudden, the Factories burst upon him, or their windows did,—hundreds of bright windows, illuminated every night in honor of Toil,—and which neither the darkness of the night,

51

nor the wildness of the storm, could obscure, and which never bent or blinked before the rage and violence around. The Factories, and factory life,—how it glowed at that moment to his eye! And even his own ideal notions thereof were more than transfigured before him, and he envied the girls, some of whom he knew, who, through that troubled winter night, were tending their looms as in the warmth, beauty, and quietness of a summer-day. The Factories appeared like an abode of enchantment.[15]

Yet, to his surprise, Judd's hero discovers that thriving Woodylin is full of misery and brutality; that its society is divided against itself; that the rich are unchristian and snobbish in their selfish vanity, while the poor are sunk in ignorance, degradation, and drunkenness. Judd does not attribute this misery to the new institutions and values of an economic society. On the contrary, his view of life made him seek the explanation of social and economic change in terms of the traditional religious categories of individual vice and virtue. His anxiety at the social dislocations of an emergent industrialism expresses itself in an obsessive concern with drunkenness, gambling, prostitution, and other personal vices. Although he is highly critical of many aspects of the new society, he seeks their cause in a breakdown of personal morality rather than in a failure of social values and institutions. Instead of questioning or qualifying the idea of individual economic advancement as a primary value, his solution to the problem of vice and misery is the gospel of self-help: encourage individuals to have faith, to work diligently at their callings, to avoid the temptations of vice, and the opportunities of American life will take care of the rest.

Thus, the self-help writers of the second half of the nineteenth century tried to interpret a dynamically changing American society in terms of a traditional religious view of life. In the attempt to resolve conflicting values, they tended to confuse economic success and moral merit in a way that earlier moralists would never have done. Franklin, for example, viewed the pursuit of wealth as a purely pragmatic matter. In order to achieve higher human ends, the individual had to free himself from the bondage of economic necessity. But, the self-help popularizers of the mid-nineteenth century resolved the pursuit of final ends and rising in society into one and the same thing. Freeman Hunt was critical of those who went to church to advertise their businesses, but he insists that "a truly religious man will give proper attention to business; and a man who conducts a business as he ought, will do it on religious principles." [16] "The destiny of mankind," says T. S. Arthur, "is a return to heavenly order and true happiness." [17] But he goes on to insist that this is to be achieved by rising to respectability and wealth through the discipline of industry, temperance, and frugality. According to Henry Ward Beecher, "the truest happiness implies the development, the education, of the social and the spiritual, as well as the physical elements of our being . . . it includes benevolence, and takes on the here and the hereafter as well." [18] Yet two pages later he asserts, "I had almost said that it is the *beau ideal* of happiness for a man to be so busy that he does not know whether he is or is not happy." [19]

It is not difficult to account for the predominantly moralistic ethos of the gospel of self-improvement. In the first half of the nineteenth century, its exponents were primarily Protestant clergymen, whose thinking reflected an ethical tradition at least two centuries old. Speaking from positions of power and prestige in the community, these men were socially and intellectually conservative. The source of their anxiety was the industrial economy which was breaking up the traditional social order and bringing new groups into positions of power and prestige. In a sense, though they preached the gospel of self-help, they were opponents of social change. With its emphasis on self-discipline and sticking to one's calling, their gospel was as much an attempt to preserve the traditional social hierarchy as to encourage young men to pursue economic success. At the same time, they sincerely believed that men would fall into vice and corruption if they were not spurred to constant effort and self-discipline. Thus, the apostles of self-help were caught in a curious paradox: men must be encouraged to pursue individual economic advancement, but they must do so without wishing to be rich or to rise dramatically in social status. The man who did not work diligently to improve his condition was corrupt and degraded, but the real purpose of industry was not wealth but moral merit.

Wealth alone is not the main and proper object of any profession. It is not, and should never be considered the chief pursuit of life. A profession which furnishes employment and support, and affords the means of mental tranquility and true honest independency, even if it should not lead to the acquisition of considerable wealth, is preferable, both for time and eternity, to that which sacrifices ease of mind, domestic happiness, or the slightest point of integrity to the acquisition of millions.[20]

This was the line of the social superior who hoped to keep the recipient of his advice in a position of contented inferiority without having to undertake the responsibility of supporting him. In a nutshell, and without giving due credit for sincerity and sympathy, this was the message of the gospel of self-improvement as it took shape in the second quarter of the nineteenth century. It is not surprising that the evidence of observers and the statistics of economic change show that the majority of Americans did not take it seriously as a guide to behavior. By the end of the third quarter of the nineteenth century, Americans were becoming increasingly unresponsive to this concept of self-improvement. Significant changes in tone and emphasis can be detected in the self-help books. Yet, as Ervin Wyllie has demonstrated in his careful study, *The Self-Made Man in America,* the self-improvement handbook retained its dominantly moralistic flavor and its message of industry, frugality, integrity, and piety throughout most of the nineteenth century. Even later, when the more frankly materialistic philosophy of success became dominant, the moralistic tradition continued in a subsidiary stream.

The persistence of this tradition suggests that the average American, although he enthusiastically accepted and participated in the economic expansion of the nineteenth century, must have felt some of the same anxiety about the mobile society that was reflected in the self-help books. Perhaps these works of popular ethics constituted a literature of reassurance rather than of inspiration and guidance. The Americans who read them probably found a psychological security in their simple moralistic formulas and in their insistence that the individual who had faith in the ways and beliefs of his fathers would ultimately be rewarded.

Self-Improvement and the Boss's Daughter: The Self-made Man in Didactic Fiction

The self-made man in the sentimental novel of the pre-Civil War era was essentially a fictionalization of the self-improvement handbooks. The authors of these novels were members of the same religiously oriented middle-class group. Some of them, like T. S. Arthur, produced both tales of didactic sentiment and self-help books; the same basic pattern of ideas dominated both fiction and non-fiction. The self-made hero was an exceptionally virtuous and industrious young man, and the

55

novel dealt with his triumphant overcoming of hardship and temptation, his diligent pursuit of a business, and his rise to respectability and affluence. There was even the same emphasis on overcoming the temptations of the flesh. In one of my favorite passages, Edwin Fairbanks, the incredibly virtuous hero of A. L. Stimson's *Easy Nat; or, The Three Apprentices. A Tale of Life in New York and Boston, but Adapted to Any Meridian* (1854), narrowly escapes the wiles of the seductive daughter of Judge Bogardus when he smells wine on her breath:

The spell was broken, and Edwin was enabled to tear himself away from the siren, who had held him for some minutes, lost to all self-consciousness by the power of her fascination. Oh! ye young ladies, seeking temperate husbands, and yet loving a little wine occasionally yourselves, be warned by the unhappy Helen's example—and always eat a sugared cubeb or two, after drinking.[21]

In novel as in handbook, industry, frugality, honesty, and perseverance were central qualities. Those who sought success by dishonest methods or through speculation were villains whose dismal fate proved the immorality and ineffectiveness of their methods. The fictional eulogists of the self-made man also stressed a properly religious attitude toward rising in society. One of the characters in T. S. Arthur's *Sparing to Spend* explains how one could safely rise in the world, if one does so without desire for wealth or worldly gratifications:

"If the love of the world be not permitted to enter our hearts, Ellen, we have nothing to fear. We may go up to a higher [social] position—may accept these added temporary blessings, and still retain that sweet tranquility of mind which is worth more than all this world has to offer." [22]

Finally, there is the same image of a stable social order, an established hierarchy which remains undisturbed by the process of mobility. In *Allen Prescott*

(1834), the story of a self-made lawyer, Mrs. S. A. L. Sedgwick describes (and doubtless agrees with) these opinions of one of her leading characters:

By birth, education, and political associations allied to those often invidiously termed the aristocracy, he was nevertheless in sentiment one of the people. He had no visionary schemes of universal equality; he saw and approved of many of these distinctions which exist even among us; but he also saw that while classes as such were susceptible of little change, there was in individuals a tendency upward that nothing could repress; that the frame of society remained unshaken, though its component parts changed their position; and his benevolence led him to co-operate with a state of things which he believed best for the mass, though he, personally, might suffer inconvenience.[23]

Nevertheless, despite these fundamental similarities, there are some revealing differences between novels and didactic handbooks. In fantasy, men will sometimes reveal deep-lying attitudes of which they are only partly conscious. Thus, in the self-help handbooks, it is universally agreed that, no matter what his birth, the individual who works diligently and honestly is as honorable, if not more so, than one who is rich and well-born. In the didactic novels, however, there are strong signs of a continuing admiration for high social status, and a covert prejudice against the common man. Often, for example, one finds a somewhat embarrassed defense of the self-made man as a hero. Timothy Flint, fearful that his readers will not respond properly to his tale of *George Mason, the Young Backwoodsman* (1829) threatens divine wrath:

[The reader] will not dare to despise the lowly tenants of the valley, where the Almighty, in his wisdom, has seen fit to place the great mass of our race. It has been for ages the wicked, and unfeeling, the stupid habit of writers, in selecting their scenery and their examples, to act as if they supposed that the rich, the titled, and the distinguished, who dwell in mansions, and fare sumptuously every day, were the only persons, who could dis-

play noble thinking and acting; that they were the only charac-
ters, whose loves, hopes, fortunes, sufferings, and deeds had
anything in them worthy of interest, or sympathy.[24]

Writers of this type of story frequently take pains to
emphasize the genteel qualities and background of their
heroes. The convention of the lost heir is employed to
show that the self-made hero, although he began his life
in poverty, is of impeccably aristocratic birth. Mrs. E.
D. E. N. Southworth daringly makes her *Ishmael*
(1863) the apparent bastard of a poor young farm girl.
Actually, through the device of a secret marriage, he is
the legitimate son of a wealthy and aristocratic planta-
tion owner. Even when the hero cannot claim aristo-
cratic birth, he usually marries into the upper classes.
Furthermore, in many sentimental novels the self-made
hero is impeccably genteel. T. H. Shreve's *Drayton: A
Story of American Life* has a hero of gentle birth whose
family has fallen on evil days. Forced to struggle
against great adversity, Drayton manages to pick up a
full-fledged classical education and all the gentlemanly
appurtenances. At one point in the story he confronts a
mere man of wealth and demonstrates his superior
cultivation:

And now, as he thought of the insolence with which he had been
treated by a man of wealth and consequence, a man whose ear
was familiar with the notes of adulation, his face flushed with
anger. When he thought of the ignorance of the man who sup-
posed a volume of Plutarch to be a trashy romance, he could
not but feel great contempt for him. Often, on such occasions,
he renewed the settled purpose of his heart to effect a triumph
over the obstacles which surrounded him, and claim of the world
that homage which wealth can not purchase and genius alone
can exact.[25]

With these qualifications, Drayton quickly finds a pa-
tron in the aristocratic Colonel Meredith, marries his
brilliant and accomplished daughter, and embarks on a

promising career in law and politics, "proud, as the majority of self-made men are, who having forced their way upward through difficulties appalling to meaner natures, feel their superiority." [26]

Drayton, George Mason, and Mrs. Sedgwick's *Allen Prescott* were probably influenced by the Jeffersonian theory of natural aristocracy, although their authors do not grasp the full complexity of Jefferson's conception of the republican community. On the contrary, the idea of mobility reflected in these novels is as limited as that of *The Farmer's Friend* (see p. 27). Society is portrayed as relatively static, with clear and fixed distinctions of rank. Those few individuals whose exceptional merit and genius fit them for a higher station are simply assimilated into the existing upper classes. If there is a significant difference in the way this conception is expressed in the novels of the period 1830–50 and in Hitchcock's *The Farmer's Friend* of the 1790's, it lies in a greater emphasis on the idea of genius surmounting all social obstacles. Influenced by the romantic idea of natural genius, *Drayton*'s author argues that

There is no condition from which superior genius will not rise. Pile up obstacles as high as Pelion on the energies of a man of true genius, and his native strength will enable him to throw off the mountain and lift his disencumbered head toward the heavens which smile upon it. And here in this land, where the will of man is as free as the wing of the swallow, we have demonstrated the great truth, that happy is the country in which genius and not hereditary right, governs.[27]

T. H. Shreve was an admirer of Andrew Jackson, and this passage bears a strong resemblance to Bancroft's romantic eulogy of Old Hickory as the natural genius from the West who "came as one free from the bonds of hereditary or established custom; he came with no superior but conscience, no oracle but his native judgement. . . . Guided by natural dialectics, he developed

59

the political doctrines that suited every emergency with a precision and a harmony that no theorist could hope to equal." [28]

It would be easy to overstate the depth of this commitment to natural genius, for it is almost invariably the case in novels of this kind that, above all, nature teaches the traditional deportment and attitudes of the upper-class gentleman. In Flint's novel, mentioned above, George Mason's sister has no instructor but the wilds of the Kentucky frontier. Strangely enough, she turns up with an instinctive comprehension of the "proprieties of deportment" and is more successful at winning the affection of the aristocratic Mr. Leonard "than if she had been trained to murder at a fashionable boarding-school." [29] The idea of natural genius seems to have been more of a literary overlay on a traditional image of social hierarchy than a deeply held conviction.

There are a number of didactic novels in which the image of a traditional social hierarchy is not as prominent. In these novels, instead of being marked out by his exceptional genius and innate gentility, the self-made hero's chief qualities are his athletic piety and his remarkable temperance. The primary concern of authors like T. S. Arthur and Sylvester Judd is the traditional middle-class Christian virtues. Embodying to an unbelievable degree the worldly asceticism of the Protestant ethic, these self-made heroes are deployed to attack the moral laxity, extravagance, and corrupt business practices of the new industrial cities. T. S. Arthur's *Sparing to Spend,* for example, is intended to

exhibit the evils that flow from the too common lack of prudence, self-denial and economy in young people at the beginning of life. . . . Extravagant expenditures—living beyond the means —is the besetting evil of social life in this country. . . . "SPARING TO SPEND" has for its aim the correction of this evil, in so far as an exhibition of its folly, and the peace, prosperity and happiness almost certain to flow from an opposite course of life, can effect so desirable an object.[30]

Arthur's *The Way to Prosper* (1851) contrasts the industry, frugality, and integrity of the Stevens brothers, who become successful printers and booksellers, with the indolence, extravagance, and speculative propensities of the Close brothers, each of whom fails miserably. Sylvester Judd's Richard Edney, in the novel named for him, is not only diligent on his own behalf, but spends much of his time exhorting indigents to industry and piety. A strong partisan of the temperance cause, he helps raid saloons and is instrumental in the formation of the Knuckle Lane Society, a club devoted to the reform of paupers by offering them hot coffee and the Gospel. No wonder he is finally rewarded with the hand of the governor's daughter!

In these novels, social distinctions based on genius or gentility are rejected explicitly. Both Judd and Arthur criticize resoundingly the pretensions of high society. One of their standard villains is the snobbish gentleman who fails to recognize the honest, if simple, virtues of the hero, and is generally punished for it by losing his wealth and position. Instead of exceptional intelligence and genteel cultivation, religious and moral merit are held to be the true basis of social distinction. "It is good sense that creates the higher orders," one of Judd's spokesmen insists. "Joined to this—sometimes leading it, sometimes enforcing it,—are education, opportunity, industry, self-denial." [31] More important than any social ties or distinctions is the higher relation of "Christian fidelity." Acting in accordance with this injunction, Richard Edney admonishes his employer for drunkenness—and gets a raise!

But whether the primary emphasis is on an ideal of gentility or the virtues of piety, industry, and temperance, the sentimental novel is dominated by a tradi-

61

tional conception of social organization and individual ethics. Yet the curious incidence of providence or luck in the novels suggests some doubts about that tradition. Although the self-help books insist that individual qualities of character are the key to success, in the novels one can hardly find a single instance where industriousness, frugality, and piety are the operative factors in the hero's rise in society. Instead, the hero saves an elderly gentleman from a runaway horse and gains a wealthy patron; or falls in love with a charming young lady who turns out to be the governor's daughter; or discovers that he is the long-lost heir to a great fortune; or is simply favored by Providence. As Raymond Williams suggests in his discussion of English novels of a similar period and type, the hero's problems are solved by a kind of magic rather than by a clearly envisioned process of cause and effect. Charting the course of his hero's career in fiction, the writer calls upon the external force of God or luck, rather than the internal factor of character, for the final accomplishment of the design. The self-made hero of Arthur's "Don't Be Discouraged" fails in business three times. He is industrious, diligent, temperate, and frugal, and yet the fates seem to be against him. But as he mulls over his disasters, a new spirit enters his soul:

He could go up into higher regions of his mind, and see there in existence principles whose pure delights flowed not from the mere gratification of selfish and sensual pleasures. He was made deeply conscious, that even with all the wealth, and all the external things which wealth could give, and for the gratification of the senses, and for the pampering of selfishness and pride, he could not be happy. That happiness must flow from an internal state, and not from any combination of external circumstances.[32]

At the very moment that he comes to this realization (and presumably has no further use for success in business) the hero receives a business proposition, and soon he becomes a wealthy merchant. Looking back over his experience, he realizes that his reverses were but blessings in disguise.

The fictional eulogists of the self-made man are never quite able to imagine their hero's career in human terms. They resort to supernatural intervention to insure the worldly success of the morally meritorious. Committed to a traditional ethic, they try to understand and explain the economic and social changes of the nineteenth century in terms of that ethic, but, lacking any real comprehension of the forces at work, they resort to idealization and literary sleight-of-hand. By transforming the ambitious individual into an ideal paragon, they hope to persuade the young, and perhaps themselves, that the traditional ethic is still operative and that society will reward the virtuous. Their novels may have reassured those who were anxious about the development of American society, but their view of society was too fanciful to have any significant influence on the behavior of Americans, or any real effect on the changes they feared.

Man on the Make: The Self-made Man in Humor and Satire

The self-help handbook and novels about the self-made man embodied a generally accepted interpretation of the mobile society, but when we turn to the literature of humor and satire we find a very different set of attitudes. In fact, one satirist of the period was so disgusted by the moralistic idealization of the self-made man that he created an elaborate burlesque of the didactic novel. Charles F. Briggs' *The Adventures of Harry Franco, A Tale of the Panic* (1839) is a minor work, worthy of more attention than it has received for its deft ridicule of the gospel of self-improvement.

63

Like most good self-made men, Harry Franco is brought up in the country, but is not an orphan, nor is his mother the heroically wise and devoted paragon who so often gives the idealized hero the moral instruction which forms his character. Harry's mother is a city-bred woman "who had picked up her ideas of human nature from novels and romances." [33] His father is a weak and completely indolent gentleman, whose moral ideas are largely limited to obsessions about table manners. Ironically, the elder Franco is ultimately more successful than his son.

The Francos, far from being industrious but unfortunate, fall into poverty through disappointment at not receiving a legacy from a distant relative. Mrs. Franco, "to solace herself, took to two articles of domestic manufacture, which owe their support chiefly to indolent old ladies, and romantic young ones; viz.; novels and snuff." [34] The education of the young Francos is left to nature. Unlike the nature which transforms George Mason and his sister into models of genteel deportment, in *Harry Franco* nature "would no doubt have led us into the street . . . had it not been that we were very proud, and our little hearts could not brook the sight of our cousins better dressed than ourselves, and, as we were taught to believe, at our expense." [35]

Inspired by the stories he has read of "adventurous boys, who had left their homes with nothing but a wallet and a mother's blessing; and of their making their fortunes, and returning with their pockets lined with gold," and not dreaming that "there were men and women in the world wicked enough to invent stories to mislead the minds of the young and simple," [36] Harry sets out to make his fortune. Recalling that, in the stories he has read, the hero frequently makes his way by saving a beautiful young heiress from a dangerous

64

predicament and then marrying her, Harry keeps his eyes open. Unfortunately, when he does encounter Georgiana de Lancey, who is both a wealthy heiress and the niece of a rich New York merchant, she is not in danger. Missing the opportunity to snatch this plum from the jaws of death, Harry at least determines to help her board a steamboat:

I resolved not to let this last opportunity escape of showing my gallantry, and seeing somebody near her, I stepped briskly past, and asked her if I should have the pleasure of assisting her out of the boat; she thanked me very sweetly, and took hold of my extended hand; but as I stepped back my foot slipped, and I fell my whole length in the bottom of the boat. When I got upon my feet again, she was gone. I hobbled on board the steamer but I could see nothing of her.[37]

Such are the adventures of Harry Franco. The hero finds that he simply cannot follow the inhumanly industrious and temperate course of the sentimental heroes, or, if he does, the result is failure. In the end, it is his indolent father's success in a land speculation scheme that makes it possible for Harry to gain the hand of the lovely Georgiana:

It appeared that, notwithstanding the hard times, the improvements in our village had been carried on; the track of a railroad had been carried through my father's garden, which had enhanced the value of his property almost a hundred fold; a joint stock company had purchased the family mansion, and altered it into a classic temple, by adding a row of wooden pillars and a pediment, and giving it a coat of white paint; it had been christened Franco Hall, and lithographed views of it were hung up in all the taverns in the country, and my sister wrote that it was to be in one of the annuals. My father had suddenly become a man of consequence, and there were rumors of his being nominated for Congress. It is wonderful how soon a man's abilities are discovered, when it is known that he made a fortunate speculation.[38]

The burlesque of the idealized self-made man in *The Adventures of Harry Franco* was the response of a sophisticated urban intellectual to the moralizing of the self-improvement tradition. In a different vein, there appeared in the more popular humorous literature of the age of Jackson a number of heroes whose characteristics and adventures embody a vigorous and amoral image of the mobile society. In these works, the mobile individual is a shrewd, enterprising, and frequently roguish operator, and his keys to success are not industry, frugality, and piety but cleverness, daring, and a keen sense of the main chance. The context in which he operates is a fluid, changing society in which every man stands up for himself and the sucker rarely gets an even break.

Major Jack Downing, the original of the cartoon figure of Uncle Sam and the first of a distinguished line of self-made political oracles, was the creation of a young newspaperman, Seba Smith. The major was first conceived in the classic mold of the shrewd country bumpkin whose naïve descriptions are in fact an ironic commentary on the political "doin's" he witnesses with amusement. Smith gradually expanded his conception, and, as Jack Downing becomes a dark-horse candidate for governor of Maine and then goes to Washington in search of a lucrative office, he appears more and more in the image of the shrewd and self-reliant young politician out to set right the tradition-bound inanities of the nation's rulers by the application of good common sense and a fervent dedication to the open society. In 1834, when Smith wrote the "Sketch of My Early Life," the transformation was complete, and Jack Downing became an embodiment of young America on the make.

In the sketch, Jack is revealed to be the scion of a respectable Down East farming family. His grandfather fought in the "fatigue of Burgwine," and his father is an industrious farmer. But Jack takes after Uncle Joshua, a shrewd but indolent Yankee who "was a clear shirk, and never would work if he could help it." [39] Uncle Joshua's laziness gives him a political bent and "by the time he was twenty-five years he knew more about politics than any other man in Downingville." [40] Now "the foremost man in Downingville," he is an inspiration to Jack, who also hates work.

I jogged along with father on the farm. But let me be doing what I would, whether it was hoeing potatoes, or pitching hay, or making stone wall, or junking and piling logs, I never could feel exactly easy. Something seemed to keep ringing in my ears all the time, and saying I was made to do something in the world besides this.[41]

Tempted "forty times to pack up and go and seek my fortune," Jack at last comes to this decision:

In the fall of the year 1829, I took it into my head I'd go to Portland. So one day I up and told father, and says I, "I'm going to Portland, whether or no, and I'll see what this world's made of yet." Father stared a little at first, and said he was afraid I should get lost; but when he see I was bent upon it he give it up, and he stepped to his chest and opened the till, and took out a dollar and give it to me, and says he, "Jack, this is all I can do for you; but go, and lead an honest life, and I believe I shall hear good of you yet." [42]

Eventually Jack goes to Washington, becomes a friend of General Jackson, receives a major's commission in the army, and spends the rest of his career trying to keep the government in the right path.

The difference between Jack and the self-made man of the didactic tradition is striking. Making no pretense of uncommon virtue or ability, he frankly pursues his own ends in his search for office. No gentleman, and with no particular desire to be one, he feels no need of education or cultural refinement. His main talents are a common-

67

sense shrewdness that enables him see the vanities of others, a plentiful share of Yankee brass, and a spread-eagle patriotism which puts to shame the pretensions of other politicians. His attitude toward the past and the traditionally authoritative classes is that of an early Andrew Carnegie bearding the Kaiser on his yacht to let him know that the day of kings and nobles is over.

Unlike Jack Downing, Davy Crockett was not a creation of fiction; in the 1830's he was a frontier politician in search of a following. He first came into the national eye as a frontier character of the half-horse, half-alligator type. The first *Life* (1833) emphasizes this aspect of the legend:

David Crockett, the subject of the following memoir, was born in Greene county, East Tennessee, of poor and respectable parentage. . . . When David became old enough to go to school his father's situation made it necessary that he should go to work. No one, at this early age, could have foretold that he was ever to ride upon a streak of lightning, receive a commission to quiet the fears of the world by wringing off the tail of a comet, or perform sundry other wonderful acts, for which he has received due credit, and which will serve to give him a reputation as lasting as that of the Hero of Orleans.[43]

Successful as a book, this *Life* was a failure as a campaign document, its intended purpose, for the next year Davy and his managers prepared another *Life,* from which the tall tales of the Crockett legend were largely eliminated. Disingenuously, Davy expressed shock and anger that the author of the earlier life, which had been written with his full knowledge and consent, should have presented him as such an outrageous character.

Despite some exaggerations and a rather large dose of anti-Jacksonian polemic, Crockett's own version of his life is a remarkably realistic document for the time. Davy makes little attempt to gloss over his repeated failures to make a living before entering politics, and though he occasionally drops into the pose of the natural man, he lays no claim to genius, outstanding virtue, or any other intellectual abilities or distinctions. Indeed, he appears remarkably like what he must have been: a crude, uneducated, but shrewd frontier politician with a keen eye for the main chance. He himself recognized that the sources of his political success lay in his personality and in his ability to turn off any serious political discussion with a joke or a tall tale. Like Jack Downing, he presents himself as a man of ordinary common sense and patriotism, honest, self-seeking, with a willingness to learn, a solid nerve, and a self-reliance embodied in his famous motto "GO AHEAD." Though Whig managers later tried to dress Davy in the ill-fitting costume of the more orthodox gospel of self-improvement, his own narrative of his career provides Americans with one of the first realistic treatments of a man of few intellectual or cultural gifts whose vigor, nerve, and ability to advertise himself made him rise from the canebrake to considerable political prominence, and ultimately to something of a national myth.

Although Sam Slick was the creation of a Canadian, he had American ancestors and almost immediately became American property. Thomas Chandler Haliburton, his creator, was a Canadian jurist who hoped to cure the lack of enterprise and the leveling tendencies of his native Nova Scotia by the application of some Yankee common sense. Sam is the peddler's peddler, the direct ancestor of those legendary salesmen who sell refrigerators to the Eskimos. A strenuous exponent of industry, Sam has his own notions about morality. "Human natur," as he sees it, is a compound of corruption, cupidity, and vanity, which the enterprising and industrious man will do his best to take advantage of. No man to give the sucker an even break, Sam transmutes the middle-class ethic of industry, economy, and integrity into a salesman's enterprise, sharpness, and "soft sawder." Frankly avowing his interest in wealth, Sam assures his readers that "your great men are nothin but rich men, and I can tell you for your comfort, there's nothin to hinder you from bein' rich too, if you will take the same means as they did." [44] And he enjoins them to

give up politics—it's a barren field, and well watched too; where one critter jumps a fence into a good field and gets fat; more nor twenty are chased round and round, by a whole pack of yelpin curs, till they are fairly beat out, and end by bein half starved, and are at the liftin at last. Look to your farms—your water powers—your fisheries, and factories. In short, says I, puttin on my hat and startin, look to yourselves, and don't look to others. [45]

Haliburton's success inspired other humorists to deal with those aspects of American enterprise ignored by the moralists of self-help. These writers developed further versions of the shrewd upstart whose nerve and sharpness enable him to triumph over the more sedate and respectable of his fellow citizens. Mrs. Ann Stephens' *High Life in New York* (1843) features Jonathan Slick, who combines Jack Downing's rural naïveté and vigor with Sam Slick's shrewd insight into "human natur." Jonathan's earthy common sense is set off against the genteel snobbishness of New York society. The satirists of the Old Southwest also delighted in the unscrupulous man on the make. J. J. Hooper's classic *Simon Suggs' Adventures* parodies the campaign biographies of self-made political figures during the Jacksonian period. Its hero is a more roguish incarnation of Sam Slick:

The shifty Captain Suggs is a miracle of shrewdness. He possesses in an eminent degree, that tact which enables him to detect the *soft spots* in his fellow, and to assimilate himself to whatever company he may fall in with. Besides, he has a quick, ready wit, which has extricated him from many an unpleasant pre-

dicament, and which makes him whenever he chooses to be so—
and that is always—very companionable. In short, nature gave
the Captain the precise intellectual outfit most to be desired by
a man of his propensities. She sent him into the world a sort of
he-Pallas, ready to cope with his kind from his infancy, in all
the arts by which men *"get along"* in the world; if she made
him, in respect to his moral conformation, a beast of prey, she
did not refine the cruelty by denying him the fangs and the
claws.[46]

With his motto, "IT IS GOOD TO BE SHIFTY IN A NEW
COUNTRY," Simon Suggs is a delightful perversion of the
idealized self-made man. His creator even takes an occa-
sional dig at the pious posturing of the gospel of self-
improvement:

"Well!" [Simon] continued, in a strain of unusual piety, as he
threw up and caught again a rouleau of dollars: "Well! thar *is*
a Providence that purvides; and ef a man stand squar' up in
what's right, it *will* prosper his endeavours to make somethin'
to feed his children on! Yes, thar *is* a Providence! I should like
to see the man would say thar ain't. I don't hold no sich. Ef a
man says thar ain't no Providence, you may be sure thar's some-
thing wrong *here"*; striking the region of his vest pocket—"and
that man will swindle you, ef he can—CERTIN!" [47]

One wonders whether Hooper knew anything of the
speculations and pious platitudes of the fabulous Daniel
Drew whose career as a Wall Street buccaneer and
staunch Methodist was beginning about this time.

There is a curious cultural paradox in the co-exist-
ence of the moralistic, socially traditional gospel of self-
improvement reflected in self-help handbooks and senti-
mental novels and the essentially amoral, antitraditional
image of the ambitious individual in works of humor
and satire. To a certain extent, of course, characters
like Sam Slick and Simon Suggs are presented crit-
ically as indictments of the selfish, amoral, speculative
spirit of the newer era, and yet even in the case of out-

and-out rogues like Simon Suggs the criticism is mild. Furthermore, the hero's hypocritical pretensions to piety and virtue are as much an object of satire as his actions. It is true that these different portrayals of the self-made man are addressed to different audiences, but the difference in audience is probably more a matter of sex and age than of social class. The sentimental novel was intended for the wholesome entertainment and instruction of women and young people and, therefore, reflected a more moralistic and religious presentation of reality than the books created primarily for an older, masculine audience. It is also true that satire and humor have traditionally exploited the vices and folly rather than the virtues of human kind. But differences in genre and literary convention will not account for this difference in presentation. The same disparity between conceptions of what constitutes success often exist within the same work. In such novels as John B. Jones's *The Life and Adventures of a Country Merchant* (1854), Bayard Taylor's *John Godfrey's Fortunes* (1865), and Richard B. Kimball's *Henry Powers* (1868), the two conflicting strands of moralistic self-improvement and untrammeled enterprise run side by side in an uneasy and tenuous balance. Jones's books deal with western businessmen and show a considerable knowledge of the attitudes, beliefs, and practices of a particularly enterprising group of Americans. His characters are far from overscrupulous and vigorously make use of all of the tricks of the trade to expand their operations and put their competitors out of business. Yet Jones assures his readers that piety, industry, and honesty are the only keys to success. In rather more sophisticated fashion, Richard Kimball tries to resolve the conflict between the pursuit of wealth through speculation and the traditional morality of piety and industry. His hero is a virtuous youth, fully trained in the gospel of self-improvement. But he does have to learn that there is a difference between the ethic he has been taught and the proper business morality, which admits that man's desire for money and his pursuit of his own advantage are reasonable goals which justify business practices. Thus, although Kimball warns his readers of the few "human spiders" waiting to trap the unwary speculator, his novel glorifies the "true-hearted, loyal men in Wall Street." [48]

The same mixture of belief in the supreme importance of piety, industry, frugality, and honesty together with completely unrestricted entrepreneurship are readily apparent in the careers and attitudes of the great American businessmen who led the way in the economic development of the United States in the nineteenth century. Some few business leaders were clearly untroubled by traditional religious or moral beliefs of any sort; the great majority were sincere adherents to the traditional middle-class gospel. Daniel Drew, whose activities made his name a byword for financial chicanery, was a pillar of the Methodist church.

The Decline of the Protestant Ethic

In his important study of *The Protestant Ethic and the Spirit of Capitalism,* Max Weber notes a number of affinities between the central values of Protestantism and the emerging spirit of business enterprise. As Weber demonstrates, the major Protestant creeds and the ethos of middle-class enterprise emphasized an individualistic spirit, the diligent pursuit of a calling, self-discipline, and temperance. Although there has been a protracted controversy over the exact historical significance of Weber's analysis—did the Protestant reformation cause the rise of capitalism or vice versa?—few scholars have questioned Weber's fundamental assertion that the Protestantism of the seventeenth and eighteenth centuries was responsive to the spirit of middle-class enterprise, and tried to erect the impulse toward economic advancement and the desire for salvation into a single coherent system of values. As Weber indicates, the coherence of this system was dependent on the concept of the divinely ordained secular calling. Diligent worldly enterprise was not inconsistent with religious salvation since the Divine Providence had assigned to each individual a secular occupation to carry out during his worldly existence. By working hard in the occupation to which God had called him, the industrious man glorified God. Even so, there had always been a certain ambiguity about the degree to which the individual was free to choose or change the profession in which he began his career. When the Protestant tradition came together with the democratic ideas of free mobility and equal opportunity, the ideological balance between the pursuit of salvation and of worldly advantage was strained to the utmost. Going beyond this middle-class Protestant tradition, Jefferson and Franklin created an essentially secular philosophy in which the ideal of common progress toward a more abundant and humane culture took the place of the goal of individual salvation, and an open society shaped by democratic social institutions replaced the image of a static, hierarchical order. But, in the first half of the nineteenth century, the Protestant tradition was too firmly fixed in the public mind to allow the open confrontation and acceptance of a society governed solely by economic and political motives. Americans accepted the challenge of material abundance, launched themselves in the pursuit of economic expansion, and created a dynamically changing society, but they wanted to be reassured that they had not departed from the traditional synthesis of religious and secular callings. Covertly, they delighted in the

74

amoral enterprise of fictional Sam Slicks and real-life Commodore Vanderbilts; overtly, they gave their approval to the idealized version of success embodied in self-improvement handbooks and didactic novels. But the gap between accepted moral attitudes and changing values was rapidly becoming too great for the traditional formulas to bridge. The coming generations would demand that these formulas be redefined.

CHAPTER III

SELF-IMPROVEMENT AND
SELF-CULTURE: Ralph Waldo Emerson

> This one fact the world hates; that the soul be-
> comes; for that forever degrades the past, turns all
> riches to poverty, all reputation to a shame, confounds
> the saint with the rogue, shoves Jesus and Judas
> equally aside.
> Ralph Waldo Emerson, "Self-Reliance"

In the early 1870's, Francis Parkman, the American historian, unleashed his considerable rhetorical powers against the self-made man:

Our civilization is weak in the head, though the body is robust and full of life. With all the practical vigor and diffused intelligence of the American people, our cultivated class is inferior to that of the leading countries of Europe; for not only does the sovereign Demos think he can do without it, but he is totally unable to distinguish the sham education from the real one. The favorite of his heart is that deplorable political failure, the "self-made man," whom he delights to honor, and to whom he confides the most perplexed and delicate interests, in full faith that, if he cannot unravel them, then nobody else can. He thinks that he must need to be a person of peculiar merit and unequaled vigor. His idea of what constitutes him is somewhat singular. He commends as self-made the man who picks up a half education at hap-hazard; but if, no matter with what exertion, he makes use of systematic and effective methods of training and instructing himself, then, in the view of Demos, he is self-made no longer.[1]

Parkman's attack represented one important tradition of criticism directed against the ideal of the self-made man. Earlier, in the age of Jackson, this tradition was embodied in the polemical novels and tracts of Parkman's favorite American novelist, James Fenimore Cooper. Like Parkman, Cooper rejected the self-made man in favor of the traditional ideal of the gentleman. Cooper believed that American society, despite its democratic political structure, had great need for a cultivated class. Such a class was "the natural repository of the manners, tastes, tone, and to a certain extent, of the principles of a country." [2] The mass of men, rightfully engaged in producing the necessities of life, have neither the time nor the education necessary to preserve and advance the standards of civilized society. "Were society to be satisfied with a mere supply of the natural wants," argued Cooper, "there would be no civilization. The savage condition attains this much. All beyond it . . . is so much progress made in the direction of the gentleman." [3]

Surprisingly, neither Cooper nor Parkman considered themselves opponents of democracy. The very book in which Cooper outlined his conception of an American gentry was entitled *The American Democrat.* In fact, Cooper considered democracy a superior form of polity, not because it eliminated hereditary status, but because he thought democracy preserved the cultivated class from the corruption inevitably incident to the exercise of political power. In a democracy, he argued, the men of wealth and leisure do not have a hereditary political position. Freed from the struggle for power, they can use their greater cultivation to guide the moral and artistic development of the community. It was his belief that, by spurning the social and intellectual leadership

78

of the cultivated class and turning instead to a ridiculous admiration of the self-made man, Americans had embarked on a path that could only lead to the barbaric plutocracy he had portrayed in his satire, *The Monikins*.

Parkman was less inclined to blame this situation on the mass of Americans. Anticipating Santayana's attack on the genteel tradition, he accused the educated class itself of having abdicated its responsibility. "The New England man of letters," he proclaimed, "was apt to be a recluse." Consequently, "the products of his mind were as pallid as the hue of his face, and like their parent, void of blood, bone, sinew, muscle and marrow." [4] Having declined the gambit of life, this emasculate gentleman had abdicated his proper function of maintaining cultural standards and had left the field to the ignorance and pretensions of the self-made man. The gentleman and scholar, Parkman insisted, must return to the political arena and win back the authority he had lost by proving his superiority in the rough and tumble of democratic politics. In effect, Parkman advised the gentleman to beat the self-made man at his own game.

As critics of the self-made man, Cooper and Parkman were American analogues to the great English tradition of Coleridge, Carlyle, Ruskin, and Arnold. Cooper's ideas tended in the direction of a cultural "establishment," although he was far from Coleridge's conception of a clerisy, supported by the government and given the function of preserving the cultural tradition. When they attacked the cultural dominance of narrow economic motives, and emphasized the importance of intellectual and artistic cultivation to the development of American culture, Cooper and Parkman were in line with Matthew Arnold. But Arnold not only anathematized the middle classes, he was, as well, a vigorous critic of the aristocracy. Cooper and Parkman were not prepared to go quite this far. They had faith in the virtue and intelligence of the class to which they belonged: the native American mercantile and landed aristocracy with its tradition of genteel cultivation and public service. Cooper's attack on the self-made man was weakened by his own snobbery and lack of political insight. That he imagined a social class which could exercise significant cultural leadership without also holding a certain degree of political power is some indication of his political naïveté. Because he came from a later generation, perhaps Parkman recognized that to lead the country the cultivated class must also gain political authority. Those who shared his views supported civil service reform as a practical political move to bring men of education and culture into the public service. And yet, insofar as it was supposed to establish the dominance of a specially educated class, this movement only achieved a partial success. The thrust of American democracy was against the ideal of gentlemanly leadership in politics and culture. However valid their criticism of the state of public culture in nineteenth-century America, Cooper and Parkman's gentleman could not unseat the self-made man from his place in the public esteem.

The Ideal of Self-Culture

Cooper and Parkman believed that ambition, particularly when it was based on the pursuit of wealth, threatened cultural standards and led inevitably to a decline in manners and morals. As patrician traditionalists, they reflected an influential minority sentiment, which, though it was rarely embodied in a significant political movement, has had an impact on the development of American culture. But the ideal of the self-made man has also had its philosophical and cultural defenders. Though their ideas ran the gamut from the relatively conventional concept of self-culture expressed by William Ellery Channing to the more radical vistas of Walt Whitman, the intellectual advocates of the self-made man agreed that political democracy and economic mobility were not sufficient until they were completed by the full development of the individual citizen's spiritual potential. For them, the ultimate democratic man was not only self-made but a significant moral and intellectual individual.

Whitman expressed this point of view in its most far-reaching form in his *Democratic Vistas* (1871). His thesis is that the democratic revolution in politics and economics is only a preliminary step in the direction of true democracy. Far from opposing the pursuit of success, Whitman insists that "the extreme business energy, and this almost maniacal appetite for wealth prevalent in the United States, are parts of amelioration and progress, indispensably needed to prepare the very results I demand. My theory includes riches, and the getting of riches, and the amplest products, power, activity, inventions, movements, etc. Upon them, as upon substrata, I raise the edifice design'd in these Vistas." [5] The first stage of "planning and putting on record the political foundation rights of immense masses of people" and the second stage of "material prosperity, wealth, produce, labor-saving machines . . . general employment, organization of great cities, cheap appliances for comfort, numberless technical schools, books, newspapers, a currency for money circulation, &c.," were only the foundation for a third stage, the emergence of a new artistic and intellectual culture:

The Third stage, rising out of the previous ones, to make them and all illustrious, I, now, for one, promulge, announcing a native expression-spirit, getting into form, adult, and through mentality, for these States, self-contain'd, different from others, more expansive, more rich and free, to be evidenced by original authors and poets to come, by American personalities, plenty of

81

them, male and female, traversing the States, none excepted—
and by native superber tableaux and growths of language, songs,
operas, orations, lectures, architecture—and by a sublime and
serious Religious Democracy sternly taking command, dissolv-
ing the old, sloughing off surfaces, and from its own interior and
vital principles, reconstructing, democratizing society.[6]

One great principle would form the basis of this final
stage, that of the fullest development of individual per-
sonality. "To democracy, the leveler, the unyielding
principle of the average, is surely join'd another princi-
ple, equally unyielding, closely tracking the first, indis-
pensable to it. . . . This second principle is individual-
ity, the pride and centripetal isolation of a human being
in himself—identity—personalism." [7]

Whitman believed that this principle could become an
actuality through the power of art. He announced a new
group of American poets, of which he considered him-
self the forerunner, who would create an image of
human personality suitable to the potential of democ-
racy. To prepare the way for these bards, a new idea of
culture was necessary:

I should demand a programme of culture, drawn out, not for a
single class alone, or for the parlors or lecture-rooms, but with
an eye to practical life, the west, the working-men, the facts of
farms and jack-planes and engineers, and of the broad range of
the women also of the middle and working strata, and with ref-
erence to the perfect equality of women, and of a grand and
powerful motherhood. I should demand of this programme or
theory a scope generous to include the widest human area. It
must have for its spinal meaning the formation of a typical per-
sonality of character, eligible to the uses of the high average
of men—and *not* restricted by conditions ineligible to the
masses.[8]

Although he looked to the future and his program had
an ambience of prophecy which would probably have
made the supporters of lyceums and mechanics' insti-

tutes a little nervous, Whitman's vision of a new American culture grew out of an age rich in cultural institutions aimed at providing intellectual and artistic as well as economic opportunities for the mass of American citizens. In 1826, for example, Timothy Claxton, an English immigrant, founded the Boston Mechanics' Institution and the *Young Mechanic,* a paper which promoted the idea of self-education for artisans and mechanics. Other institutions of the same type soon appeared, along with libraries, lecture-series, and other organizations created to give members of the working class opportunities for self-culture. Typical of these institutions were the appropriately entitled Franklin Lectures, established in Boston in 1831 to "give entertainment and instruction, upon terms so moderate, that everybody might attend them." In the same year that saw the opening of Claxton's Mechanics' Institution, Josiah Holbrook, a well-to-do farmer of Millbury, Massachusetts, founded the first American lyceum. The idea of the lyceum spread like wildfire across the country, and by 1831 the delegates of a thousand town lyceums organized the National American Lyceum in New York City. By the 1850's, institutions for self-culture blanketed the northern and western states.

Behind any broad popular movement of this sort, there is usually a considerable diversity of motives and interests. This was certainly the case with self-culture. In part, the broad interest in popular educational institutions reflected the demand for a common-school education which Americans were soon to undertake as a public responsibility. But other interests temporarily found a common ground in the self-culture movement: there were workers and farmers seeking to increase their skills or to become more successful economically; there were philanthropists who felt a moral duty to extend some of the cultural benefits they enjoyed to the

83

less fortunate; there were businessmen seeking a better trained and more docile labor force, and determined aristocrats who hoped that education would teach the rising classes to respect the leadership of their social superiors. Finally, there were men who dreamed of a society in which all men would have the opportunity to develop their spiritual and creative potential.

In one of the classic expressions of the ideal of self-culture, William Ellery Channing clearly indicated the difference between the traditional idea of self-improvement and the broader goal of self-culture. Channing believed that by creating a mobile society Americans had succeeded in resolving the age-old conflict between the rich and the poor. Where is the property in this country? he asked. "Locked up in a few hands? Hoarded in a few strong boxes? It is diffused like the atmosphere, and almost as variable, changing hands like the seasons, shifting from rich to poor, not by the violence but by the industry and skill of the latter class." [9] Since wealth is available to all who will work for it, society is stable, orderly, and generally just. The poor, since "they possess unprecedented means of bettering their lot," will never "be prepared to make a wreck of the social order, for the sake of dividing among themselves the spoils of the rich, which would not support the community for a month." [10]

Thus, according to Channing, the problems facing Americans were not political or economic, but cultural. The average American must be given the opportunity to develop his mind as well as to gain wealth or rise in society. Without education, the poor would be unfairly hampered in the natural process of self-advancement. Some might turn to improper and socially disruptive means to advance themselves. But, in Channing's mind, there was an additional, even more important reason for self-culture:

I have all along gone on the principle, that a man has within him capacities of growth, which deserve and will reward intense, unrelaxing toil. I do not look upon a human being as a machine . . . but as a being of free spiritual powers; and I place little value on any culture, but that which aims to bring out these and to give them perpetual impulse and expansion. I am aware, that this view is far from being universal. The common notion has been, that the mass of the people need no other culture than is necessary to fit them for their various trades; and though this error is passing away, it is far from being exploded. But the ground of a man's culture lies in his nature, not in his calling. His powers are to be unfolded on account of their inherent dignity, not their outward direction. He is to be educated, because he is a man, not because he is to make shoes, nails, or pins.[11]

Channing criticized those who desired self-improvement only in order to rise in the world. So low an impulse could produce only a "stinted, partial uncertain growth." [12] He insisted, however, that self-culture, properly pursued, was not without practical application. One of its chief ends was to fit men for action, but it did so not by teaching the individual how to succeed in business, but by showing him how to discover and develop the creative potential which lay deep within his soul. From this point of view, self-culture was not only a social and economic advantage but a spiritual responsibility, "a solemn duty." [13]

The advocates of self-culture shared Cooper and Parkman's concern for intellectual and artistic achievement, but they would have no commerce with a hereditary cultivated class. Believing in the tremendous creative power inherent in all individuals, the self-culture movement was, in many respects, far more sympathetic to individual mobility and social innovation than moralistic apostles of the Protestant ethic like Henry Ward Beecher and T. S. Arthur. Nowhere is this more apparent than in the thought of the most eloquent and widely read spokesman of self-culture, Ralph Waldo Emerson.

In his essays and lectures, most of which were originally created for that primary institution of self-culture, the lyceum, Emerson made an impressive synthesis of the diverse ideals of self-improvement, success, and self-culture which had developed in the early nineteenth century, shaping them into a pattern with his own transcendental philosophy.

The Individual and the Oversoul

An ardent and consistent proponent of self-improvement, Emerson chanted "welcome evermore to gods and men is the self-helping man." [14] His faith in self-culture was supported by his transcendental philosophy of the Oversoul, a universal spirit immanent in all things. Self-reliance, living in harmony with this fundamental principle of being, was, in Emerson's philosophy, the ultimate foundation of human culture. Traditional ideals of culture were as much a barrier as a means to the fullest development of the individual. The energy of the Oversoul, he proclaimed, "does not descend into individual life on any other condition than entire possession. It comes to the lowly and simple; it comes to whomsoever will put off what is foreign and proud." [15] "Build . . . your own world," Emerson declared. "As fast as you conform your life to the pure idea in your mind, that will unfold its great proportions." [16] The vigor and independence of "a sturdy lad from New Hampshire or Vermont, who in turn tries all the professions, who *teams it, farms it, peddles,* keeps a school, preaches, edits a newspaper, goes to Congress, buys a township, and so forth . . . and always like a cat falls on his feet, is worth a hundred of these city dolls" who study at college and are totally disheartened if "not installed in an office within one year afterwards in the cities or suburbs of Boston or New York." [17]

86

The rugged young self-made man, with his vigor, confidence, and constant enterprise, was, for Emerson, a symbol of the free and self-reliant spirit. Although his ultimate dream was the realization of spiritual laws in individual life, Emerson did not confine his attention solely to the realm of the ideal. His own experience had taught him that men could not satisfactorily conduct their lives without a discipline of the body and mind as well as a cultivation of the soul. Far from being an impractical idealist, Emerson tried to comprehend the lower law of things as well as the higher law of man. "We live amid surfaces, and the true art of life is to skate well on them." [18] With such a motto, Emerson became a philosopher of success as well as the apostle of true self-reliance, its higher spiritual correlative.

The Way of the World

Compared to the hymns to industry, frugality, integrity, and piety that filled much of the literature of self-improvement in his day, Emerson's ideas about worldly success were surprisingly realistic. The first requisite for success was knowledge of and obedience to the laws of the world. "Things have their laws as well as men; and things refuse to be trifled with." [19] "Success," he argued, "consists in close obedience to the laws of the world, and since those laws are intellectual and moral, an intellectual and moral obedience." [20] This meant that wealth and property were usually signs of a man's possession of worldly virtues. Of course, wealth did not always indicate that its possessor had worldly understanding and a knowledge of the laws of nature. Sometimes men received money through inheritance, sometimes through luck, sometimes through cheating and crime. Wealth and property as signs of worldly knowledge could be "counterfeit" and misleading. But, on the

87

whole, Emerson was convinced that a man who had actually earned wealth through his own labors, and not through adventitious circumstance, had demonstrated a high cultivation of his worldly understanding.

The cultivation of the understanding as a means to worldly success required, in Emerson's mind, a number of important convictions and mental qualities.

All successful men have agreed in one thing,—they were *causationists*. They believed that things went not by luck, but by law; that there was not a weak or a cracked link in the chain that joins the first and last of things. A belief in causality, or strict connection between every trifle and the principle of being, and, in consequence, belief in compensation, or, that nothing is got for nothing,—characterizes all valuable minds, and must control every effort that is made by an industrious one.[21]

Other mental qualities were equally important. Since property was an intellectual production, its acquirement required coolness, right reasoning, promptness, and patience. Better order, timeliness, and being at the right spot were far more important than industry and frugality, but perhaps the key intellectual trait of the successful man was the ability to combine long-range planning and complicated combinations of elements with a careful and detailed attention to specific facts.

In addition to these qualities of mind, success required definite traits of temperament and physique. Like all believers in self-help, Emerson insisted "there is always a reason, *in the man,* for his good or bad fortune, and so in making money." [22] Health, of course, was essential. Almost equally important were personal force and magnetism. To describe these qualitities, Emerson used a metaphor from electricity, indicating the correspondence between human and natural force; "Success goes thus invariably with a certain *plus* or positive power: an ounce of power must balance an ounce of weight." [23] Not a wholly benevolent quality, this power often appeared "in the supersaturate or excess, which makes it dangerous and destructive." "Yet," Emerson added, "it cannot be spared." [24] He observed this force in successful businessmen, and in powerful political leaders whose actions he frequently disapproved, but whose personal vigor was essential to the solution of large problems. Emerson believed that, like all things, this power was lawful and could be attained by any man who set his mind and will to the matter. To develop it, he recommended concentration, "the stopping off decisively our miscellaneous activity, and concentrating our force on one or a few points"; and "drill, the power of use and routine."

The discipline of experience or what more rugged advocates of success called "the school of hard knocks," was also important to worldly success. Poverty and debt can be demoralizing, but they can also be a source of invaluable discipline. "Debt, grinding debt, whose iron face the widow, the orphan, and the sons of genius fear and hate—debt, which consumes so much time, which so cripples and disheartens a great spirit with cares that seem so base, is a preceptor whose lessons cannot be foregone, and is needed most by those who suffer from it most." [25] "The first-class minds . . . had the poor man's feeling and mortification," Emerson said, and added that "all great men come out of the middle classes." Therefore, "the wise workman will not regret the poverty or the solitude which brought out his working talents." A poor young man may look with envy on the child of wealth, born into the lap of fortune, but he is really the lucky one, for " 'tis a fatal disadvantage to be cockered, and to eat too much cake." [26]

Napoleon was Emerson's model of worldly success and one of his "representative men." The Corsican possessed in supreme measure those qualities of temperament and understanding that Emerson considered the keys to success. He had that *"plus* condition of mind and body" to the fullest extent—"What a force was coiled up in the skull of Napoleon!" [27]—and a fully developed understanding of the laws of the world, along with all the mental qualities of the worldly success: coolness, timeliness, attention to facts, careful calculation, and the power of combining grand design with minute attention to fact. In addition, Napoleon had the inestimable advantage of being a self-made man.

To these gifts of nature, Napoleon added the advantage of having been born to a private and humble fortune. In his later days he had the weakness of wishing to add to his crowns and badges the prescription of aristocracy; but he knew his debt to his austere education, and made no secret of his contempt for the born kings, and for "the hereditary asses," as he coarsely styled the Bourbons.[28]

Napoleon, as the historical agent of the vigorous and enterprising middle classes, was the living representative of "the young and the poor who have fortunes to make" and of those who desire "to keep open every avenue to the competition of all, and to multiply avenues." [29]

Beyond Success

But if Napoleon was the supreme embodiment of worldly success, his career and character also demonstrated the final inadequacy of this ideal. "I am sorry that the brilliant picture has its reverse," Emerson said, "but that is the fatal quality which we discover in our pursuit of wealth, that it is treacherous, and is bought by the breaking or weakening of the sentiments." [30] Seen from a higher level, Napoleon was "singularly destitute of generous sentiments," was "unjust . . . egotistic and monopolizing . . . a boundless liar" with "a passion for stage effect." In short, "when you have penetrated through all the circles of power and splendor, you were not dealing with a gentleman, at last; but with an impostor and a rogue; and he fully deserves the epithet of *Jupiter Scapin,* or a sort of Scamp Jupiter." [31]

The ultimate failure of Napoleon was not caused by personal vice, but was inevitable in the present state of human culture. The democratic system of opportunity for all was, according to Emerson, the best for the present. From a higher point of view, the advocates of free mobility differed only in degree from the defenders of established wealth "because both parties stand on the one ground of the supreme value of property, which one endeavors to get, and the others to keep." [32] Wealth and power were goals of a lower ideal of success which "the eternal law of man and of the world" would not permit to lead anywhere but to frustration.

As long as our civilization is essentially one of property, of fences, of exclusiveness, it will be mocked by delusions. Our riches will leave us sick; there will be bitterness in our laughter, and our wine will burn our mouth.[33]

What success might be like in a world whose institutions and social organization were more in accordance with the higher laws of the Oversoul, Emerson could hardly predict. He was certain, however, that men could achieve a higher success than wealth and power:

At present, man applies to nature but half his force. He works on the world with his understanding alone. He lives in it and masters it by a penny-wisdom; and he that works most in it is but a half-man, and whilst his arms are strong and his digestion good, his mind is imbruted and he is a selfish savage.[34]

In his late essay on "Success," published in *Society and Solitude,* Emerson attempted to set down some of the canons and methods of true success as opposed to the "haggard, malignant, careworn running for luck" that had come to be "the popular notion of success" in Amer-

91

ica. The true success would be marked by self-reliance and self-trust, sensibility, or homage to beauty and truth, and what Emerson called an embracing of the affirmative. Although the examples he chose of the latter quality sound a little like Norman Vincent Peale— "Don't be a cynic and disconsolate preacher. Don't bewail and bemoan. Omit the negative propositions. Nerve us with incessant affirmatives"—his conception was no facile optimism. He stated it more impressively when he insisted that the questions to ask of a man in evaluating his true success were

what does he add? and what is the state of mind he leaves me in? Your theory is unimportant; but what new stock you can add to humanity, or how high you can carry life? A man is a man only as he makes life and nature happier to us.[35]

The Present and the Future

In the long run, Emerson believed that the American system of opportunity and the traditional conception of hereditary aristocracy were both based on the false principles of property and exclusiveness. However, he was certain that of the two systems, the open society was best because it made property and power fall into the hands of the most vigorous and progressive men, those Jefferson called the natural aristocracy. In spite of the growth of democracy, the fact of aristocracy was "as commanding a feature of the nineteenth century, and the American republic, as of old Rome, or modern England," [36] Emerson insisted. A society based on exclusiveness must inevitably have an aristocracy, but let it be a real one. "We must have kings, and we must have nobles. Nature provides such in every society,—only let us have the real instead of the titular. Let us have our leading and inspiration from the best." [37]

Unfortunately, men are more easily influenced by the

prestige of wealth and fashion than by genius and vir-
tue, and have an "inextinguishable prejudice . . . in
favor of a hereditary transmission of qualities." Emer-
son believed, as Jefferson did, that most aristocracies
were artificial. "The persons who constitute the natural
aristocracy," Emerson explained, "are not found in the
actual aristocracy, but only on its edge; as the chemical
energy of the spectrum is found to be greatest just out-
side of the spectrum." [38] The natural aristocracy is con-
stituted largely of self-made men, too busy making their
way to become "society's gentlemen." The artificial
aristocracy cannot long defend its ranks against the in-
roads of the "class of power." "A natural gentleman
finds his way in, and will keep the oldest patrician out
who has lost his intrinsic rank." Thus, the typical his-
tory of aristocracy, unless protected by hereditary bar-
riers and legal prescriptions, was in accordance with
the rule of from shirt-sleeves to shirt-sleeves in three
generations. "Fashion . . . is virtue gone to seed. . . .
Great men are not commonly in its halls. . . . They are
the sowers, their sons shall be the reapers, and *their*
sons, in the ordinary course of things, must yield the
possession of the harvest to new competitors with
keener eyes and stronger frames." [39]

In his discussion of the natural aristocracy, Emerson
largely ignored the fundamental Jeffersonian idea of
the democratic political community with its social insti-
tutions shaping and directing the process of mobility.
Indeed, Emerson's politics were sublimely negative.
Perhaps his fundamental political principle was that
the state must follow the character of the citizen, a
truism insofar as it suggests that there are basic limits
to the complete freedom of action of any government,
but clearly false insofar as it denies that institutions
shape men as much as men shape institutions. His
thought was subtler than most of his contemporaries',

93

his faith in the potential of a democratic culture was a profound conviction, and he clearly recognized how far the American reality was from his ideal; yet, Emerson's philosophy was marked by the same fundamental weakness which limited the effectiveness of the self-culture movement as a whole: its inability to take politics seriously. Like many other advocates of self-culture, Emerson was greatly concerned about some of the political and economic developments of his day. He was a vigorous critic of the individualistic, self-seeking ethos which he saw as characteristic of American business:

The general system of our trade, (apart from the blacker traits, which, I hope, are exceptions denounced and unshared by all reputable men,) is a system of selfishness; it is not dictated by the high sentiments of human nature; is not measured by the exact laws of reciprocity; much less by the sentiments of love and heroism, but is a system of distrust, or concealment, of superior keenness, not of giving, but of taking advantage.[40]

Emerson also felt that the American political system had not lived up to its promise. The leaders of the Democratic party, he said, "have not at heart the ends which give to the name of democracy what hope and virtue are in it," while the Whigs were "timid, and merely defensive of property."[41] "'Tis a wild democracy," he once exploded, "the riot of mediocrities and dishonesties and fudges. Ours is the age of the omnibus, of the third-person plural, of Tammany Hall."[42]

Yet, believing that the development of human society was a one-way process in which the renovation of individuals had to precede the creation of new social institutions, Emerson was content to let the future take care of itself. His overriding faith in the power of the Oversoul and the greatness of the American destiny made him fearful of political action which might impede progress by erecting artificial barriers to the natural flow of power and ability. He and most of his fellow advocates of self-culture had a zeal for education and for the creation of the widest possible opportunities for all men. But, suspicious of or uninterested in politics, they failed to realize that no system of education could go very far beyond the existing social and political values of the community. Thus, the self-culture movement had a tendency to attack the problem of democratic culture at the wrong level. Although the mechanics' institutes and the lyceums of the age of Jackson as well as the Chautauquas of the later nineteenth century made the idea of self-culture a vital popular tradition, leaders and spokesmen were rarely able to grasp the political implications of their endeavor. Along with Emerson, they encouraged Americans to cultivate their souls, and created institutes, lecture series, and correspondence courses to help them do it. But they waited upon history to bring about the rich democratic culture of which they dreamed.

From Self-Reliance to Positive Thinking

Just as the legend of Lincoln was the highpoint of the self-made man, so Emerson's philosophy was, in terms of breadth and scope of vision, the zenith of self-culture in America. No political leader after Lincoln embodied so dramatically or profoundly the ideal of mobility. As he was apotheosized in legend, Lincoln was the common man made great. The poverty-stricken youth who had to educate himself by the fitful flame of an open fire became one of the great leaders of history and the martyr-savior of the open society which had made his achievement possible. By his side, the conquests of Napoleon seemed temporary and insignificant, for Lincoln's success was spiritual rather than worldly. It was, as the legend portrayed it, a victory of the human spirit, a testament to the greatness and worth of the individual, rather than a political triumph. Lincoln's individual greatness became a fulfilment of the ideal of the self-made man in its highest and deepest aspiration. It summed up both the popular dream of fame and fortune and the philosopher's vision of free moral and spiritual growth which had found expression in the self-culture movement. Later nineteenth-century publicists tried to make the Lincoln legend stretch to fit other political and economic leaders. Horatio Alger, having treated Lincoln in a book entitled *Abraham Lincoln, the Young Backwoods Boy; or, How a Young Rail Splitter Became President,* wrote a companion volume, *From Canal Boy to President; or, The Boyhood and Manhood of James A. Garfield.* But Garfield, a self-made man, was hardly a Lincoln. Nor, for all his greatness as an industrial organizer, was Andrew Carnegie, although when he wrote his Franklinesque *Autobiography* he attempted to display his career as an illustration of the ideals of self-improvement and self-culture. The trouble was, first of all, that Lincoln was not a typical figure but unique, a historical combination of individual genius and special circumstance which could hardly be duplicated. As a symbol of American aspirations and ideals, he was supreme; but as a literal model for aspiring young men, his career, particularly after it had been idealized by the apostles of self-improvement, was hardly typical of the increasingly complex industrial society of the late nineteenth century.

Lincoln had no successors as the ideal self-made hero; Emerson was the last important American thinker to express the ideals of self-improvement and self-culture without serious reservations. As a lyceum lecturer in constant demand, Emerson was able to maintain himself in direct and continuous communication with the hopes and dreams of the mass of his fellow countrymen. In succeeding generations, America's most important cultural leaders—the philosophers, writers, and social critics of the late nineteenth century—became increasingly critical of the popular ideal of self-improvement. Their attacks did not immediately shake the faith of the majority, but the fruitful interplay between popular aspirations and serious philosophy, which had been a part of the self-culture movement, gradually ceased to exist. It is unlikely that many of Emerson's contemporaries were able to follow all the turns of his thought; and many believed him to be a particularly eloquent apostle of the traditional gospel of work and win. And yet Emerson's ideas and terms made a deep impact on the popular imagination. His conception of the Oversoul and his belief that the truly self-reliant individual could be transformed by uniting himself with powerful universal forces, were simplified and popularized in the "New Thought" movement of the early twentieth century. In this movement, Emersonian self-reliance was metamorphosed into personal magnetism and made the key to a financial success available to all. In *The Conquest of Poverty*, a New Thought tract that ironically led to the indictment of the author for fraudulent use of the mails, the influence of Emerson, in debased and perverted form, was clear:

What! Can a person by holding certain thoughts create wealth? Yes, he can. A man by holding certain thoughts—if he knows the Law that relates effect and cause on the mental plane—can actually create wealth by the character of the thoughts he entertains. . . . The weakest man living has the powers of a god folded within his organization; and they will remain folded until he learns to believe in their existence, and then tries to develop them.[43]

And somewhat later, in the 1920's, Roger Babson, one of the popular philosophers of success, announced that the basic law of getting on in the world was none other than

97

"The Law of Action and Reaction"—the Emersonian idea of compensation.

What is the biggest thing in the world? Some may suggest "The World War." Another may suggest the "United States Steel Corporation," another the "Republican Party," and still another, some power that has shaped the destinies of the world. But my own answer to the question is different, as I believe that the biggest thing in the world is the *law of action and reaction,* namely, *for every action there is an equal and opposite reaction.*[44]

Emerson cannot be held responsible for the way in which self-elected followers oversimplified and distorted his ideas. Nor should we forget that there were other important lines of Emersonian influence, those running through Whitman into twentieth-century American art, literature, and music, and through William James and John Dewey into the philosophies of pragmatism and progressive education. But neither Whitman, James, nor Dewey had the kind of direct and immediate relationship with the popular tradition of self-improvement that Emerson did. The popular tradition continued to develop without significant impact from the most creative intellects of the period. By a process somewhat similar to the one by which Jeffersonianism had hardened into the fixed and increasingly sterile ideology of agrarianism, the ideal of self-culture became narrower and more rigid, its apostles repeating over again their oversimplified version of Emerson's philosophy and failing to respond to the challenges of modern society. In the end, Emerson's vigorous philosophy dwindled into the ritualistic self-deception of New Thought and its twentieth-century offshoots, while America's cultural leaders turned away from the exciting adventure of self-culture to a more traditional and formal conception of education.

98

CHAPTER IV

FROM RAGS TO RESPECTABILITY:
Horatio Alger

> Luke Walton is not puffed up by his unexpected and remarkable success. He never fails to recognize kindly, and help, if there is need, the old associates of his humbler days, and never tries to conceal the fact that he was once a Chicago Newsboy.
>
> Horatio Alger, *Luke Walton*

Today his books are read more often by cultural historians than by children, and such erstwhile classics as *Struggling Upward* and *Mark, The Matchboy* are no longer on the shelves of libraries, but the name of Horatio Alger has become synonymous with the self-made man. American businessmen who commission brief biographies often are described in the following manner:

The Horatio Alger quality of William J. Stebler's rise to the presidency of General American Transportation Corporation makes one almost pause for breath.[1]

There is even a Horatio Alger award presented annually by the American Schools and Colleges Association to eight Americans who have reached positions of prominence from humble beginnings. In recent years, this award, a bronze desk plaque, has been presented to such leading industrialists and financiers as Benjamin F. Fairless, retired chairman of the United States Steel Corporation; James H. Carmichael, chairman of Capital Airlines; and Milton G. Hulme, president and chairman of a large investment banking firm in Pittsburgh. The creator of *Ragged Dick* has become a familiar idol to Americans concerned about the decline of what they refer to as "individualistic free enterprise." *Advertising Age* in December, 1947, tired of "government interference" in business, begged for a new Horatio Alger to inspire American youth with the independence and enterprise of their fathers.

Many of those who parade under Alger's mantle know little about their hero beyond the fact that he wrote books about success. They would probably be startled if they read one, for Alger was not a partisan of "rugged individualism," and only within limits an admirer of pecuniary success. For a patron saint of success, his life was rather obscure. Born in 1832 in Revere, Massachusetts, he was trained for the ministry at the insistence of his domineering father. He soon gave this up when he found he could support himself by writing children's books. He published a collection of sentimental tales in 1856, and his first widely popular juvenile, *Ragged Dick,* was published serially in Oliver Optic's (William T. Adams) *Student and Schoolmate* magazine, and as a book, in 1867. Alger moved to New York about 1866 and, aside from an occasional trip West and to Europe, spent most of his life in and around the Newsboys' Lodging House, an institution which figures in many of his stories. Its superintendent, Charles O'Connor, was one of his few close friends. Alger, whose books made fortunes for several publishers, died a relatively poor man. He sold most of his books outright for small sums, and spent what money he received in acts of spontaneous and unflagging charity to help almost anyone who applied to him. His amazingly rapid composition of books like *Grit, the Young Boatman of Pine Point* and *Jed, the Poorhouse Boy* was interspersed with occasional efforts at a serious novel, desultory participation in various reform movements—New York Mayor A. Oakey Hall, member of the Tweed ring, once named him chairman of an anti-vice commission—and brief forays into education (he sometimes tutored boys in Greek and Latin to supplement the income from his books).

Alger's death in 1899 did not put an end to the publication of Alger books. Publishers hired ghosts like Edward Stratemeyer, later the author of the Rover Boys series, to capitalize on Alger's popularity. Inevitably, there were signs of a reaction. Parents began to protest against what they considered the false values and unreality of the Alger stories, and a number of libraries removed his books from the shelves. They were republished less often in the second decade of the twentieth century, and, after World War I, sales declined rapidly. At the centennial of Alger's birth, in 1932, a survey of New York working children [2] showed that less than 20 per cent of the "juvenile proletariat" had ever heard of Alger; only 14 per cent had read an Alger book; and, even more threatening, a "large number" dismissed the theory of "work and win" as "a lot of bunk." A similar survey taken in the forties revealed that only 1 per cent of 20,000 children had read an Alger book.[3]

Alger and his Predecessors

There was a marked difference between Alger's work and that of his most important predecessor in the field of juvenile fiction. Jacob Abbott, author of the "Rollo" and "Caleb" books, began his extremely successful career as a writer of children's books in the early 1830's with a long, rather heavily theological, tome discussing the Christian duties of young boys and girls. A strong emphasis on evangelical Protestantism remained the central element in his work. Alger, on the other hand, was not so concerned with the role of religion in the lives of his young heroes. There were other important differences between the Abbott boy and the Alger boy. A firm believer in the ethic of industry, frugality, integrity, and piety, Abbott rarely made ambition itself a significant element in his stories. Rollo and Caleb were not poor boys but the scions of well-to-do middle-class families. The typical Abbott book concerns everyday events from which Rollo or Caleb learns an important moral lesson. In *Rollo at Work,* for example, the hero learns how to work through a Lockean course of instruction which instils in him a progressively greater capacity for sustained effort.

Unlike Alger, Abbott chose to write about younger boys from well-established families for whom social mobility was not a significant problem, and his stories reflect the more conservative social views of the upper middle-class audience for which he wrote. As he presents American life, there are rightful and fundamental class distinctions, each class has its particular role, and there is relatively little movement between classes. At the same time, there is no conception of a leisure class in the Abbott books, and, in terms of worldly luxuries, the gulf between the higher and lower ranks is not great. According to Abbott, since every rank has its proper work, there should be no idlers.

In Alger's stories, on the other hand, rising and falling in society are characteristic phenomena. This is not the first appearance in American children's literature of the idea of mobility. Even in the period of Abbott's dominance, some juvenile authors began to write tales anticipating those of Alger. An interesting halfway house can be seen in the works of Mrs. Louisa M.

Tuthill in the period 1830–50. Like Abbott, Mrs. Tuthill generally wrote about boys from well-established families, not the street boys who were Alger's favorite subjects. As an adherent of the Jeffersonian ideal of natural aristocracy, Mrs. Tuthill believed that American institutions properly encouraged the rise of talented and virtuous young men to whatever positions of eminence their merits entitled them. In her *I Will Be a Gentleman,* for example, she attacks the idea of hereditary distinction:

Having no hereditary titles in the United States, there can be no higher distinction than that which belongs to moral worth, intellectual superiority, and refined politeness. A republican gentleman, therefore need acknowledge no superior; he is a companion for nobles and kings, or, what is better, for the polite, the talented, the good. Since such are an American's only claims to distinction, it becomes the more important for him to cultivate all those graces which elevate and dignify humanity. No high ancestral claims can he urge for his position in society. Wealth he may possess, and there are those who will acknowledge that claim; but if the possessor have not intelligence and taste to teach him how to use his wealth, it will only make him a more conspicuous mark for ridicule. Those glorious institutions of New England, common schools, afford to every boy the opportunity to acquire that intelligence and taste, and his associates there are from every class of society. There is no unsurmountable obstacle in any boy's way; his position in society must depend mainly upon himself.[4]

Mrs. Tuthill puts the same limits on rising in society as the didactic novelists of the same period. The candidate for distinction must be talented, virtuous, and refined, although he need not spring from an aristocratic family tradition. This emphasis on gentility and refinement, however acquired, also has an important role in the Alger books. Alger constantly emphasizes neatness, good manners, and the proper clothes, and yet his conception of gentility is far less elevated than Mrs. Tuthill's. In spite of her frequent protestations that the way was open to all, Mrs. Tuthill's heroes spring from respectable families who have the means to educate their children.

Most of the children's literature of the pre-Civil War period deal, with the offspring of secure, middle-class families, but the orphaned boy of the city streets is not without his bards. As early as 1834, a putative autobiography of a bootblack who rose from poverty to be a member of Congress was published with the delightful title *A Spur to Youth; or, Davy Crockett Beaten*. In the following year, Charles F. Barnard published *The Life of Collin Reynolds, the Orphan Boy and Young Merchant*. In this tearful tale, dedicated to the pupils of the Hollis Street Sunday School in Boston, the hero is orphaned when his mother dies and his father goes to sea. Undaunted, he determines to support himself by peddling candy, peanuts, and sundries on the New York ferries. In good Alger fashion, he soon meets the wealthy Mr. J., who is impressed by the boy's history, his industry, and his enterprise and adopts him. Entering Mr. J.'s store, Collin is doing well when the opportunity to sigh forth a highly sentimental deathbed scene proves more attractive to his creator than the fulfilment of material promise. Poor Collin is disposed of in a fall from a horse.

Even closer to the Alger formula is J. H. Ingraham's *Jemmy Daily: or, The Little News Vender*, published in 1843. Ingraham, a hack writer of astonishing fertility, made sentimental romance out of almost any subject. Ingraham's treatment of the newsboy foreshadowed both Alger's characteristic material and his method of treating it. Jemmy Daily and his noble mother, reduced to starvation by a drunken father, are saved when, in a chance encounter, the lovely daughter of a wealthy merchant gives Jemmy food and a sixpence. As a newsboy, Jemmy manages to support his mother. When father becomes intolerable, Jemmy and his mother leave him, a shock which happily reforms the drunkard. The rest of the story concerns Jemmy's fight with a bully and his foiling of the quack Dr. Wellington Smoot's lascivious designs on his mother. Once reformed, the father is granted a convenient death, and Jemmy takes over the family, becoming a clerk under the benevolent tutelage of Mr. Weldon. Jemmy's reward is the promise of a junior partnership and the hand of Mr. Weldon's daughter, the girl who had originally befriended him.

The difference between Ingraham's tale and the typical Alger story is largely a matter of emphasis. The plot and characters are essentially the same, but Ingraham stresses religious conversion and "the great moral temperance reform, which is without question one of the agents of God in ameliorating the condition of fallen man." [5] Jemmy Daily's rise in society and his gradual acquisition of respectability are not as important to him as they were to Alger.

In the 1850's, as urban phenomena became of increasing interest and concern, newsboys and bootblacks were common figures in popular fiction. A. L. Stimson's *Easy Nat* includes an Alger-like street boy adopted by a benevolent farmer, and Seba Smith's wife, a sentimental novelist of considerable popularity, published a long novel, *The Newsboy,* in 1854. [6] This is a typical romantic adventure, containing as one of its many plots the narrative of a poor newsboy's rise to some prominence, through, as usual, the patronage of a benevolent merchant. One writer in the 1850's went so far as to proclaim the newsboy the symbol of a new age:

Our clarion now, more potent than the Fontabrian horn, is the shrill voice of the news-boy, that modern Minerva, who leaped full blown from the o'erfraught head of journalism; and, as the news-boy is in some respects the type of the time—an incarnation of the spirit of the day,—a few words devoted to his consideration may not be deemed amiss.[7]

Alger had considerable precedent for his dramatization of the street boy's rise to social respectability. Nor was he the only writer of his time to employ this subject. In fact, Alger neither created the Alger hero nor was he his only exponent. A flood of children's books by such authors as Oliver Optic, Mrs. Sarah Stuart Robbins, Mrs. Madeline Leslie, and the Rev. Elijah Kellog dealt with the rise to moderate security of a poor boy. Alger, however, outsold them all. Somehow he was able to seize upon just those combinations of characters and plot situations that most engrossed adolescent American boys of the nineteenth century.

Alger's Message

Alger's contemporary position as a symbol of individualistic free enterprise has obscured the actual characteristics of his stories. A number of misconceptions must be cleared away before we can get to the heart of the Alger version of what constitutes success. Here, for example, is a typical interpretation of the Alger hero in a recent book:

Alone, unaided, the ragged boy is plunged into the maelstrom of city life, but by his own pluck and luck he capitalizes on one of the myriad opportunities available to him and rises to the top of the economic heap. Here, in a nutshell, is the plot of every novel Alger ever wrote; here, too, is the quintessence of the myth. Like many simple formulations which nevertheless convey a heavy intellectual and emotional charge to vast numbers of people, the Alger hero represents a triumphant combination—and reduction to the lowest common denominator—of the most widely accepted concepts in nineteenth-century American society. The belief in the potential greatness of the common man, the glorification of individual effort and accomplishment, the equation of the pursuit of money with the pursuit of happiness and of business success with spiritual grace: simply to mention these concepts is to comprehend the brilliance of Alger's synthesis.[8]

This passage illustrates several important misconceptions concerning Alger's books. In the first place, Alger's heroes are rarely "alone and unaided," and do not win their success entirely through individual effort and accomplishment. From the very beginning of his career, the Alger boy demonstrates an astounding propensity for chance encounters with benevolent and useful friends, and his success is largely due to their patronage and assistance. In the course of his duties Fred Fenton, the hero of *The Erie Train Boy,* meets a wealthy young girl named Isabel Archer—presumably named in homage to Alger's literary idol, Henry James—who gives him money to pay his mother's rent. In addition, he encounters an eccentric miner, who later helps him sell some land belonging to his late father, and the uncle of a wealthy broker, who gives young Fred his chance in business. Alger's heroes are well aware of their indebtedness to these patrons, and modestly make no pretense of success through their own efforts, although Alger assures his readers that they deserve their advancement. Ragged Dick, congratulated on his achievement by one of the innumerable wealthy men who befriended him, replies: " 'I was lucky,' said Dick, modestly. 'I found some good friends who helped me along.' " [9]

Nor did the Alger hero rise "to the top of the economic heap." Some years ago a writer for *Time,* in a mathematical mood, calculated that the average Alger hero's fortune is only $10,000. Usually the hero is established in a secure white-collar position, either as a clerk with the promise of a junior partnership or as a junior member of a successful mercantile establishment. None achieve anything resembling economic or political prominence. Moderate economic security would best summarize the pecuniary achievements of the typical Alger hero, in spite of such tantalizing titles as *Fame and Fortune, Striving for Fortune,* and *From Farm to Fortune.* For example, at the end of *Fame and Fortune,* the hero is in possession of a magnificent income of $1,400 a year, plus the interest on about $2,000 in savings. In Alger's mind, this was "fame and fortune."

We may admit that Alger's representation of economic reality was highly sentimentalized, but it is unfair to call him an uninhibited adulator of wealth who equated spiritual grace with business success. The true aim of the Alger hero is respectability, a happy state only partially defined by economic repute. Nor was Alger unaware that many men were successful as the result of questionable practices. He may have lacked knowledge of these practices, but Alger frequently reminded his readers that many wealthy and successful men were undeserving of their fortunes. One of his favorite villains is the wealthy, unscrupulous banker who accumulates wealth by cheating widows and orphans. On the whole, Alger's formula is more accurately stated as middle-class respectability equals spiritual grace.

Alger was no more an unrestrained advocate of the "potential greatness" of the common man than he was of the uninhibited pursuit of financial success. His heroes are ordinary boys only in the sense of their lowly origin. In ability and personal character they are far above average. Many boys in the Alger books are unable, in spite of their earnest efforts, to rise above a lowly position. Micky McGuire, a young slum boy who is a secondary character in the *Ragged Dick* series, is reformed at last through the efforts of Dick and his patron Mr. Rockwell. But the old maxim "No Irish Need Apply" still held for Alger.

110

Micky has already turned out much better than was expected, but he is hardly likely to rise much higher than the subordinate position he now occupies. In capacity and education he is far inferior to his old associate, Richard Hunter, who is destined to rise much higher than at present.[10]

Who, then, is the Alger hero, and what is the nature of the adventures in which he is involved? Alger has two types of heroes. The first, and probably the more popular, is the poor, uneducated street boy—sometimes an orphan, more frequently the son of a widowed mother —who rises to moderate affluence. The second is a well-born and well-educated middle-class youth whose father dies, leaving the son to fend for himself. In some cases a villainous squire or distant relative attempts to cheat the hero out of his rightful legacy, but, in the end, the hero is restored to his inheritance or succeeds in rising to his proper place.

Alger made desultory attempts to vary the character of his hero in each story, but such an achievement was beyond his skill, and the reader could be certain that, whatever the situation, and whether the hero smokes or uses slangy language, the same solid core of virtue is present. Alger's heroes, who range in age from around twelve to eighteen, are in the tradition of the didactic novels of self-improvement. One must give Alger some credit for making his young paragons a little less earnest and more lively than the placid prigs of T. S. Arthur. The Alger hero might begin as an intemperate spendthrift like Ragged Dick, but soon he becomes a master of the traditional virtues of industry, economy, integrity, and piety. He is manly and self-reliant—two of Alger's favorite words—and, in addition, kind and generous. Never a genius, he is usually a boy of above-average intelligence, particularly in the area of mathematics, and is also a strenuous devotee of self-culture. The Alger hero is never snobbish or condescending; in-

111

deed, he is the veritable apotheosis of modesty. Thoroughly democratic in his tastes, he befriends other poor boys and is uniformly courteous to people of all classes. The Alger hero demonstrates to a high degree those traits that might be called the employee virtues: fidelity, punctuality, and courteous deference. It is upon these latter traits that Alger places the greatest stress.

Against his hero, Alger sets three types of boys who serve as foils to the hero's sterling qualities. One of these may be called the lesser hero. He is usually a slightly younger and less vigorous edition of the major figure. The lesser hero often has greater advantages than his friend, but he lacks the enterprise, the courage, and the self-reliance of the hero, and frequently depends on him for protection against the harsh urban world, enabling the hero to demonstrate his courage and generosity. Another boy who appears in almost all the Alger books is the snob. Insisting that he is a gentleman's son, the snob looks down his nose at the hero's willingness to work at such lowly trades as that of bootblack or newsboy. Sometimes the snob is the son of a rich but grasping relative of the hero's, envious of his greater capabilities and endeavoring to get him into trouble. The young snob shows the obverse of all the hero's virtues: he is lazy, ignorant, arrogant, and unwilling to work because he considers it beneath his station. He is overtly contemptuous and secretly envious of the hero's successes. Alger delights in foiling this little monster, usually by arranging for his father to fail in business, thereby forcing the snob to go to work at a salary lower than the hero's.

Another type appearing somewhat less frequently in the Alger books is the poor boy who lacks the intelligence and ability of the hero and is more susceptible to the corruption of his environment. Often he becomes involved in plots against the hero, but is usually won over when he recognizes his true manliness and forgiving character. Although sometimes reformed through the hero's efforts, the Micky McGuire type is doomed to remain in a subordinate but respectable position by his lack of intelligence and enterprise. Curiously enough, these dim-minded characters are Alger's most interesting and vivid creations, and foreshadow the "bad boy" heroes of later juvenile books. In addition, they frequently represent immigrant groups—Irish, Italians, Germans—who, not all bad, play a distinctly inferior role in Alger's version of America.

The adult characters vary no more than the boys in the typical Alger book. The central adult figure is the benevolent businessman whose chance encounter with the hero gives him his big opportunity. Like all adults in Alger, this figure is thinly characterized, his major traits being the ability to recognize and reward the hero's potentialities. He is called upon to deliver long homilies on the virtues requisite to success. Generally, he is a merchant or a highly reputable stockbroker. In his business dealings he is honest and upright, scorning all but the most elevated commercial practices. In effect his role is to serve as an ideal adoptive father for the hero.

The second most important male adult in the Alger books is the villain, who usually has some important hold over the hero. Sometimes he is a mean stepfather, more often a grasping uncle or cousin who becomes the hero's guardian, and frequently a cruel, miserly squire who holds a mortgage on the family property. Whatever his mask, he invariably attempts to assert his tyrannical authority over the hero, and fails. One is tempted to describe him in Freudian terms as the overbearing father-figure whose authority the adolescent hero rejects and overthrows.

Few of the Alger heroes are orphans; the majority

have a widowed mother dependent upon them for sup-
port. Here Alger differs appreciably from his predeces-
sors. The Alger mother stands in a very different rela-
tionship to her doughty young offspring than do the
mothers in the novels of T. S. Arthur. The "Arthurian"
mother is pre-eminently a source of moral authority, an
instructor and preceptor, whose gentle commands the
young hero is expected to obey. In Alger, the mother
rarely commands or instructs; although she presumably
has some hand in her son's development, her authori-
tative function is mentioned only rarely. On the con-
trary, she is both a dependent and an admiring on-
looker. Always gentle and supremely confident in her
son's ability, she never criticizes or disciplines. Indeed,
occasionally she is weak and indecisive, qualities which
might lead the family into difficulty were it not for the
manly self-reliance of her son. Characteristic of the
Alger version of maternity is this interchange between
Paul the peddler and his mother:

"You see, mother, Phil would be sure of a beating if he went
home without his fiddle. Now he doesn't like to be beaten, and
the padrone gives harder beatings than you do, mother."
"I presume so," said Mrs. Hoffman, smiling. "I do not think
I am very severe."
"No, you spoil the rod and spare the child." [11]

The benevolent merchant, the villainous father-figure,
and the gentle and appreciative mother are at the center
of most Alger books. They are joined by a variety of
minor figures, all of whom can be traced to the tradi-
tional stereotypes of the sentimental novel: the warm-
hearted Irish woman, poor and crude, kind and gener-
ous, who helps the hero escape from the villain; the
snobbish female with aristocratic pretensions; the
"stage Yankee" who appears in an occasional novel as a
friend of the hero; and a variety of minor villains, such

as the miserly moneylender, the petty swindler, and, in the Western stories, the stagecoach robber.

From such material, together with carefully accumulated local color—the books are filled with detailed descriptions of New York City—Alger constructed his tales. Almost invariably, they follow the same formula: by an amazing series of coincidences, and a few acts of personal heroism and generosity, the hero escapes from the plots laid by his enemies—usually an unholy alliance between the snobbish boy and the villainous father-figure—and attains the patronage of the benevolent merchant. In generating the action, chance and luck play a dominant role. Alger was apparently aware that the unbelievable tissue of coincidences which ran through his stories put some strain on the tolerance of his youthful readers. In *Struggling Upward,* for example, Linton Tomkins, the lesser hero, chances upon practically every other character in the book in the course of a twenty-minute promenade. Somewhat amazed at this feat, Alger can only remark that "Linton was destined to meet plenty of acquaintances." [12] At the book's conclusion he confesses:

So closes an eventful passage in the life of Luke Larkin. He has struggled upward from a boyhood of privation and self-denial into a youth and manhood of prosperity and honor. There has been some luck about it, I admit, but after all he is indebted for most of his good fortune to his own good qualities.[13]

However much the hero's good qualities may have been involved, and they often seem incidental, Alger is obsessed with luck. The chapter which contains the crucial turning point of the book is invariably entitled ———'s Luck, and every accession to the hero's fortunes stems from a coincidence: the land thought to be worthless suddenly becomes valuable because a town has been built around it; the strongbox which the hero saves from thieves turns out to belong to an eccentric and wealthy old man who rewards the hero; the dead father's seemingly worthless speculation in mining stock is in fact a bonanza.

Alger's emphasis on luck resembles that found in the stories of T. S. Arthur and other apostles of the self-made man in the pre-Civil War era. Like them, he represents American society as an environment in which sudden and unaccountable prosperity frequently comes to the deserving like manna from heaven. To some extent, this reliance on luck or Providence is a literary shortcoming. Both Alger and Arthur turned out books at a tremendous rate; sloppiness and inadequacies in plotting and motivation could be concealed in part by defending coincidence. Furthermore, accident, luck, and chance have always played a large role in folk and popular literature, for they allow for exciting plot manipulation and the maintenance of suspense. It is equally true that the form which the accidental takes in a given work is some indication of the beliefs of an author and his intended audience.

In the case of Arthur and his contemporaries, the accidental assumes the form of the more or less direct intervention of Divine Providence. God acts to reward the deserving, punish the evil, and convert the doubting to a faith in his powers. Alger ignores the religious implications of the accidental. In his stories, luck is seemingly independent of the divine, inhering in the particular social environment of America, with its absence of hereditary class distinctions and the freedom it allows. Because most of the great merchants had been poor boys themselves, they were always on the lookout for deserving young men to assist. If the hero has the daring and self-assurance to seize one of his many opportunities to come to the attention of a benevolent patron, and is also blessed with the virtues of industry, fidelity, and good manners, he is certain to get ahead.

116

Religion itself does not play a major role in the life of the Alger hero. His heroes pray and go to Sunday School willingly enough, but Alger places greater stress on their obligations to others—loyalty to family and employer, and personal assistance to the less fortunate. His books encourage humanitarianism in their emphasis on practical good works and frequent insistence that Americans extend opportunities for worldly success to the juvenile proletariat of the cities. Although, like most writers in the tradition of self-improvement, Alger attributes success and failure to qualities within the individual, he occasionally points out to his young readers that a stifling and corrupting environment can be a major cause of vice and failure. An important factor in the rise of his streetboy heroes is their removal from the streets, where, if they remain, moral decay and poverty are certain. Alger can hardly be granted a profound understanding of the contemporary scene, but sympathy for the underprivileged is strong in his books. Judging from the prominence of his themes, there is as much evidence that Alger was an important influence on future reformers as a popular model for incipient robber barons.

Luck is not the only element in the success of the Alger hero. He has to deserve his luck by manifesting certain important traits which show him to be a fit candidate for a higher place in society. He carries the full complement of middle-class virtues, but these are not solely industry, frugality, and piety. Far more important are those qualities of character and intellect which make the hero a good employee and a reputable member of middle-class society. To his hero's cultivation of these qualities Alger devotes much of his attention. The hero has to learn how to dress neatly and modestly, to eliminate slang and colloquialisms from his speech, and to develop a facility with the stilted and pretentious language that Alger took to be the proper medium of verbal intercourse among respectable Americans. In addition, he has to educate himself. Alger's conception of the liberally educated man is also closely tied to social respectability. It is particularly desirable for the hero to have a neat hand and mathematical ability, but it is also important that he show a smattering of traditional culture. A foreign language is usually the prescribed curriculum. Ragged Dick studies French, for example. Since a foreign language plays no part in the hero's economic life, it is apparently intended by Alger as a certificate of a certain kind of respectability. The ability to learn French or Latin, although he might never have an opportunity to use such a skill, shows that the hero has a respect for learning as an end in itself and is no mere materialist. Thus, the Alger hero is a pale reflection of the ideal of self-culture as well as a devotee of rising in society.

Inner attainments are marked by characteristic external signs. The most crucial event in the hero's life is his acquisition of a good suit. The good suit, which is usually presented to the hero by his patron, marks the initial step in his advancement, his escape from the dirty and ragged classes and his entry upon respectability. It immediately differentiates the hero from the other bootblacks, and often leads to a quarrel with such dedicated proletarians as Micky McGuire. A second important event follows on the first: he is given a watch. The new watch marks the hero's attainment of a more elevated position, and is a symbol of punctuality and his respect for time as well as a sign of the attainment of young manhood. Alger makes much of the scene in which his hero receives from his patron a pocket watch suitably engraved.

Perhaps the most important group of qualities which operate in the hero's favor are those which make him the ideal employee: fidelity, dependability, and a burning desire to make himself useful. In a common Algerine situation, the hero, entrusted with some of his employer's money, is confronted by a villainous robber. At great risk to his own life, he defends his employer's property, preferring to lose his own money, or even his life, rather than betray his patron's trust. Under lesser stress, the hero demonstrates his superiority over the snobs by showing his willingness to perform any duties useful to his employer, and by going out of his way to give cheerful and uncomplaining service without haggling over wages. In *Fame and Fortune,* Roswell Crawford, a snob, is fired from his position as errand boy in a dry goods store when he not only complains of being required to carry packages—work too low for a "gentleman's son"—but has the additional temerity to ask for a raise. Ragged Dick, on the other hand, generously offers to carry Roswell's packages for him. Needless to say, Dick receives a raise without asking for it, because his patron recognizes his fidelity and insists on a suitable reward.

Emphasis on fidelity to the employer's interests is perhaps the worst advice Alger could have given his young readers if financial success was of major interest to them. Contrast the Alger hero's relations with his employers and Benjamin Franklin's as described in the *Memoirs.* Franklin keeps his eyes on his own interests when he works for his brother, and for the Philadelphia printers, Bradford and Keimer; indeed, he shows considerable satisfaction at his ability to turn Keimer's faults to his own benefit. By studying the inadequacies of his former employer he is able to make his own business a success. The Alger hero would never resort to such a self-serving device.

Placed against Emerson and his philosophy of self-reliance, Alger is simply another exponent of the idealized version of the self-made man found in the novels of

T. S. Arthur, Sylvester Judd, and other sentimentalists of the 1840's and 1850's. His understanding of social mobility is on the same level of abstracton and idealization. Emerson, in comparison, has a much more profound understanding of the implications of social mobility and the actual characteristics likely to lead to economic and social advancement, as well as a broader ideal of self-culture. It is as true of Alger as of Arthur that he presents the mobile society through the rose-colored glasses of the middle-class ethical tradition of industry, frugality, and integrity, and the sentimental Christian version of a benevolent Providence.

The great attainment of Alger's hero is to leave the ranks of the "working class" and become an owner or partner in a business of his own. Yet few of Alger's heroes have any connection with such enterprises as mining, manufacturing, or construction, the industries in which most of the large fortunes of the late nineteenth century were made. Alger's favorite reward is a junior partnership in a respectable mercantile house. This emphasis is a throwback to the economic life of an earlier period, when American business was still dominated by merchants whose economic behavior in retrospect seemed refined and benevolent in comparison to the devastating strategies of transcontinental railroad builders, iron and steel manufacturers, and other corporate giants. Alger's version of success is, in effect, a reassertion of the values of a bygone era in an age of dramatic change and expansion.

Alger's Popularity

Today one would hardly expect adolescent boys to respond to Alger's vision of a dying past. His popularity with many older Americans—a phenomenon that continues into the present time—is certainly nostalgic.

Alger is a teacher of traditional manners and morals rather than an exponent of free enterprise. His fictions embody the values that middle-class Americans have been taught to revere: honesty, hard work, familial loyalty; good manners, cleanliness, and neatness of appearance; kindness and generosity to the less fortunate; loyalty and deference on the part of employees, and consideration and personal interest on the part of employers. These "bourgeois virtues" are strenuously displayed by the Alger hero and his benevolent patron, along with that strong respect for education and self-culture which is a considerable part of the middle-class heritage. On the other hand, the Alger villains represent those vices particularly reprehensible to many nineteenth-century Americans: they have aristocratic pretensions and try to adopt the airs of the leisure-class; they frequent theaters and gaming houses and are intemperate; they are disloyal to their families and often try to cheat their relatives; they are avaricious, miserly, and usurious; and they lack integrity and are unscrupulous in business affairs. The conflict between middle-class virtues and vices is played out against a background of unlimited opportunities in which the virtues ultimately show themselves to be indispensable and the vices trip up their possessors.

At the time when Alger wrote, traditional commercial practices and ethics had been undermined by economic expansion. A lifetime of hard work often left a man worse off than when he began. The growing gulf between millionaire and employee and the increasing development of complex economic hierarchies were so circumscribing individual ownership and control that a clerk was better off working for others than attempting to found and operate his own business. Alger reasserts an older economic model, one that had begun to be out of date as early as 1830, but which still lingered in the minds of Americans as the ideal form of economic organization: a multiplicity of small individual businesses or partnerships. He certainly had little idea of the actuality of business enterprise in his day—nowhere in his novels do industrial corporations or the character types they produce appear—but he does have enough personal knowledge of New York City to give a certain plausibility and contemporaneity to his representation of American life. He is able to present the traditional pattern of middle-class economic ideals in late nineteenth-century dress and fill the bustling streets and thoroughfares of a nineteenth-century industrial metropolis with a nostalgic reincarnation of the ideal *eighteenth-century* merchant and his noble young apprentice. This moral and economic anachronism is an important source of Alger's popularity with adults. When, a generation or so later, the accumulation of social and economic change made it no longer tenable, even in fantasy, the books began to come down from the library shelves, classed as unrealistic and misleading, perhaps even dangerous, fairy tales.

Although parents encouraged their children to read Alger because he seemed to reassert the validity of hard work, economy, integrity, and family loyalty, this is probably not the source of his popularity with young boys. There were a great many reasons why children liked Alger. He writes of places that they were interested in. In these locales he places a set of characters whose activities have enough of the fantastic and unusual to be exciting, yet always retain enough connection with the ordinary activities of American boys to encourage an emotionally satisfying empathy. Alger's glorification of financial success has been overemphasized by commentators, but many of his young readers enjoyed dreaming of the day when they would be rich enough to buy gold watches, good clothes, and have others dependent on their beneficences. Furthermore,

Alger has a simple and unsophisticated sense of justice, which punishes the enemies of boyhood. The snobs, the bullies, the uncles and spinster aunts who do not like boys get their comeuppances in ways that must have appealed to a juvenile audience. Alger is hardly a master stylist, but his narrative and dialogue are simple, clear, and relatively fast-moving; and his diction, if formal and stilted, is not arcane or difficult.

These elements were undoubtedly important factors in Alger's popularity with his juvenile audience; and there was a further dimension to the Alger formula. Legion are the dangers of Freudian interpretation of literary works, but Alger cries out for this kind of treatment. Consider the following brief summary, which can apply with variations to almost any of the Alger books: an adolescent boy, the support of a gentle, loving, and admiring mother, is threatened by a male figure of authority and discipline. Through personal heroism he succeeds in subverting the authority of this figure and in finding a new male supporter who makes no threats to his relationship with the mother and does not seek to circumscribe his independence. The pattern is too obvious to require extended comment. When we recall that the late nineteenth century was an era of relatively strict paternal discipline and control, it does not seem far-fetched to suggest that the Alger books may have been appreciated as phantasies of father-elimination. The rapid decline in the popularity of Alger books after World War I probably resulted in part from the changing character of familial relationships in the twenties and thirties. When new ideals of parent-child relationship became generally accepted, the Alger hero's victory over the villainous father-figure must have lost much of its bite.

CHAPTER V

THE SELF-MADE MAN
AND INDUSTRIAL AMERICA:
The Portrayal of Mobility
in the Nineteenth-Century Novel

> So many great fortunes are now made, every year, by lucky strokes, or by a sudden rise in the values of property over the vast field opened, in our day, to enterprise and speculation . . . that the old mode . . . by slowly "working one's way up," by frugality, the practice of industry and by the display of punctuality and integrity merely, may be said to have fallen into disrepute.
>
> E. L. Godkin, *North American Review,* July, 1868

> If you tell a single concrete working man on the Baltimore and Ohio Railroad that he may yet be the president of the company, it is not demonstrable that you have told him what is not true, although it is within bounds to say that he is far more likely to be killed by a stroke of lightning.
>
> Richard T. Ely, *Social Aspects of Christianity,* 1889

Horatio Alger's juvenile phantasies of mobility in America surely reflect the social ideas of some of his contemporaries. Many nineteenth-century adults thrilled to the adventures of a grown-up model of the Alger hero in the novels of popular writers like Mrs. E. D. E. N. Southworth. However, the moralistic ideal of success characteristic of the earlier nineteenth century was shaken, in the seventies and eighties, by social change.

There was no single beginning point for the social,

economic, and ideological revolutions which so drastically transformed American society in the nineteenth century. Even in the thirties and forties, the synthesis of self-improvement was clouded with ambiguities. But the rate of change was accelerated after the Civil War. From 1865 on, more and more Americans were immediately and directly affected by the two major social developments of the nineteenth century: the creation of more complex and more centralized social organizations: cities, corporations, and political institutions; and the growing importance of groups other than the native Protestant middle class of western European background. Both of these developments rapidly broke up the social patterns that had given birth to the ideal of self-improvement. The ideal itself was transformed as it was taken up by new groups and revised to meet new conditions and needs.

It is this complex process of criticism and transformation of the ideal of self-improvement under the impact of the changing social conditions of the later nineteenth century which I shall discuss in this and the succeeding chapter. As a basis for an analysis of the different ways in which Americans understood and criticized the nature of mobility in their new industrial society, I have examined a large number of novels published between 1860 and the end of the century, including the works of major writers like Twain and Howells and those of forgotten but then popular authors like Mrs. Southworth and E. P. Roe.

Alger for Grownups: Mrs. Southworth's Ishmael

Broadly speaking, the treatment of the self-made man in the late nineteenth-century novel reflects two different approaches to the problem of the new American society. Many Americans shared E. L. Godkin's belief that the dislocations of emergent industrialism were largely a function of moral decline and the erosion of traditional ideals. What was needed, they argued, was a reassertion of the traditional gospel of self-improvement and an attack on those individuals and groups whose ideas and goals seemed to be in conflict with the tradition. Others, like Richard T. Ely, came to feel that the accepted conception of success was false and misleading; that the new industrial society could not be understood and controlled in the terms of received economic, social, and ethical thinking. They insisted that Americans re-examine their political and religious assumptions and develop new philosophies of social policy and individual conduct.

Mrs. E. D. E. N. Southworth's sentimental novels illustrate the persistence of the traditional ideal of self-improvement in its simplest form. In 1863–64, Mrs. Southworth, already one of the nation's most popular writers, published *Self-Made, or Out of the Depths*, as a serial in the *New York Ledger*. This long and unusually turgid tale was republished in 1874 and soon thereafter appeared in book form as a two-volume novel under the titles *Ishmael* and *Self-Raised*. One of the best-sellers of the period, it was still being reissued at the beginning of the twentieth century. Street and Smith, the publishers, claimed that "there is hardly a reader in America who has not read this author's 'Ishmael' and 'Self-Raised.' They are classics of the people, and no author of popular fiction has ever been more justly praised, nor held a more secure position in the hearts of American readers than Mrs. Southworth."

The strongest impression that *Ishmael* and its sequel make upon the contemporary reader is equally true of most of Mrs. Southworth's novels—complete and unadulterated absurdity. Yet they obviously appealed to a great many readers, for they were preferred to the nov-

els of Dickens, which they resembled in a superficial
way. The key to *Ishmael*'s great popularity probably lay
in Mrs. Southworth's ability to articulate in fiction the
fondest hopes of her readers, providing a vicarious ful-
filment of dreams which had little chance of realization.
That she was so concerned with the particular aspira-
tions of her own period perhaps provides some explana-
tion for her later decline in popularity during the twen-
tieth century.

Ishmael and *Self-Raised* were largely based on the
formula of the idealized self-made man as worked out by
writers like Timothy Flint, Sylvester Judd, and T. S.
Arthur. It was transmuted, however, into Mrs. South-
worth's own peculiar blend of Dickens, Scott, and
Susanna Rowson's *Charlotte Temple*. Like the earlier
bards of self-improvement, Mrs. Southworth is firmly
convinced that America is a land of opportunity where
the rise of virtuous and talented men to fame and for-
tune is an "illustration of the elevating influence of our
republican institutions."[1] Her hero's story is intended
as an example to youth, to show that "there is no depth
of human misery from which they may not, by virtue,
energy, and perseverance, rise to earthly honors as well
as to eternal glory."[2]

Mrs. Southworth's Ishmael is a paragon of industry,
economy, and piety, who combines the worldly virtues of
Franklin's Poor Richard with sentimental Christianity.
Despite these basic similarities, there are a number of
important differences between *Ishmael* and its predeces-
sors. The earlier novels were predominantly didactic,
full of specific illustrations of moral precepts. If any-
thing, they avoided exciting adventure and dramatic
achievement. Furthermore, these novels were based on
contemporary situations. They sentimentalized the life
and characters they represented, but there was always a
recognizable connection between the problems faced by

the hero of a novel of T. S. Arthur and those confront-
ing an ordinary young American in his career. Verisimil-
itude was important to Arthur because he wanted his
books to move his readers to specific moral activity—the
exercise of greater economy, resistance to the tempta-
tions of high life and the theater, and the swearing off of
beverages stronger than water. In fact, one finds in the
novels of men like Arthur the first tentative fumbling to-
ward the treatment of social subjects like lower-class ur-
ban life that was to become so important to the "realists"
of the late nineteenth century. Arthur sought to impress
a view of life on his young readers, and he realized that
to do so he must explain many of the disturbing phenom-
ena of life with his own moral and religious apparatus.
Therefore, his heroes are usually ordinary young men
confronting common social and occupational problems.

In *Ishmael,* on the other hand, Mrs. Southworth not
only places her story in an earlier period—the golden
age of the early nineteenth century—but makes the cir-
cumstances of Ishmael's career so extraordinary and
unusual that they bear little resemblance to those of her
audience. Through most of the book Ishmael believes
himself a bastard and an orphan. His mother is the wife
of the wealthy and aristocratic Herman Brudenell, but
the marriage has been kept a secret. When his mother
dies in childbirth, Ishmael is brought up by his aunt.
His pristine virtues soon bring him to the attention of
various wealthy and well-established individuals, and he
is given the opportunity for a classical education in the
best gentlemanly style. Hardly has he completed his
studies when his heroic rescue of the lovely Claudia Mer-
lin from runaway horses wins him the patronage of
Judge Merlin. Industriously completing a law course
while serving as the judge's private secretary, Ishmael
soon becomes a lawyer and immediately wins fame at the
bar for his brilliant defenses of persecuted women. He is

129

on his way to fame when his career is sidetracked by another problem. The lovely Claudia—the stereotyped brunette of sentimental fiction—has half-encouraged Ishmael's admiration, but, preferring to make an aristocratic marriage, she accepts the proposal of the noble Lord Vincent. Vincent turns out to be a villain, interested only in Claudia's large fortune. Most of Ishmael's attention in the second volume is devoted to the rescue of Claudia and the foiling of Vincent's artful designs. By the end of the two volumes, Ishmael has not only attained great fame and become one of his country's leading statesmen but has outwitted the leading aristocratic villains of Europe and gained the hand of his true love—the *blonde,* a simple and loving girl who has been his admirer from childhood.

American children in the nineteenth century were repeatedly told, and may have believed, that each and every one of them had a perfectly good chance of becoming President, but it seems doubtful that adult readers of *Ishmael* considered his career within the bounds of possibility. Ishmael's achievement is worked out against the background of an idealized version of an earlier social structure which bears little resemblance to any historical reality and none at all to the world in which later readers lived. Thus the novel is more the celebration of a glorious past than a straight look at the contemporary world. By focusing attention on the glorious achievements of a self-made man in the early nineteenth century, Mrs. Southworth creates a setting into which her readers could escape from the harsher realities of the Gilded Age and a fictional experience in which all the old verities of the middle-class ethic and evangelical Protestantism continue to operate. The middle-class reader, perplexed by strikes, monopolies, large corporations, and the demands of groups adhering to foreign religious and social ideas, finds reassurance that the real meaning of America lies in the values of individualism, hard work, and piety that his parents had taught him, and finds emotional relief in the triumph of an archetypal figure who, embodying these values, wins unblemished fame, fortune, and love.

Beyond Alger: The Revolt of the Old Middle Class

Mrs. Southworth's sentimental Algerism is by no means entirely typical of the popular novels of the later nineteenth century. As the public became more aware of the corruption, chicanery, and social dislocations of the Gilded Age, Algerism was increasingly restricted to works of moral instruction for children. A new group of popular writers created novels for adult audiences which, while reasserting the validity of the ideal of self-improvement, vehemently criticized the new urban, industrial society for its transgression of the traditional faith. The major impulse of these works is an assault on the new social and economic groups—immigrants and organized labor on one hand and the power of large industrial and financial organizations on the other—whose actions do not fit the older pattern of self-help. Unable to conceive of society in any other way than as an aggregation of individuals seeking their individual ends, these popular writers attribute the social problems of the Gilded Age to the folly and cupidity of particular individuals or groups—to the failure of capitalists and working men to follow the prescribed course of industry, frugality, integrity, and piety; to the corrupting influence of the urban masses; to the dangerous folly of immigrants who are unable to understand the true character of American life.

E. P. Roe's *Barriers Burned Away,* a best-seller of the 1870's, is an early example of the revolt of the native

131

middle class. In this novel, Dennis Fleet, the hero, is the son of a New Englander who has moved to the West. When his father dies, Dennis goes to Chicago seeking a job in order to support his destitute mother and sisters. In Roe's description of the city, the reader senses the fear and suspicion with which he, like many rurally oriented Americans, views the ways of life of a burgeoning industrial metropolis. Dennis finds the city a cruel and heartless place. In spite of his eagerness to work, his noble virtues, and his intelligence, he is unable to find a job. But his faith is unwavering and, on the verge of starvation, he discovers that God's Providence is still active, even in the city. When he attempts prayer as a means of seeking employment, Dennis' pleas are answered almost immediately. Getting temporary employment as a snow shoveler for a large and prosperous department store, Dennis is soon on the inside, first as a janitor and then as a clerk. Moreover, his artistic abilities soon bring Dennis to the attention of the wealthy Ludolph, owner of the store.

Ludolph is intended to represent the corrupting influence of foreign ways. A German, he has emigrated to Chicago hoping to make his fortune, return to Germany, and marry his beautiful daughter Christine to a great nobleman. A convinced aristocrat and an atheist, he has trained his daughter to be both. In addition to her aristocratic pretensions, Christine dreams of becoming a great artist, and it is in this connection that Dennis enters her life. She shows him a painting that she has copied from the work of a fine artist, expecting Dennis to praise it highly. He immediately recognizes it as a lifeless copy and tells her so. Furious that he has seen her weakness, Christine encourages Dennis to fall in love with her and then rejects him as a boorish pretender. Dennis falls into a decline at this treatment, and Christine, thinking him dying, remorsefully discovers

132

that she has fallen in love with him. At this point, the great Chicago fire intervenes, Christine is converted, Dennis recovers, the atheistic Ludolph dies in an attempt to save his wealth, and the two lovers are united to start life anew with every barrier burned away.

In *Barriers Burned Away,* the enemies of self-improvement are carefully identified. Resentment at the prestige accorded former members of the working class who accumulate large sums of money in business appears in the characterization of the Browns. Mr. Brown "was a mighty brewer, but he and his were in character and antecedents something like the froth on their own beer."[3] His daughter, a snob, deliberately reminds Dennis of his low station, while Miss Winthrop, her name indicating her role as a symbol of good old American respectability, is uniformly courteous and readily willing to recognize Dennis's merits. Successful foreigners like Ludolph are portrayed very unsympathetically. The city, too, with its extremes of luxury, fashion, and extravagance, is antagonistic to traditional middle-class social ideals. When Dennis first arrives in Chicago, he innocently expects to find there the same kind of recognition of his respectable native origin that he has always experienced in the country, but Roe warns the reader that Dennis

would learn, to his infinite surprise, that even in a Western democratic city men would be welcomed in society whose hand no pure woman or honorable man ought to touch, while he, a gentleman by birth, education, and especially character, would not be recognized at all. He would discover that wealth and the indorsement of a few fashionable people, though all else were lacking, would be a better passport than the noblest qualities and fine abilities. As we follow him from the seclusion of his simple country home into the complicated life of the world, all this will become apparent.[4]

In Roe's hands, the literary idealization of the self-made man is transformed into a phantasy defeat of those

133

forces which are identified as hostile to the prestige and traditional ideals of the native middle-class. This attitude becomes even clearer as the century draws to a close. In 1896, Ella Wheeler Wilcox, a novelist whose plots, characters, and general attitudes indicate her descent from Roe and Mrs. Southworth, published *An Ambitious Man*. In this novel, the hero, Preston Cheney, "a self-made youth with an unusual brain and an overwhelming ambition," finds himself in a society which no longer resembles that happy Utopia of his forefathers when merit and ability assured a rapid rise to security and respectability:

His brain, his strength, his abilities, his ambitions, what were they all in the strife after place and power, compared to the money of some common-place adversary? Preston Cheney, the native-born American directly descended from a Revolutionary soldier, would be handicapped in the race with some Michael Murphy whose father had made a fortune in the saloon business, or who had himself acquired a competency as a police officer. America was not the same country which gave men like Benjamin Franklin, Abraham Lincoln, and Horace Greeley a chance to rise from the lower ranks to the highest places before they reached middle life. It was no longer a land where merit strove with merit, and the prize fell to the most earnest and the most gifted. The tremendous influx of foreign population since the war of the Rebellion and the right of franchise given unreservedly to the illiterate and the vicious, rendered the ambitious American youth now a toy in the hands of aliens, and position a thing to be bought at the price set by un-American masses.[5]

Perhaps the most sweeping indictment of the new American society at the hands of a writer still devoted to the ideal of self-improvement can be found in a novel with an amazing title: *An Iron Crown: or, The Modern Mammon. A Graphic and Thrilling History of Great Money-Makers and How They Got Millions. Both Sides of the Picture—Railway Kings, Coal Barons, Bonanza*

Miners and Their Victims. Life and Adventure from Wall Street to the Rocky Mountains. Board of Trade Frauds, Bucket-Shop Frauds, Newspaper Frauds, All Sorts of Frauds, Big and Little. Although of no literary value, this novel should be compared to Sylvester Judd's *Richard Edney,* which resembles it in encyclopedic portrayal of the reform interests of the 1830's and 1840's.[6] The difference in attitude concerning the source of social evils is striking. Judd, a sincere and serious man in his reform interests, sees very little wrong with the constitution of society, beyond some fear at the growth of cities. In his mind, reform is primarily a matter of freeing the individual from personal vice and thereby enabling him to support himself and become a respectable member of society. T. S. Denison, author of *The Modern Mammon,* feels that almost everything is wrong with the society around him and has a number of very specific proposals for political action aimed at remedying the dangerous situation. In contrast with Judd, he has little hope that individuals, no matter how virtuous and industrious they are, can change the social situation without organized political action. This does not mean that he rejects the ideal of self-improvement, however. His reform proposals are aimed at the creation of a society in which industry, frugality, integrity, and piety will win their proper rewards, and shrewdness, dishonesty, and the manipulation of "un-American" masses will meet with the obliquity they deserve.

Denison vehemently attacks the monopolistic corporation, unchecked speculation, the unrestrained pursuit of great wealth by individuals, and the political corruption of the illiterate urban masses. His heroes are those who through industry, perseverance, and fair dealing try to acquire moderate wealth and to use it in such a way as to benefit society. All of his central characters are self-made men, but some of them arrive at their

135

wealth by dishonesty, corruption, speculation, and mo-
nopoly, while others follow the traditional path of hon-
est industry. In terms of financial accumulation, the
former are infinitely more successful. One "was brought
up a poor farmer's son, among the hills of Western
Massachusetts. His humble origin, like that of so many
men eminent in American history, has no effect in cur-
tailing his visions of a different and vastly exalted
sphere of action for the future." [7] Henry Ingledee
leaves home "to do for himself" at the age of twenty-one.
By thirty he is a successful merchant in an obscure
town in the far West. "At the age of fifty he was worth
fifty millions, and a railway king of world-wide celeb-
rity." [8] Denison finds little to admire in this rapid rise
to wealth and fame. On the contrary, he insists and at-
tempts to demonstrate in his narrative that "It might
have been better for him had he still been a country
school teacher; it certainly would have been much bet-
ter for the country." [9] Ingledee, for all his great success,
is a man of very small merit:

Mr. Ingledee, the many fold millionaire, who almost swayed
the finances of a continent, and who played with railway systems,
as the angler plays with a struggling fish before landing him, had,
with all his force of character, an exceedingly small soul ani-
mated by unworthy and ungenerous motives. He was the very
incarnation of selfishness which is perhaps the most despicable
of human vices. He lived, toiled and dreamed to pile up more
millions, no matter how, and to keep them all in the family in
the person of a worthless son.[10]

His wealth cannot truly be said to be the result of his
own efforts, for much of it is due to luck and chance.
The result of Ingledee's endeavors, a massive and mo-
nopolistic corporation, has the effect of limiting the op-
portunities of other individuals, preventing them from
working honestly to achieve security and respectability.
   Denison strongly condemns those men who seek wealth

and power as the sole ends of life and praises the pursuit of success by the traditional means of industry, frugality, and integrity.

Lest someone may construe these remarks as an attack on all wealth, let me say that large fortunes may be honestly made in legitimate ways. A man by a lifetime of close attention to business, combined with prudent economy, may become very wealthy, and remain strictly honest. I am in sympathy with honest wealth. It is a blessing to the community when in the right hands. It is not a blessing in the hands of monopolists. It is dangerous to give any man too much power. These monopolists of modern days are the successors of the military plunderers.[11]

In contrast to his gallery of unscrupulous self-made men, Denison sets two characters who might well have been lifted out of the pages of T. S. Arthur and Horatio Alger. Arthur Wilson, an honest and industrious young man from the country, fails to succeed in corrupt New York City, but, going West, he makes a lucky strike and discovers a rich mine. Unfortunately, his natural good sense is temporarily overpowered by a desire for millions. Bringing his capital to New York, Arthur Wilson starts a brokerage business. He soon learns his lesson. Fleeced by Wall Street wolves, he manages to save a small amount from the wreckage. With this he retires to New Jersey where he goes into business in a small way and presumably lives happily ever after.

The other wholesome type begins his career as a newsboy, the sole support of his widowed mother and younger brother. Pipe Malley's rise closely resembles that of the typical Alger street boy—although Alger was less likely to make his hero a young Irishman—and Denison glorifies his achievement in similar fashion:

[Pipe Malley] was slowly rising in the world, with increasing prosperity. He wore better clothes, and persistently attempted to improve his speech and manners. Though he was not an ex-

137

traordinary young man yet, only those who have been what Pipe Malley the newsboy was, and have afterward risen in life, can realize what the true self-made man has to encounter in his struggle with the world. To rise unaided from poverty and ignorance to eminence, requires abilities little short of genius.[12]

According to Denison, the city with its illiterate masses is the second major source of danger to American society. Easily corrupted by men like Henry Ingledee, the political machinery of the city has become a plutocracy run for the benefit of selfish monopolists who amass their millions by restricting the opportunities of more honest and respectable men. Only in the country, despite the hardships of rural life, are the true traditions of American democracy preserved intact. One of Denison's spokesmen advises:

Go back to the country. You may never be a rich man, but you will always be sure of honor and a competence by reasonable effort. The country is nature's smiling workshop, the city is a vast treadmill, where every toiler is a beast of burden chained to his post. In the country the self-respecting poor man is an esteemed member of society. The alluring pleasures of city society are not for the poor man, nor even for the man of moderate means.[13]

With eschatological rhetoric Denison predicts that the extension of urban corruption to the country will be a sign of the doom of traditional American institutions:

God forbid that this monster of political corruption should ever crawl from his slimy den in our great cities to fasten on the honest rural districts. When he does so unrebuked, the grandest experiment ever tried, of government by the people and for the people, will be recorded in the book of time as a failure. The weeping genius of liberty, with heavy heart and eye that fondly dwells on history's brightest page, will sadly close forever the record of the last republic, and man's greatest opportunity is lost till the cycles of time shall change the very face of civilization itself.[14]

Algerism on the Run: Mark Twain

Roe and Denison's formula of corrupt politicians, avaricious monopolists, and benighted promoters *vs.* the long-suffering and noble middle class had a great appeal for Americans, the majority of whom, after all, considered themselves as members of that saving remnant. Both Populist and Progressive reform movements tended to attribute the evils they fought to the dominance of the "interests" over the "people." As Woodrow Wilson puts it:

the originative part of America, the part into which the ambitious and gifted working man makes his way up, the class that saves, that plans, that organizes, that presently spreads its enterprises until they have a national scope and character,—that middle class is being more and more squeezed out by the processes which we have been taught to call processes of prosperity.[15]

But, however effective it was as a popular rallying cry, the attack on the "interests" and the cry of moral degeneration was not enough to satisfy many Americans, who found themselves unable to accept the easy assumption that renewed faith in an older social ideal could solve the problems of a rapidly changing society. In the work of the most significant American novelists of the period —Mark Twain, William Dean Howells, and Henry James—the middle-class attack on the surface phenomena of trusts, political corruption, and industrial exploitation is superseded by an attempt to understand the deeper cultural implications of the new industrial society, a more critical view of the traditional ideal of self-improvement, and a questioning of the middle class's claim to be the sole repository of virtue in America.

Mark Twain's earliest social and political satires re-

139

flect the accepted middle-class view of the new social phenomena. For example, "The Revised Catechism," printed in the *New York Tribune* in 1871, is a humorous version of E. L. Godkin's lament that the values of industry, honesty, and piety have been replaced by the philosophy of grab:

Q. What is the chief end of man?

A. To get rich.

Q. In what way?

A. Dishonestly if we can, honestly if we must.

Q. Who is God, the only one and True?

A. Money is God. Gold and greenbacks and stocks—father, son and the ghost of the same—three persons in one; these are the true and only God, mighty and supreme; and William Tweed is his prophet.

Q. How shall a man attain the chief end of life?

A. By furnishing imaginary carpets to the Court-House; apocryphal chairs to the armories, and invisible printing to the city . . . .

Q. Who were the models the young were taught to emulate in former days?

A. Washington and Franklin.

Q. Whom do they and should they emulate now in this era of enlightenment?

A. Tweed, Hall, Connely, Camochan, Fisk, Gould, Barnard, and Winans.

Q. What works were chiefly prized for the training of the young in former days?

A. Poor Richard's Almanac, The Pilgrim's Progress, and The Declaration of Independence.

Q. What are the best prized Sunday-school books in this more enlightened age?

A. St. Hall's Garbled Reports, St. Fish's Ingenious Robberies, St. Camochan's Guide to Corruption, St. Gould on the Watering of Stock, St. Barnard's Injunctions, St. Tweed's Handbook of Morals, and the Court-House edition of the Holy Crusade of the Forty Thieves.

Q. Do we progress?

A. You bet your life.[16]

140

At the same time, Twain ridicules the Algerine conception of success through virtue. His "The Story of a Bad Little Boy" and "The Story of a Good Little Boy," written about 1865, show how the moral injunctions of the self-improvers, scrupulously followed, can only lead to an early and inglorious doom. The good little boy, Jacob Blivens,

had a noble ambition to be put in a Sunday-school book. He wanted to be put in, with pictures representing him gloriously declining to lie to his mother, and her weeping for joy about it; and pictures representing him standing on the doorstep giving a penny to a poor beggarwoman with six children, and telling her to spend it freely, but not to be extravagant, because extravagance is a sin.[17]

When Jacob leaves home to make his way in the world, he carries with him for recommendation a Sunday School tract indorsed "To Jacob Blivens, from his affectionate teacher." He can hardly believe his senses when his application for employment is brusquely refused. After several misadventures, Jacob is blown sky-high by nitroglycerin while hunting up bad little boys to admonish, and

thus perished the good little boy who did the best he could, but didn't come out according to the books. Every boy who ever did as he did prospered except him. His case is truly remarkable. It will probably never be accounted for.[18]

Going to the source of the moral injunctions which he felt were ridiculous when applied too seriously, Twain offers his opinion of "The Late Benjamin Franklin."

The subject of this memoir was of a vicious disposition, and early prostituted his talents to the invention of maxims and aphorisms calculated to inflict suffering upon the rising generation of all subsequent ages. His simplest acts, also, were contrived with a view to their being held up for the emulation of boys forever—boys who might otherwise have been happy. It was in this spirit that he became the son of a soap-boiler, and probably

141

for no other reason than that the efforts of all future boys who tried to be anything might be looked upon with suspicion unless they were the sons of soap-boilers. . . . His maxims were full of animosity toward boys. Nowadays a boy cannot follow out a single natural instinct without tumbling over some of those everlasting aphorisms and hearing from Franklin on the spot. . . . That boy is hounded to death and robbed of his natural rest, because Franklin said once, in one of his inspired flights of malignity:

> "Early to bed and early to rise
> Makes a man healthy and wealthy and wise." [19]

Twain's main complaint is not against Franklin but against the belief of parents that they can force their children to be geniuses by making them do what Franklin did. No matter how rigidly a program of hard work, "studying by moonlight, and getting up in the night instead of resting until morning," is applied, Twain points out, it will not "make a Franklin of every father's fool." Franklin's "execrable eccentricities of instinct and conduct" are merely signs of his own genius and not the creators of it.[20] In Twain's mind, Franklin was able to follow the extraordinary and exhausting course of action he enjoins because of his own remarkable capacities. It is absurd to expect the average youth to follow such a course of action, which, without genius, will not help him to get ahead.

Twain also became increasingly dubious of another of the major assumptions of self-improvement: that a man's success or failure in life is entirely the result of his own character and effort. Like many of his contemporaries, Twain accepted the deterministic ideas current in the late nineteenth century. Gradually he became convinced that a man was what his heredity and education had made him. In his earlier books, he is inclined to allow some freedom of moral choice, but by the time he came to write "What is Man?" Twain was sure that any notion of a free will, or disinterested moral choice, was illusory.

Nor did Twain have any illusions about the benevolence of men of wealth and the industry, perseverance, and integrity with which they had made their money. His early western experiences and his own business ventures gave him perhaps more of an insider's view of American business than any other writer of comparable stature. The satirical descriptions of mining, railroad promotion, land speculation, and the corrupt relationship between business and politics in *Roughing It* and *The Gilded Age* are evidence enough that he was not an unqualified admirer of wealth.

Yet, despite these sentiments, Twain could also say to an assembly of successful men at a dinner in celebration of his sixty-seventh birthday:

> Our institutions give men the positions that of right belong to them through merit; all you men have won your places, not by heredities, and not by family influence or extraneous help, but only by the natural gifts God gave you at your birth, made effective by your own energies; this is the country to live in.[21]

One might conclude that this was on Twain's part a momentary lapse into acceptable public rhetoric, but there is too much evidence that his attitude toward success was thoroughly ambiguous. Twain admired and respected many individuals who, from his satirical comments on American business, he might have been expected to condemn. H. H. Rogers, of Standard Oil, was one of Twain's close personal friends. General Grant, in some minds the living symbol of the Gilded Age, was an admired hero and warm friend. Twain was less intimate but friendly with Andrew Carnegie and other leading industrialists. His own business ventures were notoriously inconsistent with his satirical attacks on speculation and the frantic quest for financial success. Indeed,

Twain's intermittent pursuit of great wealth through such varied ventures as gold and silver mines and a type-setting machine had a certain resemblance to the activities of one of his own most famous fictional creations, Colonel Beriah Sellers, that archetypal image of the unsuccessful promoter.

Twain's ambivalence toward the pursuit of wealth helped him to view post-Civil War America with a combination of sympathy and outrage. His descriptions and satires of this period are much more convincing than works like Denison's *The Modern Mammon* or Kimball's *John Powers, Banker,* both of which cover ground similar to that of Twain and Charles Dudley Warner's *The Gilded Age. The Gilded Age,* despite its many flaws and the structural confusion engendered by dual authorship, is a classic of American social satire. Washington Hawkins, Colonel Sellers, and Senator Dilworthy transcend the caricatures and stereotypes that marked the middle-class attack on the "new society." Hawkins and Sellers were ordinary men of the best intentions, caught up in the glowing rhetoric of material progress and individual self-improvement. In pursuit of their dreams they were led step by step into participation in the grossest and most corrupt of activities, the wholesale bribery of Congress. Their personal morality was exemplary, and their good will toward others never in doubt, but their inability to see the public implications of their actions and their susceptibility to the dream of personal fortune and social progress preached by those they looked upon as moral authorities made them totally incapable of responsible political and economic action.

On the other hand, Senator Dilworthy seems a completely self-conscious rogue. Yet, even he cannot be totally condemned when seen as a product of the society from which he springs. The popular tradition of self-improvement gave him a perfect rationalization for his devious activities. Had he not risen from obscurity and poverty to fame and wealth through his own efforts? What if his methods seemed open to question by narrow-minded moralists? Had not the improvements he supported been in the public interest? Dilworthy might have recalled Emerson's assertion that self-seeking American businessmen were doing more for the benefit of humanity than Florence Nightingale and all the other humanitarians put together, and congratulated himself as a public benefactor, which in fact he frequently did. In this character, Twain caught a great deal of the self-made millionaire's justification of his acts. The reader senses the author's outrage, but he also detects a kind of admiration and respect for the pure brass that shines through his behavior.

Hawkins, Sellers, and Dilworthy were products of a society running out of control, its traditional checks removed by the dislocations of a frightful war. With old institutions uprooted, and social life transformed by the chaos of rapid economic expansion, the old values had been forgotten. What had become of the society "where there is no fever of speculation, no inflamed desire for sudden wealth, where the poor are all simple-minded and contented, and the rich are all honest and generous, where society is in a condition of primitive purity, and politics is the occupation of only the capable and the patriotic"? [22] The old ideal of the moral pursuit of wealth had been replaced by new visions of sudden and massive enrichment. The "silver fever" and railroad promotion now ruled the minds of men. In such an environment, blind optimists like Sellers came to the fore with enthusiastic projects for the creation of fortunes, which other men, equally bemused by the fever of speculation, eagerly took up. Stone's Landing, a squalid settlement on a sluggish backwater, became a great commercial center in the minds of its promoters. Shrewder men, who saw in this blind enthusiasm the opportunity for real profit, took up the promotion, milked it for what it was worth, and abandoned the naïve enthusiasts who originated the scheme. Stone's Landing reverted to the bullfrogs and mud turtles, and Colonel Sellers went on to more fantastic and visionary schemes. The result was that continuous cycle of boom and bust that Twain portrays so graphically in *The Gilded Age* and *Roughing It*.

In such a social environment, the man who achieved the greatest wealth and the highest social position was likely to be the most corrupt, dishonest, and hypocritical. Senator Dilworthy, whose successful career was based on bribery and political influence, posed as a benefactor of the community, a guardian of the public interest, and a self-made man who owed his achievements to his regular attendance at Sunday School. The Honorable Patrique Oreille, "a wealthy Frenchman from Cork," had through "industry" and "economy" been "enabled . . . to start a low rum shop in a foul locality, and this gave him political influence," an influence which he parlayed into "fame and great respectability." He soon became a contractor and a friend of the great William Weed, made a fortune by furnishing "shingle-nails to the new courthouse at three thousand dollars a keg and eighteen gross of 60-cent thermometers at fifteen hundred dollars a dozen," and traveled to France to learn how to speak English with a foreign accent. Returning to the United States, he and his family established themselves as members of Washington aristocracy.[23]

In spite of his satiric assaults on the traditional glorification of self-made man, Twain was never able to resolve his ambivalence toward the ideal of the poor boy making a fortune and arriving at a respected social position. *The Gilded Age* resembles Denison's *The Modern Mammon* when it turns from satire and criticism to the presentation of the hopeful side of American civilization. Its hero—the creation not of Twain but of Charles Dudley Warner—is the noble young Philip Sterling who succeeds through industrious perseverance and personal merit. As a character and a symbol, he might as well have been borrowed from an earlier romance, for he embodies the traditional doctrine that the moral efforts of an honest, industrious, and God-fearing young man are sure to be rewarded with prosperity and happiness. Thus, in *The Gilded Age,* the reassertion of the traditional version of self-improvement, an ideal whose inapplicability had been demonstrated throughout the rest of the novel, is presented as the standard by which the other characters are to be judged.

Twain's frequent attacks on Algerism suggest that he was not convinced that the re-establishment of Poor Richard as a guide for American youth would do much to solve the problems of nineteenth-century America. Less and less able to see the values he cherished embodied in any group or individual in contemporary American society, Twain developed the fictional formula so characteristic of his later years: the use of a central figure from outside the world of the novel to demonstrate the failure of all groups.[24] In *A Connecticut Yankee at King Arthur's Court,* he chooses for this "transcendent" figure a character in the comic tradition of the self-made go-getter. Hank Morgan, the Connecticut Yankee, has been rightly compared to Jack Downing and Davy Crockett, for he possesses many of the virtues and vices of these American heroes. Together with the same indifference to traditionally established authority that Jack Downing manifests in his willingness to advise the President and other exalted leaders, Hank has all the practical knowledge and skill a man

can want. He might know next to nothing about Came-
lot, and nothing at all of medieval history and culture,
but he knows to the minute the time of an eclipse in the
sixth century. He is "nearly barren of sentiment," but he
has immense skill with his hands and boundless knowl-
edge of the soft side of human nature.

This industrialized Sam Slick is confronted with one
of the most traditional, static, and aristocratic societies
in history. His initial reaction is characteristic:

If . . . it was really the sixth century, all right, I didn't want
any softer thing: I would boss the whole country inside of three
months; for I judged I would have the start of the best-educated
man in the kingdom by a matter of thirteen hundred years and
upward.[25]

At first the Yankee is dazzled by the possibilities of get-
ting ahead. He is in an environment that any man who
had to make his way in the world might find ideal:
"Look at the opportunities here for a man of knowledge,
brains, pluck and enterprise to sail in and grow with the
country. The grandest field that ever was; and all my
own." [26] But his dreams of personal success are soon
soured by his growing acquaintance with the facts of
history, an acquaintance pressed upon him by his con-
tact with the institutions and people of sixth-century
England. A confirmed believer in self-help, he is shocked
by the power of traditional institutions:

It is pitiful for a person born in a wholesome free atmosphere to
listen to their humble and hearty outpourings of loyalty toward
their king and Church and nobility; as if they had any more
occasion to love and honor king and Church and noble than a
slave has to love and honor the lash, or a dog has to love and
honor the stranger that kicks him! Why, dear me, *any* kind of
royalty, howsoever modified, any kind of aristocracy, howsoever
pruned, is rightly an insult; but if you are born and brought up
under that sort of arrangement you probably never find it out
for yourself, and don't believe it when somebody else tells you.

It is enough to make a body ashamed of his race to think of the sort of froth that has always occupied its thrones without shadow of right or reason, and the seventh-rate people that have always figured as its aristocracies—a company of monarchs and nobles who, as a rule, would have achieved only poverty and obscurity if left, like their betters, to their own exertions.[27]

The Yankee forgets his own chance for aggrandizement in his shock at these social conditions, and he determines to reform England. With the assistance of a few men of intelligence and ambition who have begun to question the values of their society, he establishes a "man-factory" to train some of the more capable youths in technology and democracy. But this underground movement faces die-hard opposition at every turn. The Yankee becomes increasingly pessimistic and less able to envision the success of the reforms he has initiated. He comes to believe that human beings are less independent of tradition, less capable of reform than he has thought.

We speak of nature; it is folly; there is no such thing as nature; what we call by that misleading name is merely heredity and training. We have no thoughts of our own, no opinions of our own; they are transmitted to us, trained into us. All that is original in us, and therefore fairly creditable or discreditable to us, can be covered up and hidden by the point of a cambric needle, all the rest being atoms contributed by, and inherited from, a procession of ancestors that stretches back a billion years to the Adam-clam or grasshopper or monkey from whom our race has been so tediously and ostentatiously and unprofitably developed. And as for me, all that I think about in this plodding, sad pilgrimage, this pathetic drift between the eternities, is to look out and humbly live a pure and blameless life, and save that one microscopic atom in me that is truly me; the rest may land in Sheol for all I care.[28]

The Yankee's great plans are a failure. The forces of hereditary right and prescriptive order are roused to vehement opposition. The Yankee succumbs, tired and despairing, to the cheap tricks of the bogus Merlin. The charlatan, easily overcome as an individual, is irresistible when he carries the whole weight of mankind's stupidity and folly behind him.

Insofar as *A Connecticut Yankee in King Arthur's Court* is an attack on hereditary aristocracy, Twain is beating a dead horse. It is possible that his inability to make up his mind about the social developments of the nineteenth century encouraged him to turn away from America to assault a society and a principle of social organization of whose evil he was convinced, and yet it is unlike Twain to skip over the defects of America in order to twist the lion's tail. After *The Gilded Age, Life on the Mississippi,* and *Huckleberry Finn,* it is difficult to believe that suddenly he became convinced that democracy as practiced in late nineteenth-century America was that much superior to English aristocracy. If *A Connecticut Yankee* is a step on the road to the bitter pessimism of *The Mysterious Stranger,* it should also be interpreted on another level than that of an attack on aristocracy. The Yankee represents a rational democratic society in which position is in accordance with moral and intellectual merit. One of his dearest reforms, for example, is the establishment of an army officered not by men of hereditary standing, but chosen through a rigorous system of competitive examination. His "man-factory" resembles the Jeffersonian educational ideal: the training of men for social leadership without reference to social status. On the other hand, the Yankee's opponents stand for position and influence gained through heredity, corruption, and chicanery. King and nobles possess their power through the willingness of the masses to respect and admire the magic of birth. The church has gained power through its ability to play on the fears and superstitions of the people and its willingness to enter into corrupt alliances with king and aristocracy to exploit the people. Lesser figures like Merlin, and the traveling magician whom the Yankee encounters in the Valley of Holiness, exemplify the principle of fraud, a skill at trickery and manipulation of the popular mind. Against these avenues to power and privilege, the Yankee asserts honest industry, technological skill, and respect for the worth of the individual. Such weak weapons enable him to hold out for a time, but the ingrained superstition and stupidity of the masses, including most of the Yankee's own trained men, eventually overwhelm him. The republic which he hopefully proclaims after Arthur's death does not succeed, and England settles back into centuries of barbaric slumber.

Seen in this light, *A Connecticut Yankee,* for all its charm and humor, is a bitter and despairing parable of the inevitable defeat of a society based on the ideal of a free citizenry governed by men of virtue and talent chosen from and by the people. The Yankee's fate is a fictional embodiment of Twain's growing skepticism at the capactiy of men to govern themselves and to select their leaders by a rational process. With the mass of men incapable of self-government, a society based on the principles of self-improvement—on free and unlimited individual mobility without the adventitious prerogatives of birth and the superstitious admiration of men for hereditary masters—must inevitably fail.

Every man is a master and also a servant, a vassal. There is always someone who looks up to him and admires and envies him; there is always someone to whom he looks up and whom he admires and envies. This is his nature; this is his character; and it is unchangeable, indestructible; therefore republics and democracies are not for such as he; they cannot satisfy the requirements of his nature. The inspirations of his character will always breed circumstances and conditions which must in time furnish him a

151

king and an aristocracy to look up to and worship. In a democracy he will try—and honestly—to keep the crown away, but Circumstance is a powerful master and will eventually defeat him.[29]

Like many of his contemporaries, Twain associates the meaning of American democracy with the idea of self-improvement. Democracy means a society in which all men, no matter what their origin, have a chance to rise as far as their merits will take them. But Twain cannot deny that nineteenth-century America has made a mockery of this ideal: the young are told that merit consists in following the injunctions of narrow-minded teachers, while in practice they soon learn to emulate the corruption and chicanery of those who manage to amass large sums of money. The public in general worships not the man of integrity and genius. but the man who tells the biggest lies, who inflames their naïve desires for sudden and easily gained prosperity, while filling his own pockets. Free mobility has failed to create a decent democratic society, but what can take its place? Recognizing its inadequacies, Twain still clings to this ideal as the only meaningful definition of democracy. In his last novels and sketches, he ceases to cope with the specific problems of American democracy and pours his disillusionment into the somber but powerful tales of boundless human corruption and blindness that form the marrow of *The Myterious Stranger,* "The Man that Corrupted Hadleyburg," and *What is Man?*

William Dean Howells and the Self-made Man

William Dean Howells' first published fiction was an Alger story. "A Tale of Love and Politics, Adventures of a Printer Boy," appeared in the *Ashtabula Sentinel* of September 1, 1853. Howells was sixteen years old, and the story, which told of the success of a poor, young orphan boy, may well have reflected its author's own dreams. Seven years later, as a rising young Ohio journalist, Howells, in a campaign biography of Lincoln, emphasized Lincoln's importance as a symbol of self-improvement and encouragement to "the rustic boy, who is to be President in 1900." But Howells' romance with Algerism was not destined to last. As his experience of the world expanded, in his rise from printer's devil to become one of the most important literary figures of his age, Howells increasingly rejected the traditional ideal of self-improvement. In many ways his early experience paralleled that of Twain—both were westerners who eventually found successful literary careers in the East—but Howells had little emotional ambivalence toward success. By the time he wrote his major novels, Howells had not only come to view the new industrial society with a critical eye, but had begun to feel that the ideal of individual economic and social advancement was a major cause of social dislocation and individual unhappiness.

This theme was a central one in the series of novels dealing with self-made men which Howells began to write in the early 1880's. In *A Modern Instance* (1882), Howells describes the rise and fall of a young newspaperman. His portrayal of Bartley Hubbard is a straightforward representation of a highly believable American type: a young man of quite ordinary talents and of a weak and vacillating character, driven by a strong desire for wealth and position which overpowers his rudimentary moral principles. Hubbard began life as an orphan, but, unlike the orphans of T. S. Arthur and Horatio Alger, whose early trials and tribulations were a source of moral discipline, Hubbard's early insecurity and difficulty stunt his moral development. While his enforced independence teaches him a certain kind of self-reliance, it is manifested in a brassy determination

153

to succeed and a complete indifference to the rights and wishes of others.

In his portrayal of Bartley Hubbard's sordid career, Howells emphasizes his belief that the desperate pursuit of success can only destroy such an individual. Beginning his rise in a small town in Maine, Hubbard's desire for status drives him to court Marcia Gaylord, a judge's daughter. On his way up, he moves to Boston, but here, his increasing experience of urban society makes him believe that the simple and relatively uncultured Marcia will be an encumbrance to his ambition. At the same time, his early successes make him overconfident. He becomes more and more ready to undertake anything that promises personal advantage, no matter how unscrupulous it may be. His lack of insight and principle make it impossible for him to recognize the response of others to his increasing corruption. His career ends with his desertion of his wife, a sordid divorce case, and his flight to the West, where he is shot by an irate victim of his scandalous libels. Yet, sordid and unsavory as he is, Hubbard is not portrayed as a villain. More than anything else, he is the victim of his desire to get ahead. At almost any point until his final desertion of Marcia, Hubbard might have saved himself by giving up his frantic pursuit of success, but this motive is so deeply ingrained in his character that he cannot stop. *A Modern Instance* is a sharp commentary on what must have been a characteristic tragedy of many young Americans and the precursor of Dreiser's still more somber study of a comparable man in *An American Tragedy*.

In his next major novel, *The Rise of Silas Lapham* (1885), Howells shows an increasing concern with the nature of the social order through which the ambitious individual has to make his way. The story of Silas Lapham is another tragedy of an individual's rise and fall; it is also, in part, the tragedy of a society where the lines of social class prevent communication and understanding between men. In the world of Silas Lapham, the barriers of taste, education, and social position cannot be "burned away" as they were in the sentimental world of E. P. Roe, for they are ingrained by years of habit and training.

Howells' attitude toward class is strikingly different from that of the earlier sentimental novelists of self-improvement. These writers, although conscious of class distinctions, attributed to their heroes an innate knowledge of the tastes, manners, and attitudes they would need to occupy a higher social position. Only men like Cooper, frankly devoted to the ideal of the gentlemen, emphasized the gulf of manners and taste between the established upper classes and the self-made man. Yet Cooper's viewpoint is essentially that of the upper class to which be belonged, and he is unable to treat a self-made man with the same sympathy and admiration that he reserves for the American gentlemen.

Howells, on the other hand, portrays both aristocrat and upstart with sympathy and understanding. His deep democratic convictions and his own experience as a self-made intellectual cause him to sympathize with those who seek to rise from obscurity, while his cultural interests and his friendship with upper-class Brahmins like James Russell Lowell give him insight into the attitudes and values of the established aristocracy. Furthermore, his knowledge of nineteenth-century European literature and thought also help him to see the force of class distinctions in the behavior of Americans. *The Rise of Silas Lapham,* for example, was probably influenced by Balzac's similar novel which traces the rise and fall of a self-made man, *La Grandeur et Décadence de Cesar Birotteau.* In this novel, Balzac offers the history of a clever, uneducated man from the provinces who is drawn into risky speculations and forced into bankruptcy. Faced with ruin, his integrity reasserts itself, and he devotes the rest of his life to paying off his creditors.

Like Cesar Birotteau, Silas Lapham's difficulties begin when he tries to enter upper class society. At first, Lapham naïvely expects that his wealth will easily establish his equality with the less affluent but aristocratic Coreys. He rapidly discovers that the Coreys exist in a world of manners and tastes far beyond his understanding. When he is invited to dinner at their mansion, his social inexperience leads him to drink too much wine, to bore the company with long harangues, and to appear in the eyes of these proper Bostonians as a drunken boor. When his desperate speculations fail and the extravagant new house he has built as a wedge into society burns down, Lapham discovers that he has overrated his business ability. Only after the threat of financial ruin has driven him out of a false position can his true qualities as a man emerge. By this time, however, his energies have been squandered in a wasted effort to achieve a social position that could hardly have been conducive to his happiness.

In *The Minister's Charge* (*1887*), Howells turns to an assault on that staple of the self-improvement novel, the legend of the young country boy who makes his fortune in the city. The novel deals with the misadventures and ultimate return to the country of a young farmer, Lemuel Barker, who is persuaded to seek his fortune in Boston when the minister of the title, the Reverend David Sewell, misguidedly encourages the young man by praising his execrable poetry. Howell's criticism of the traditional ideal of self-improvement in *The Minister's Charge* is double-edged. Lemuel Barker's misadventures are a gloss on the absurdity of the Alger pattern. Lem's strenuous morality, self-reliance, and pride only serve to get him into one scrape after another, until he realizes that he is not equipped to succeed in the complex and bewildering social order of a large city. Surrounded by benevolent members of the upper class who are delighted to befriend and assist him, Lem is no more able to profit from their good intentions than they are able to discover the right way of helping him. Totally different backgrounds and training create one contretemps after another between Lem and his anxious benefactors. Representatives of cultivated Boston like Sewell and Corey have a romantic admiration for self-made men—Sewell's library is filled with pictures of famous men and women who began life as poor farmers —but not the slightest idea of what to do with such a phenomenon when he appears on their doorstep.

The Minister's Charge also reflects Howells' belief in the dominant influence of social institutions on individual behavior. In defeat, Silas Lapham is able to rise above the corrupting force of his environment, but Lemuel Barker is incapable of such an achievement. His only salvation lies in escaping to the rural society from which he had come. For T. S. Arthur, Lem's diligence, self-reliance, and integrity would have insured his success in any milieu. For Howells, these qualities, however admirable, cannot help a young man find a place in a social order which nothing in his past experience has prepared him to understand.

Howells extends his critique of individual mobility to its ultimate point in his most important novel, *A Hazard of New Fortunes* (1890). In the America of this novel, most individuals are completely bound by the social system. Those who do succeed, do so only by chance and raw force. By the time they arrive at the top, they are hopelessly corrupt. In old Jacob Dryfoos, Howells draws one of the first significant fictional portraits of the self-made millionaire. Dryfoos' fortune has been accumulated through crude, raw force, great shrewdness, and the luck of finding deposits of natural gas on his farm. But his very success ultimately destroys him. Desiring social position, Dryfoos leaves the Indiana countryside where he has made his fortune and moves to New York. City. His wife, a simple, country-loving woman, is desperately unhappy at the bewildering complexities of city society. His daughter, Christine, undisciplined, raw, and supremely confident in her father's wealth, power, and indulgence of her whims, is marred for life and prepared for her pathetic marriage to "a nobleman full of present debts and duels in the past." [30] More tragically, Dryfoos rapidly becomes estranged from his beloved son, and, in effect, hounds him to his death by forcing him to give up his hopes of becoming a minister. The most powerful of Howells' self-made men, Dryfoos is man enough to recognize his failure when his son dies. Ultimately, Dryfoos gains the social success he has so eagerly coveted, but it no longer has any meaning for him. With nothing left to him worth living for, he can only reflect that "it don't make a great deal of difference what we do or we don't do, for the few years left." [31]

The Aesthetic Wasteland: Henry James and the American Scene

Like Howells, but from a very different point of view, Henry James incisively attacks the American ideal of individual economic advancement. As early as *The American* (1877), James created a self-made millionaire, Christopher Newman. Suddenly realizing the sterility of his endless pursuit of wealth, he flees to Europe in search of a more meaningful form of existence. In *The Ambassadors* (1903), James dissects the middle-class ethos of success and respectability, and, as late as *The Ivory Tower*, unfinished at his death in 1916, he is still examining the meaning of success in a tale which thrusts a young American trained in European social and aesthetic values into a social context where the pursuit of wealth is the dominant standard. In these and other novels and stories James relentlessly explores the narrow and stultifying effect upon the individual of the emphasis on the single motive of pecuniary gain.

America, as James sees it, is a great commercial democracy in which the search for individual economic advancement has been a more powerful and dominant force than in any other society.

What prevails, what sets the tune, is the American scale of gain, more magnificent than any other, and the fact that the whole assumption, the whole theory of life, is that of the individual's participation in it, that of his being more or less punctually and more or less effectually "squared." [32]

But the very intensity with which Americans pursue success, the fact that "the business-man in the United States, may, with no matter what dim struggles, gropings, yearning, never hope to be anything *but* a business-man," creates a social and aesthetic wasteland, "the boundless gaping void of 'society.' " [33] How this void can be filled is the great problem of American civilization.

Americans are slowly becoming aware of their need for the amenities and refinements of civilization, but their imaginative horizons are bounded by the fact that their ideal of individual achievement demands the acquisition of wealth. Nevertheless, they feel their way toward civilization. One aspect of this development is the powerful social role given to women. Men, immersed in business, leave all other areas of life to their women, who "pounce" upon American social and cultural life. The American woman's undisputed control of the social life of the community gives her a unique position, but, unfortunately, her inexperience and lack of cultural sophistication encourage her to impose on society an oversimplified and circumscribed code of behavior. Unable to develop the taste and sensitivity, the richness and diversity that are essential to a truly civilized life, the American woman, abandoned by her success-pursuing husband, supports the sterile ethos of middle-class respectability.

Guided by the narrow economic ideal of individual achievement rather than by a broad conception of human potentialities, the attempt of Americans to develop a civilization is little more than "the grope of wealth." [34] Undirected by experience, history, and "the long, the immitigable process of time," [35] wealth alone cannot create the manners, tastes, and graces of civilized society. The pecuniary short-cut to culture reveals its true spirit, according to James, in the waste, extravagance and tastelessness of late nineteenth-century architecture and in the aimless, vacuous, gregarious society typified by the indiscriminate mob gathered in the great American hotels. The "hotel spirit" became the leading social manifestation of that "pecuniary power" which James sees in almost apocalyptic vision "so beat its wings in the void, and so look round it for the charity of some hint as to the possible awkwardness or possible grace of its motion." [36] It is the inevitable social expression of a society with no other basis for discrimination, no other barrier to intercourse and association than monetary success and the inexperienced female's definition of respectability. It is

an expression of the gregarious state breaking down every barrier but two—one of which, the barrier consisting of the high pecuniary tax, is the immediately obvious. The other, the rather more subtle, is the condition, for any member of the flock, that he or she—in other words especially she, be presumably "respectable," be, that is, not discoverably anything else.[37]

Freely open on equal terms to all who possess the neces-
sary wealth, hotel society is exceedingly democratic,
since the ability to pay is widespread. Hotel society
achieves a kind of "perfect human felicity" and has "the
admirable sign that it was, precisely, so comprehen-
sively collective—that it made so vividly, in the old
phrase, for the greatest number." [38] But it does so at
the sacrifice of all individual taste, diversity, and
privacy.

The domination of the ideal of pecuniary gain and its
resultant social manifestations make life in America a
chamber of horrors for those sensitive and discriminat-
ing individuals who wish to live a life that transcends
the narrow pursuit of success. The problem of this
group, James feels, is of particular significance:

The relation of this modest body to the country of their birth,
which asks so much, on the whole—so many surrenders and
compromises, and the possession above all of such a prodigious
head for figures—before it begins, in its wonderful way, to give
or to "pay," would appear to us supremely touching, I think, as
a case of communion baffled and blighted, if we had time to work
it out. It would bathe in something of a tragic light the vivid
truth that the "great countries" are all, more and more, happy
lands (so far as any can be called such) for any, for every sort
of person rather than the middle sort. The upper sort—in the
scale of wealth, the only scale now—can to their hearts' content
build their own castles and move by their own motors; the lower
sort, masters of gain in *their* degree, can profit, also to their
hearts' content, by the enormous extension of those material
facilities which may be gregariously enjoyed; they are able to
rush about, as never under the sun before, in promiscuous packs
and hustled herds, while to the act of so rushing about all felicity
and prosperity appear for them to have been comfortably re-
duced. The frustrated American, as I have hinted at him, scrap-
ing for *his* poor practical solution in the depleted silver-mine of
history, is the American who "makes" too little for the castle and
yet "minds" too much for the hustled herd, who can neither

achieve such detachment nor surrender to such society, and who most of all accordingly, in the native order, fails of a working basis.[39]

Toward a New Social Ethic

Ranging from E. P. Roe's middle-class resentment at the power of new economic and ethnic groups, through Howells' sense of the inadequacy of traditional ethical ideals to resolve the problems of a new social order, to Henry James's cosmopolitan critique of the narrowness and inhumanity of the dominant American values, the sources of literary assault on American life and ideals were too diverse for it to coalesce into a single program of social action. Much of the resentment and frustration which produced the attack on the new urban industrial society was channeled into the political reform movements of Populism and Progressivism. Some of it was drawn off when farmers and workingmen found it possible to employ the new social techniques of organization and co-ordination to improve their economic situation. Nativist and anti-immigration movements early in the twentieth century were still another manifestation of the critical mood of the era. Perhaps most important of all, the long swell of prosperity between 1896 and the Great Depression temporarily allayed the doubts and uncertainties of the 1870's and 1880's and encouraged a new faith in the ideal of individual advancement.

A small but important minority of Americans rejected the ideal of individual self-improvement as the foundation of a democratic social order and began to search for another principle of social organization and individual ethics. As Jane Addams, the humanitarian reformer, observes at the end of the nineteenth century:

All about us are men and women who have become unhappy in regard to their attitude toward the social order itself; toward the dreary round of uninteresting work, the pleasures narrowed down to those of appetite, the declining consciousness of brain power, and the lack of mental food which characterized the lot of the large proporton of their fellow-citizens. These men and women have caught a moral challenge raised by the exigencies of contemporaneous life; some are bewildered, others who are denied the relief which sturdy action brings are even seeking an escape, but all are increasingly anxious concerning their actual relations to the basic organization of society. The test which they would apply to their conduct is a social test. They fail to be content with the fulfillment of their family and personal obligations, and find themselves striving to respond to a new demand involving a social obligation; they have become conscious of another requirement and the contribution they would make is toward a code of social ethics.[40]

In counterpoint to the new assertion of the ideal of individual success, American intellectuals, philosophers, humanitarians, and writers began to take up the challenge outlined by Jane Addams. In religious thought, the idea of a social gospel; in politics, the concepts of social democracy and the general welfare state; in social reform, the movements for regulatory legislation to control working and living conditions in the industrial metropolis; in education, the philosophy of John Dewey, all bore the impress of a new kind of thinking about the relationship between the individual and the social order. Their formulations of the new social ethic were as diverse as the criticisms of American life which had provoked them, but these thinkers agreed with Jane Addams' basic rejection of the ideal of individual success:

The man who dissociates his ambition, however disinterested, from the cooperation of his fellows, always takes the risk of ultimate failure. He does not take advantage of the great conserver and guarantee of his own permanent success which associated efforts afford. Genuine experiments toward higher social conditions must have a more democratic faith and practice than those which underlie private venture. Public parks and improvements, intended for the common use, are after all only safe in the hands of the public itself; and associated effort toward social progress, although much more awkward and stumbling than that same effort managed by a capable individual, does yet enlist deeper forces and evoke higher social capacities.[41]

CHAPTER VI

PHILOSOPHERS OF SUCCESS

> The old nations of the earth creep on at a snail's
> pace; the Republic thunders past with the rush of the
> express. The United States, the growth of a single
> century, has already reached the foremost rank among
> nations, and is destined soon to out-distance all others
> in the race. In population, in wealth, in annual sav-
> ings, and in public credit; in freedom from debt, in
> agriculture, and in manufactures, America already
> leads the civilized world.
>
> Andrew Carnegie, *Triumphant Democracy*, 1886

If Mark Twain blasted it as the Gilded Age, Andrew
Carnegie saw the later nineteenth century as the era of
Triumphant Democracy. William James excoriated
American worship of the bitch-goddess Success, but the
very vehemence of his epithet suggested the extent to
which success was a magic word to many of his contem-
poraries. Although the social and economic changes of
the post-Civil War era threatened the position of many
groups, the rise of industry brought unprecedented
prosperity to businessmen, to the new urban middle
classes, and to many immigrants. For these groups the
dream of rags to riches had as much attraction as ever.
Even critics of the Gilded Age were more concerned
with the failure of the new America society to live up to
its promise of individual opportunity than with the
shortcomings of the ideal itself. Only more radical
utopians like Bellamy or the later Howells had enter-

167

tained the possibility of a co-operative or collective principle of social organization. Clearly, the way was open for a reformulation of the ideal of self-improvement and a reassertion of faith in American opportunities. New institutions, spokesmen, and forms of self-help literature expressed a new philosophy of success. Responding to industrialism, to a generation of criticism, and to the impact of new ideas, the philosophers of success transformed the traditional Protestant synthesis of religious and secular values into an ideology of individual material achievement. From the decisive defeat of southern and western Populism in 1896 until the great crash of 1929, success was a word to conjure with. Through the era of Progressive reform and "the age of normalcy," the philosophers of success projected their message to a wide and devoted audience through books, magazines, and speeches, and helped to shape the attitudes of a generation of Americans.

The Transformation of the Protestant Ethic

There was considerable continuity between the traditional ideal of self-improvement and the new philosophy of success. In many respects—its insistence that the key to success lay in individual character, its emphasis on the productive and self-disciplinary virtues of work, economy, and temperance, and its basically religious orientation—the philosophy of success was, as Ralph Henry Gabriel, Irvin Wyllie, and others have pointed out, a refurbishing of the Protestant ethic.

The new gospel was not simply a recapitulation of the old. The first apostles of the self-made man had established a rather tenuous balance between religious and secular values based on the idea of the diligent pursuit of a divinely ordained calling as a sign of moral and spiritual excellence. But this balance had depended on a static society in which the dominant occupations, like

those of the small farmer, the artisan, and the shop-
keeper, involved a direct relationship between individ-
ual effort and the resultant product. In such a society, it
was possible to believe that hard work and frugal living
would invariably lead to a certain degree of security.
Indeed, we have seen how the exponents of self-improve-
ment, intent upon striking the proper balance between
the individual's religious and secular callings, were
often highly critical of speculation, occupational mobil-
ity, the growth of the factory system, and other emer-
gent patterns of industrial organization which they be-
lieved to be a threat to the traditional social and moral
order. The virtues appropriate to a society in which
most men were farmers, artisians, or petty capitalists
were not so evidently relevant in a society of large or-
ganizations. The qualities which made a man a good
farmer, blacksmith, or small merchant were not neces-
sarily the same as those of a successful executive in a
large industrial or financial corporation. Even more
important, the petty capitalist's ideas of ethical conduct
and political responsibility were not equally acceptable
to men seeking to create a nationwide railroad system,
to make millions in stock speculations, or to establish
gigantic industrial combinations. As the second group
won more authority and prestige, the popular philoso-
phy of self-improvement gradually changed, accommo-
dating itself more closely to the needs of business enter-
prise and the large corporation. The main trend in the
development of ideas of self-help was away from the
earlier balance of political, moral, religious, and eco-
nomic values and in the direction of an overriding em-
phasis on the pursuit and use of wealth.

This trend was, to some extent, simply a response to
the attitudes of the average American, whose commit-
ment to the traditional gospel of self-improvement had
rarely interfered with his pursuit of his own economic
advancement. With its emphasis on sticking to a calling

and achieving prosperity in the station to which God had assigned one, the ethic of self-improvement had reflected the anxious attempts of an established elite to control the development of a materialistic society. The average American had accepted this synthesis of values because it embodied the voice of tradition. But he had rarely hesitated to ignore it when its injunctions ran counter to his economic interests. After the Civil War, the tremendous growth of productive and distributive facilities held out the promise of a better life for all men. Furthermore, the rise of industry had made the possession and control of wealth an increasingly desirable and imperative goal. Americans looked to the exponents of self-improvement to provide more practical instruction and less moralizing. This pressure from the audience was clearly operative when Andrew Carnegie attempted to explain the principles of success to a group of students at the Curry Commercial College in Pittsburgh on June 23, 1885. Carnegie was about to give these eager young seekers the old prohibition against liquor and speculation, but he prefaced these injunctions with the following assurance:

Let me indicate two or three conditions essential to success. Do not be afraid that I am going to moralize or inflict a homily upon you. I speak upon the subject only from the view of a man of the world, desirous of aiding you to become successful business men. You all know that there is no genuine, praiseworthy success in life if you are not honest, truthful, fair-dealing. I assume you are and will remain all these, and also that you are determined to live pure, respectable lives, free from pernicious or equivocal associations with one sex or the other. There is no creditable future for you else. Otherwise your learning and your advantages not only go for naught, but serve to accentuate your failure and your disgrace. I hope you will not take it amiss if I warn you against three of the gravest dangers which will beset you in your upward path.[1]

If Americans of the late nineteenth century were convinced of the desirability of individual economic success, they were also concerned that economic abundance seemed to be arriving in such an uneven way. The political and economic weakness of farmers and wage earners as compared to the organized power of capital made the gulf between rich and poor wider than it had been before. Many members of these groups came to feel that their economic opportunities had been restricted by the progress of industrial development. To explain and justify this situation, the philosophers of self-help increasingly accepted the idea that individualistic competition was the basic mode of human life. This, too, involved a transformation of the traditional concept of self-improvement. The older philosophy, stressing individual effort and achievement, did not place great emphasis on competition. Rather, it encouraged the individual to seek prosperity and advancement by fulfilling the duties of his station, duties which involved social and moral obligations as well as individual benefits. As the tempo of social change increased, it became apparent that not every individual, no matter how industrious, would be able to achieve a significant measure of economic advancement. Nobody could be more diligent than the steel worker with his exhausting ten- or twelve-hour day or the farmer with his back-breaking round of labor from sunup to sundown. Yet, if the ordinary farmer or industrial worker managed to feed and clothe his family and achieve a minimal economic security, he could consider himself lucky. Farmers and workers may have exaggerated the extent to which their situation had declined since the halcyon days of the early Republic, but it was still perfectly evident that these groups had not profited from the industrial transformation of America as much as businessmen whose activities did not exemplify so clearly the traditional virtues of industry, frugality, integrity, and temperance. In fact, business leaders, who frequently attempted to justify their activities in terms of the traditional Protestant ideal,

171

sometimes ran into amusing logical difficulties. Judge
Gary, chairman of U.S. Steel Corporation, was once
asked by a Senate committee to define hard work. As
James Prothro remarks, "he fell somewhat short of pre-
cision" when he explained, "it is hard work to work
hard whatever one does, and to the extent one does work
hard he, of course, is doing hard work. That is perfectly
evident." [2]

In spite of occasional difficulties in fitting tradi-
tional rhetoric to the needs of big business, there was no
doubt that individual economic advancement now lay
primarily in the area of business enterprise. Rural
areas, where farmers and small merchants still domi-
nated the culture, understandably held longer to the
traditional gospel of self-improvement, for, if it did not
help improve their economic status, at least it proved
their moral superiority. In the cities, and among the
younger generation, self-improvement meant moving in-
to the new world of industry and business. In this world,
the individual was inevitably in conflict with others. In
the large organization, only a few could expect to rise to
the top. The older image of a static society in which every
man was able to improve himself by diligence, no matter
what his calling, gave way to a conception of a dynamic,
changing society in which individuals competed with
one another for a limited number of prizes.

The vogue of Herbert Spencer and Social Darwinism
undoubtedly provided some of the success-philosophers
with a quasi-scientific rationale for the definition of the
self-improving individual as a dynamic competitor. One
does not have to look far in the success literature of the
turn of the century to find Darwinian clichés. Elbert
Hubbard climaxed his highly popular inspirational
tract, "A Message to Garcia," with a warning that "no
matter how good times are, this sorting continues; only,
if times are hard and work is scarce, the sorting is done

finer—but out and forever out the incompetent and unworthy go. It is the survival of the fittest. Self-interest prompts every employer to keep the best—those who can carry a message to Garcia." [3]

As Irvin Wyllie has shown, the success-philosophers rejected many of the implications of Darwinian theory. While Darwinists like William Graham Sumner advocated full competition between individuals and classes, arguing that only through the survival of the fittest could society progress, the success-philosophers, insofar as they accepted the idea of the struggle for survival, luxuriated in the cosmic optimism of popular Darwinians like John Fiske, who interpreted evolution as God's benevolent plan for human progress. To explain the coexistence of progress and poverty—the growing gap between millionaire and wage earner—the philosophers of success developed their own theory of competition. According to them, the successful competitors were those individuals whose energy, initiative, and willingness to work created prosperity and opportunities for others. Not only were such individuals entitled to a greater share of worldly goods, but, in a free, democratic society where property moved in accordance with natural laws, they would inevitably get them. Furthermore, the ideologists of success refused to believe that some individuals were inherently more fit than others. Reasserting the traditional maxim "where there's a will there's a way," they insisted that there were more opportunities than ever for a man who was determined to get ahead. Failure, they insisted, was largely caused by defects in the individual's character and will. The impact of Social Darwinism on success was, largely, superficial. The naturalistic view of the evolutionary process questioned the efficacy of the individual will and the morality and benevolence of the American social order. Advocates of success were prepared to admit that some few successful

173

millionaires had gained their wealth by following the law of the jungle, but these were the exceptions. "Ninety-eight out of one hundred of the rich men of America are honest," insisted Russell Conwell. "That is why they are rich. That is why they are trusted with money. That is why they carry on great enterprises and find plenty of people to work with them. It is because they are honest men." [4]

The self-culture movement was another important ideological source of the philosophy of success: The earlier apostles of self-improvement had emphasized the importance of a common-school education and religious training, but they did not usually recommend a broader intellectual cultivation for most men, because they were afraid it might instil tastes and attitudes inimical to diligence and piety. The self-culture movement had challenged this view by insisting that democracy required the greatest possible development, both intellectual and spiritual, of the individual personality. The idea of personality development was, in turn, a central theme of the philosophy of success. Where the fulfilment of the individual's creative and spiritual potential was a primary goal of self-culture, success treated the process of personality development as the acquisition of those qualities of will and personal magnetism which would make the individual an effective participant in the struggle for success. This emphasis on individual achievement also influenced the characteristic institutions of self-culture. After the Civil War, merchantile colleges and business schools which emphasized training in the ethos and techniques of business and social success grew far more rapidly than the old-fashioned mechanics' institutes and lyceums. The process was a gradual one. Even in the late nineteenth century, the broader ideal of self-culture was still strong enough to produce a major popular institution in the Chautauquas, which combined religion, politics, liberal education, success training, and entertainment in remarkable fusion. Chautauquas, however, were the last stand of the ideal of self-culture in anything like its original form. The popular educational institutions of the late nineteenth and early twentieth centuries placed an increasing emphasis on vocational and success training, eliminating those broader aspects of human development which the proponents of self-culture had considered essential.

New spokesmen and new kinds of self-help literature also accompanied the emergence of the philosophy of success. Clergymen were the primary spokesmen for the traditional gospel of self-improvement, and their books were modeled on sermons. Indeed, many of them, like Henry Ward Beecher's popular *Lectures to Young Men,* were simply published versions of successful sermons. Following the tradition of the Protestant sermon, these books were logically organized and detailed expositions of the virtues and qualities associated with the ideal of diligent pursuit of a calling, together with instruction in how to resist the temptations of idleness, intemperance, extravagance, and "making haste to be rich." In the 1850's, however, business journalists like Freeman Hunt and Edwin T. Freedley began to publish books of advice. After the Civil War the successful businessman became the leading oracle of self-help. Finally, toward the end of the century, there emerged what might be called the "success specialist," the individual who, like Orison Swett Marden, made a career as a philosopher and teacher of success techniques.

The form of self-help literature also changed as the philosophy of success developed. The sermon, with its detailed discussion of the virtues, was replaced by the inspirational parable with its dramatic story of success or failure. T. S. Arthur's *Advice to Young Men* gave

175

way to Russell Conwell's "Acres of Diamonds," Elbert
Hubbard's "A Message to Garcia," W. W. Woodbridge's
"That Something," and Frederic Van Rennselaer Dey's
"The Magic Story." Short biographies, showing how
well-known figures in business, politics, and the profes-
sions had won their way from poverty to fame and for-
tune, also became a primary method of the new success-
teaching. In both parable and biography the emphasis
was the same: the magic and wonder of success. Where
the apostles of self-improvement had concentrated their
attention on moral discipline and the rejection of temp-
tation, the success philosophers stressed the possibility
and the thrill of achievement. Even the sermon was
transformed from the careful exposition of virtues and
vices to a quasi-scientific explanation of the "laws of
success" and the ease and certainty of their application.
As the success-philosophers portrayed it, self-improve-
ment was no longer the piecemeal ascetic discipline pre-
scribed by T. S. Arthur but a dynamic assertion of will
and a tapping of mysterious and yet scientifically con-
trollable inner energies.

Finally, the spokesmen of the philosophy of success
found an important new forum in the popular middle-
class magazines which were developing at the turn of
the century. *The Saturday Evening Post,* under the
editorship of George Horace Lorimer, and *Success,* un-
der Orison S. Marden, reached new heights of circula-
tion with their many-sided treatment of the theme of
business success. The importance of the success theme in
the formula of these magazines and their imitators
(*Colliers* and the *American*) suggests a close connec-
tion between the new urban middle class, the major
audience for these publications, and the new philosophy
of success. Under Lorimer's editorship, and with the
help of his immensely popular series, "Letters from a
Self-Made Merchant to his Son," the *Post* presented the

176

philosophy of success in a way that caught the mood of
the middle class. Circulation increased to a million in
little over a decade. *Success* was less successful. In its
first few years, *Success* attempted to develop a formula
which combined the older gospel of self-improvement
with the newer philosophy of success. It published au-
thors like Ella Wheeler Wilcox whose point of view was
still dominated by the traditional Protestant synthesis
and who proclaimed that a desire for fame and fortune
was "all greed,—and the most foolish phase of greed,"
together with such paeans to success as Dey's "The
Magic Story." The result was confusion. On one page
the young man learned that the road to success was
'rough and rocky; on the next, that "the surest way to
win success is to get into the right niche, in a congenial
environment where we can work without friction, and
where all our powers will find quick and responsive ex-
pression." At one point he was informed that education
was necessary for an age of specialization, and, at an-
other, that character was all. One author criticized the
piratical spirit of business and informed his readers
that "one of the greatest dangers that threaten Ameri-
can institutions, today, is commercialism." Another an-
nounced that the businessman was the true hero of the
age. If one article stressed the necessity for industry,
honesty, and integrity, another insisted that originality,
boldness, and initiative were more important. But, by
1907, after the fashion of the *Post, Success* dropped the
traditional gospel. One sign of the change was the ap-
pearance of a regular feature, "Hints to Investors," in a
magazine, which, only five years earlier, had stated that
speculation was more contemptible than gambling. An-
other was the beginning of departments giving instruc-
tion in various forms of social success, "the art of con-
versation," fashion, and other aspects of culture. But,
most important of all, the traditional Protestant virtues

no longer held the center of the stage. The new philosophy of success had even conquered *Success*.

Acres of Diamonds

Russell Conwell's popular parable of the old Persian farmer who sells his farm, wanders over the world, and eventually dies without learning that the diamond mine he so passionately sought is right in his own backyard exemplifies the major theme of the philosophy of success. In an earlier period, this story might have been brought forward to illustrate the principle of sticking to one's calling. When Conwell informed his audience that the old Persian's diamond farm was none other than the great Golconda mine, it was clear that he had another lesson in mind. If the old farmer had just had the sense to seize the opportunity which awaited him, he could have escaped from farming forever by becoming the richest man in the world.

This was the main answer to the critics of the new American society. Far from eliminating or restricting individual opportunities, the social and economic changes of the late nineteenth century had multiplied opportunities for success. "There never was a place on earth more adapted than the city of Philadelphia to-day, and never in the history of the world did a poor man without capital have such an opportunity to get rich quickly and honestly as he has now in our city," insisted Conwell.[5] He and his fellow philosophers sought to prove this assertion by piling up instance after instance of individuals who had parlayed a discovery or a new idea into millions, and of others who had failed to notice a chance for riches right under their feet. Where critics of industrial society shared Henry George's fear that, under the system of competition and pre-emption, progress and poverty went hand in hand, the advocates of success saw only progress. In their view, the day was coming when opportunities would be so many and so great that every man might become a success:

The morning cometh! The day of greater things is close to us. The young man now entering on life is most surely to see far greater changes and more decided advances in science, labor, art, and religion than have been hinted at in the prophetic dreams of our fathers. The light we now have is only the gray of dawn compared with the ascending day which the young people of to-day will see before they die. The avenues to the best success are being cleared and made wider so that thousands can achieve greatness where only scores could win in the last generation. The chances for riches are many times greater now for the poor people than they were even a decade ago; but the increase of opportunity is by the hundred-fold in each ten years. There is now reasonable hope for the hitherto most hopeless, as the gates to wisdom, to love, to wealth, and to happiness swing open so easily that they turn at the touch of almost any man.[6]

But if opportunities were actually growing, why did so many people believe that the path to success was becoming narrower and narrower? Why was there so much social bitterness and poverty? Why so many failures? Many of the advocates of success were ready to admit that the new industrial society had its shortcomings and that some reforms might be necessary, but, on the whole, they found the cause of failure in the weaknesses of the individual character.

The philosophers of success did not emphasize the same personal qualities singled out by the earlier proponents of self-improvement. As Elbert Hubbard put it, not the temptations of the flesh but "incapacity for independent action . . . moral stupidity, . . . infirmity of the will, [and] unwillingness to cheerfully catch hold and lift"[7] were the major causes of individual failure, and his fellow prophets agreed. "What is it that keeps the under dog down? What is it that the upper ten possesses that the under ten thousand does not have?" asked W. W. Woodbridge in another popular success parable. His answer was "Faith, Confidence, Power, Ambition and more. For greater than all, is 'THAT SOMETHING,'" which could best be defined as the capacity to say "I WILL." This was the great secret, "the talisman of success, which [you should] write upon your memory in letters of fire." [8]

The philosophers of success admitted that many Americans were poor and unhappy. But their failure was neither caused by a basic defect in the new social system nor was it a matter of personal immorality. Rather it was simply a failure of nerve, of self-confidence, of initiative. If the new industrial age had produced a greater division between rich and poor, it was because the mass of Americans, losing their courage, had become dependent upon those who still possessed the determination to win. The earlier apostles of self-improvement had assured their followers that the individual who worked hard and avoided extravagance, drink, strange women, and gambling, was certain to rise to respectability and security in his vocation. The success-philosophers, although insisting that the traditional virtues were still necessary, believed that industry and temperance were not enough. More important than all the self-disciplinary virtues was "THAT SOMETHING"—the *inner potency* of the individual who was determined to succeed. Even the man who had repeatedly failed, even the drunkard, could retrieve himself and certainly win success if only he discovered "THAT SOMETHING." One of their favorite parables, a story repeated over and over again in the literature of success, told of the individual who, after falling into abject poverty and degradation had, by a simple act of will, completely reversed his fate and become a resounding success.

180

This theme of energy, initiative, and confidence was the dominant one of the new-model self-made man presented by George Lorimer in his popular *Post* series "Letters from a Self-Made Merchant to his Son." Obviously based on Franklin's Poor Richard, Lorimer's self-made man bears an even closer resemblance to the enterprising go-getter of Southwestern humor. Doubtless one reason for Old Gorgon Graham's popularity is the fact that his style is modeled on that of Davy Crockett, Sam Slick, and Simon Suggs, updated and made slightly more respectable.

Lorimer's "Letters" also gain authority from the fact that his hero, John Graham, a pork baron, is easily recognized as a fictional version of the well-known Chicago meatpacker, Philip Armour, for whom Lorimer had worked before joining the Curtis organization as editor of the *Post*. The letters of the title are Graham's meaty discourses to his son, Pierrepont, who, in the course of the series and its sequel, attends Harvard, goes to work for his father's company, and gains the qualities of a successful businessman. The essence of Graham's attitude toward success is clear from the advice he gives his son:

I don't want to bear down hard on you right at the beginning of your life on the road, but I would feel a good deal happier over your showing if you would make a downright failure or a clean-cut success once in a while, instead of always just skimming through this way. It looks to me as if you were trying only half as hard as you could and in trying it's the second half that brings results. If there's one piece of knowledge that is of less use to a fellow than knowing when he's beat, it's knowing when he's done just enough work to keep from being fired. Of course, you are bright enough to be a half-way man, and to hold a half-way place at a half-way salary by doing half the work you are capable of, but you've got to add dynamite and ginger and jounce to your equipment if you want to get the other half that's coming to you. You've got to believe that the Lord made the first hog with the

Graham brand burned in the skin, and that the drove which rushed down a steep place was packed by a competitor. You've got to know your goods from A to Izzard, from snout to tail, on the hoof and in the can. You've got to know 'em like a young mother knows baby talk, and to be as proud of 'em as the young father of a twelve-pound baby boy, without really thinking that you're stretching it four pounds. You've got to believe in yourself and make your buyers take stock in you at par and accrued interest. You've got to have the scent of a bloodhound for an order, and the grip of a bulldog on a customer. You've got to feel the same personal solicitude over the bill of goods that strays off to a competitor as a parson over a backslider, and hold special services to bring it back into the fold. You've got to get up every morning with determination if you're going to get to bed with satisfaction. You've got to eat hog, think hog, dream hog—in short, go the whole hog if you're going to win out in the pork-packing business.[9]

As portrayed in the injunctions of Old Gorgon Graham, success requires, above all, the will to win. Although he appeals frequently to religion and morality as support for his activities, avoiding failure is the principal goal of his ethic, and whatever seems likely to lead to this end is justified. Religion, politics, ethics, all fall into line as adjuncts to success in the pork-packing business, and the individual becomes whatever he has to be to win and keep the customer. What is good for the pork-packing business is good for the country.

The older gospel of self-improvement had assumed the importance of social respectability and gentility, but Graham is utterly indifferent to social and cultural values. High society, as he sees it, is composed of impotent and indolent snobs whose grandfathers sold whiskey to the Indians. Education is useful, but only because it teaches a young man how to think quickly and outwit his competitors. Shrewd, driving, and religiously dedicated to the packing and sale of pork, John Graham is the ideal economic man, deeply committed to material progress and able to see little of value beyond the grimy environs of the Chicago stockyards.

Emphasis on will-power, self-confidence, energy, and initiative can be attributed in part to a belief that the social discontent of the late nineteenth century indicated a dangerous degeneration in moral fiber caused by the deleterious influence of new immigrant groups and the importation of foreign social philosophies. The full emergence of the philosophy of success thus coincided with the outburst of nativism which characterized the turn of the century. The literature of success also reflected the ideal of strenuosity which was so prominent in the politics of the first years of the twentieth century. But if the success-philosophers were concerned at the decline of individual initiative, they were also aware that the large organization was becoming the dominant element in American life. The imperatives of attracting attention in a large organization and winning notice and patronage among myriad competitors put a further premium on self-confidence and dynamic personality. By the end of the nineteenth century, self-help books were dominated by the ethos of salesmanship and boosterism. Personal magnetism, a quality which supposedly enabled a man to influence and dominate others, became one of the major keys to success. The "New Thought" movement, influenced by the popular pseudo-sciences of phrenology, animal magnetism, spiritualism, and mesmerism—and by Emerson's philosophy of self-reliance—attempted to codify in scientific form the "laws" of personal magnetism. This movement, and its strong influence on later exponents of success from Roger Babson to Dale Carnegie and Norman Vincent Peale, symbolized the final breakdown of the old ideal of self-improvement before the demands of a new social and economic order. In the complexity and impersonality of modern industrial life, men were no longer satisfied that the old verities of individual diligence, self-discipline, honesty, and piety would lead to "Acres of Diamonds." As Americans demanded new techniques to follow the elusive beacon of happiness, the industrious republican of Enos Hitchcock's *The Farmer's Friend* and the pious, Christian self-improver of T. S. Arthur's novels became the rugged and grasping John Graham of Lorimer's "Letters," the ready audience for Conwell's lectures, and the dynamo of magnetic force who "owed it all" to the "New Thought" movement.

True and False Success

They concerned themselves with qualities of personality rather than the traditional moral virtues, with the pursuit of wealth rather than the diligent performance of the duties of one's station. Still, advocates of the philosophy of success insisted that true success was moral and religious as well as material. Russell Conwell's most famous maxim was the oft-quoted "if you can honestly attain unto riches in Philadelphia, it is your Christian and godly duty to do so," but Conwell placed considerable stress on the word "honestly." [10] He vigorously denied that money is the root of all evil, pointing out that the Bible insists that "the *love* of money is the root of all evil." [11]

The success-philosophers differed in their estimate of how many American millionaires had made their money dishonestly. Conwell believed that no more than 2 per cent were other than God-fearing, upright men. "The Pirate Flag in Business," which was published in *Success* in 1901, argued that American business was "now directed almost exclusively to selfish ends, and the result is the chaotic state of our society, internal and external." [12] But most writers took a middle position: there were all too many American businessmen who sought success on false principles, but the system itself was sound, and the great majority of our prominent men won their positions through a rigorous adherence to the true principles of success, the only guarantees of security and happiness.

What were these true principles? On this point the philosophers of success had more than a little difficulty, and their statements were frequently ambiguous. But they were agreed that the mere accumulation of money or power was not true success. In 1901, *Success* magazine assured its readers that "we shall never have a true measurement until we cease to gauge a man's worth by his bank account or his business." [13] Roger Babson reiterated the same point in 1923. "Although fundamental economic law is a great factor in determining whether or not we are successful, we must not make the mistake of assuming a wrong definition of success. Success is not land, money, popularity, attention, or even influence. Success is that 'something' much more enjoyable than any of these things. Success is a spiritual quality, an inward satisfaction, which cannot be measured by material things." [14] Yet, *Success* devoted most of its space to showing its readers how other people had become rich and influential, and Roger Babson was an investment counselor who specialized in advising large numbers of Americans how they might make money on the stock market. The apostles of success were caught between their enthusiasm for acres of diamonds—their commitment to the accumulation of wealth—and the traditional belief that Mammon was an ally of Satan.

Three propositions were advanced to resolve this dilemma. The first was the argument that money is an indispensable power for good. "Providence," as one success counselor put it, "has endowed man with the organ of *acquisitiveness,* as phrenologists term it, for wise and beneficent purposes, and that the civilization, refine-

185

ment, virtue, wisdom, and happiness of every community are largely dependent on its exercise, is a proposition which few persons will controvert." [15] Russell Conwell agreed. "We preach against covetousness," he said, "and oftentimes preach against it so long and use the terms about 'filthy lucre' so extremely that Christians get the idea that when we stand in the pulpit we believe it is wicked for any man to have money—until the collection-basket goes around." The correct doctrine, he went on, is that

money is power, and you ought to be reasonably ambitious to have it. You ought because you can do more good with it than you could without it. Money printed your Bible, money builds your churches, money sends your missionaries, and money pays your preachers. . . . The man who gets the largest salary can do the most good with the power that is furnished to him. Of course he can if his spirit be right to use it for what it is given to him.[16]

Critics of business had often asserted that, however philanthropic the wealthy industrialist might be after he had made his money, the process of acquisition was not only corrupting in itself but led the successful man to degrade the working man beyond relief of benefactions. The success-philosophers had an answer to this: the idea of service. "To make money honestly is to preach the gospel," Conwell insisted. "The foundation principle of godliness and the foundation principle of success in business are both the same precisely." [17] The successful businessman was the one who provided the community with the services it needed. Some of the more ardent advocates of success went so far as to make of this business hero a Christ-like figure, atoning with his sacrifice of ease and comfort for the laziness, stupidity, and weakness of will of the mass of mankind. "Nothing is said about the employer who grows old before his time in a vain attempt to get frowsy ne'er-do-wells to do intelligent work; and his long, patient, striving after 'help' that does nothing but loaf when his back is turned," lamented Elbert Hubbard.[18] Not only did the successful businessman give service to humanity by providing jobs and opportunities for his fellow men, his pursuit of success was the indispensable ingredient of human progress. Charles Perkins, president of the Chicago, Burlington, & Quincy Railroad, offered a definition of business as service which the success-philosophers fully indorsed:

Have not great merchants, great manufacturers, great inventors, done more for the world than preachers and philanthropists? . . . Can there be any doubt that cheapening the cost of necessaries and conveniences of life is the most powerful agent of civilization and progress? Does not the fact that well-fed, well-warmed men make better citizens, other things being equal, than those who are cold and hungry, answer the question? Poverty is the cause of most of the crime and misery in the world—cheapening the cost of the necessaries and conveniences of life is lessening poverty, and there is no other way to lessen it, absolutely none. History and experience demonstrate that as wealth has accumulated and things have cheapened, men have improved . . . in their habits of thought, their sympathy for others, their ideas of justice as well as of mercy. . . . Material progress must come first and . . . upon it is founded all other progress.[19]

Note how this statement echoes Emerson's similar comment on the importance of railroad builders, although Emerson is careful to indicate that praise for such progress is due to a benevolent and universal moral law and not to its business allies.

The ideal of service was instrumental in defining two worldly heroes: the great manufacturer and the technological innovator or discoverer. Andrew Carnegie and Thomas A. Edison were the darlings of the success cult; financiers like J. P. Morgan were viewed with considerably less enthusiasm, and speculators like Jay Gould

187

were frequently condemned outright. From the point of view of success, the virtues of Carnegie and Edison were spectacular. Both were self-made men, and Carnegie, in particular, was a frequent writer on success. His famous article on "Wealth" in the *North American Review* in 1889 was a highly influential exposition of the ideals of service and philanthropy. Carnegie's "gospel of wealth," as his ideas soon became known, not only expresses the basic attitudes of the success-philosophers, but shows how their ideals had guided the behavior of one of the most successful men of the day. Edison's success was the perfect illustration of Russell Conwell's "Acres of Diamonds" philosophy, for, citing such examples as the invention of the safety pin, Conwell claimed that the surest way to success was through the discovery of some extremely simple but highly useful product. The phonograph, the electric light, and Edison's other inventions not only improved the lives of millions but brought great wealth to their inventor.

Finally, the apostles of success insist that wealth, properly pursued, not only required character but was a school for it:

The very labor a man has to undergo, the self-denial he has to cultivate, in acquiring money, are of themselves an education. They compel him to put forth intelligence, skill, energy, vigilance, zeal, bring out his practical qualities, and gradually train his moral and intellectual powers.[20]

In this argument, the philosophy of success again reflects Emerson, but where Emerson clearly distinguishes between the prudential and calculative level of character and the higher faculty of transcendent Reason, the success philosophers do not. In their view, the state of ultimate spiritual fulfilment is precisely that quality of character necessary to insure success. Self-reliance and "success potency" are one and the same thing.

The man who pursues wealth as a power for good, as a means of service to his fellow man, and in order to build a noble character, need not fear the corruption of money or power. As Orison Swett Marden sums up the true and false principles for *Success* magazine in November, 1907:

. . . if your aim is sordid, if there is nothing but money, mere property, in your purpose, of course fire may burn it and earthquake destroy it. But if your aim has been to make yourself a larger, completer man, to make the world a little more decent place to live in, to help your fellow men, if you have regarded your vocation as a great life school for man building, nothing can touch the results of your efforts.[21]

Don't Shoot the Millionaire: Success, Business, and Politics

In "Wealth and its Uses," Andrew Carnegie wrote: "It will be a great mistake for the community to shoot the millionaires, for they are the bees that make the most honey, and contribute most to the hive even after they have gorged themselves full."[22] Spokesmen for success were not, as has been assumed, unalterably opposed to reform. Like most Americans of the time, they were concerned about the development of large corporations, monopolies, and trusts. In particular they distrusted the financial manipulation and speculative profiteering which so often accompanied the process of consolidation. In 1901, a writer for *Success* magazine bitterly attacked these practices:

The business world has become so one-sided in its preoccupation with mere questions of gain that its highest ideal, to-day, is to get something for nothing. The man who can "make" a million or two "on the street" in a day, without rendering any service to mankind, is considered pre-eminently a "successful man." As no man can get something without earning it, unless some one

189

else earns it without getting it, the result is that the main occupation of the business world now is to get away other people's earnings from them.[23]

Both *Success* and *The Saturday Evening Post,* along with their hymns to success, vigorously raked the muck of Wall Street. Lorimer's "Letters from a Self-Made Merchant to his Son," for example, ran next to Frank Norris' assault on grain speculation, *The Pit,* and David Graham Phillips' exposé of "Swollen Fortunes." In the same period, *Success* accompanied Orison Marden's advice on getting ahead with a series of articles on the financial chicanery of Thomas Lawson. Most striking of all, in 1906, *Success* magazine helped to organize a "people's lobby" to buttonhole legislators in support of

the perfection of the Railway Rate Law, and the extension of the power of the Interstate Commerce Commission; increase of Federal control over corporations doing interstate business; Government control of coal and oil lands; inheritance taxation; income taxation; currency reform; publicity for election expenses; means for prevention of railroad accidents; and the abolition of child labor.[24]

The success-philosophers were not averse to adding their voice to the public demands for progressive reforms. Indeed, their advocacy of certain specific reforms suggests that the success philosophy was one of the major threads of continuity between the era of progressive reform and the "age of normalcy" which followed it. Perhaps when Americans responded so eagerly to the call for "normalcy" they were not reacting against reform but moving forward in the belief that the reforms enacted under the Roosevelt and Wilson administrations had eliminated the threat of the trusts and controlled the chicanery of the speculators.

Success philosophers reassured their countrymen that American society was basically sound and that the new industrialism was entirely benevolent. As they attributed failure and poverty to individual inertia and weakness of will, so they argued that monopolies, trusts, financial chicanery, and exploitation were the result of individual adherence to false principles of success. Consequently, they violently opposed the idea that reform should change society in any way. In their view, the proper principle of legislation was to restrain the activities of unscrupulous and corrupt individuals at both the higher and lower ends of the economic order. Their legislative package included prohibition as a means of restraining individual moral corruption among the working class and anti-trust, railroad regulation and banking reforms to restrict the activities of unscrupulous monopolists and financial manipulators. Apart from these proposals, the advocates of success looked upon legislation as a last resort, and were profoundly suspicious of politics. Socialism, they proclaimed, was all very fine in theory, but, if Americans could not respond properly to the ideal of individual success, how could one expect socialism to work?

To those who propose to substitute Communism for this intense Individualism [replied Andrew Carnegie, taking a quick glance at human history] the answer . . . is: The race has tried that. All progress from [primitive savagery] to the present has resulted from its displacement. Not evil, but good, has come to the race from the accumulation of wealth by those who have had the ability and energy to produce it. . . . [Socialism] necessitates the changing of human nature itself—a work of eons, even if it were good to change it, which we cannot know.[25]

Elbert Hubbard put it more succinctly: "If men will not act for themselves, what will they do when the benefit of their effort is for all?"[26]

A further reason for avoiding all but the most essential legislation was the equivocal state of American politics. Jefferson and Franklin had made political lead-

191

ership the apex of their idea of the free society. The apostles of the self-made man venerated Jackson, Clay, Webster, and Lincoln as the apotheosis of American democracy. But the philosophers of success shared Sam Slick's view that politics was a "barren field" and the most degrading of vocations. Generally, they exempted the Presidency and the major cabinet posts from their anathema, but otherwise the average legislator and the regular politician were, in their opinion, the lowest of the low. "Young man," Russell Conwell thundered,

won't you learn a lesson in the primer of politics that it is a *prima facie* evidence of littleness to hold office under our form of government? Great men get into office sometimes, but what this country needs is men that will do what we tell them to do. . . . If the great men in America took our political offices, we would change to an empire in the next ten years.[27]

No statement could be further from the Jeffersonian conception of democracy, but, adhering as they did to this view of the American political process, it is not surprising that the success-philosophers were reluctant to advocate sweeping political and economic reforms.

The philosophy of success included positive as well as negative reasons for confidence in the business community. For every unscrupulous monopolist there were, according to the exponents of success, a hundred wealthy businessmen who had followed the true principles of honesty, energy, service, and philanthropy. These men were the natural aristocracy of America and their work had been of incalculable benefit to mankind. Not only had they used their energy and skill to make available at lower prices the necessities of life and to advance human progress by creating new products and new opportunities for their fellow citizens, but they were administering their accumulated wealth to help others on the road to success. As Andrew Carnegie put it in his "gospel of wealth," the millionaire had accumulated his money because of superior skill in the administration of wealth. Was it not logical to conclude that it was he who could best be trusted to use it for the maximum benefit of the many? Like Carnegie, the philosophers of success looked forward hopefully to the time when, under the sway of the true ideals of success, service, and philanthropy,

we shall have an ideal State, in which the surplus wealth of the few will become, in the best sense, the property of the many, because administered for the common good; and this wealth, passing through the hands of the few, can be made a more potent force for the elevation of our race than if distributed in small sums to the people themselves.[28]

Neither apologists for big business, nor opponents of every kind of governmental regulation, the philosophers of success viewed the new industrial society with more complacency than criticism, more optimism than fear. They accumulated their biographies of self-made men to demonstrate that the growth of business was essentially a growth of opportunities, not only quantitatively but qualitatively. They fervently preached that the ordinary man's chance to succeed grew better every year, and, to those who complained of the restrictive effects of bigness, answered, "this bigger system grows bigger men." [29] "Much as has been said of the danger of trusts, they are not as powerful as is supposed," *Success* assured its readers.[30] Russell Conwell was even more certain that the dangers of big business were being rapidly eliminated: "Young man, the history of the breaking up of the trusts by that attack upon 'big business' is only illustrating what is now the opportunity of the smaller man. The time never came in the history of the world when you could get rich so quickly manufacturing without capital as you can now." [31]

Finally, to those who argued that the coming of the millionaire raised the specter of hereditary aristocracy and the gradual eating away of the American system of free mobility, the success-philosophers reasserted unflinchingly the old maxim "from shirtsleeves to shirtsleeves in three generations." Under the American system of democracy, the pampered son of the rich man has no advantage over the poor boy in the race for success. Carnegie and a number of others went so far as to argue that the discipline of poverty was actually a better preparation for success than inherited wealth. Indeed, no fantasy was so dear to the philosophers of success as their belief in the deleterious effect on the individual of hereditary wealth:

The youth who is reared in a luxurious home, who, from the moment of his birth is waited on by an army of servants, pampered and indulged by overfond parents, and deprived of every incentive . . . is more to be pitied than the poorest, most humbly born boy or girl in the land. Unless he is gifted with an unusual mind, he is in danger of becoming a degenerate, a parasite, a creature who lives on the labor of others, whose powers ultimately atrophy from disuse.[32]

That such pathetic creatures could form the basis of an aristocracy in America was, of course, impossible to believe. They were lucky if they did not end up on Skid Row.

In sum, the gospel of success regarding the growth of big business was a message of reassurance and vibrant hope. The long wave of prosperity after 1896, together with the sense of security created by the enactment of a number of measures designed to punish monopolists and financial manipulators, lent authority to the message. Businessmen, by no means the monolithic alliance of "special interests" that their critics sometimes made them out to be, but confused and divided themselves by the dynamic changes accompanying the growth of industry, rallied eagerly to the standard of success. Organizations like the Chamber of Commerce and the National Association of Manufacturers, glad to have a set of principles on which small and large businessmen, producers and distributors, manufacturers and merchants, bankers and borrowers, could agree, elevated the philosophy of success to the status of an official business creed. As a result, the philosophy of success became, through the 1920's, more and more identified with the particular policies of the business community. But this in effect meant the end of the philosophy as a broad, popular ideology, for when the nation picked itself up from the shambles of 1929, business found itself almost alone in the temple of success.

The Man Nobody Knows: Success and Religion

> Every one of His conversations, every contact between His mind and others, is worthy of the attentive study of any sales manager.
> Bruce Barton, *The Man Nobody Knows*

Many of the critics of success responded more violently to the emotional fervor of its disciples than to the pattern of ideas which they expressed. When Sinclair Lewis attacked the success cult, it was clearly its fanatical zeal and its confusion of cosmic ideals and sordid business realities which most excited his ire. So, too, William James was disturbed by the cultish aspects of the success philosophy when he bitterly denounced success as a bitch-goddess.

Much of the literature of success lends support to the charge that its devotees had a tendency to equate success and salvation. Popular parables of success like "That Something" and "The Magic Story" certainly treated failure and success in terms which the Christian tradition had reserved for damnation and salvation. In these stories, the hero, having been pushed by failure into an ultimate state of moral and physical degradation, experiences a moment of illumination which trans-

195

forms his personality and makes him a dynamo of success. In "The Magic Story," a degraded failure in the fitful sleep of moral exhaustion has a vision in which his better self speaks to him:

I am he who you were, and whom you have cast out for other company. I am the man made in the image of God, who once possessed your body. Once we dwelt within it together, not in harmony, for that can never be, nor yet in unity, for that is impossible, but as tenants in common who rarely fought for full possession. Then, you were a puny thing, but you became selfish and exacting until I could no longer abide with you, wherefore I stepped out. There is a plus-entity and a minus-entity in every human body. . . . To the plus-entity of a man, all things are possible. The world belongs to him,—is his estate. He fears naught, dreads naught, stops at naught; he asks no privileges, but demands them; he *dominates,* and cannot cringe; his requests are orders; opposition flees at his approach; he levels mountains, fills in vales, and travels on an even plane where stumbling is unknown.[33]

After the vision, the hero wakes a changed man:

Thereafter, I slept again, and, when I awoke, I seemed to be in a different world. The sun was shining and I was conscious that birds twittered above my head. My body, yesterday trembling and uncertain, had become vigorous and filled with energy.[34]

The result is quick and certain. "From that moment, I was a successful man, and ere long possessed another shipyard, and had acquired a full competence of worldly goods." [35]

Such rhetoric reflects a translation of the traditional Protestant conception of conversion through the force of saving grace into the terms of success, with the assistance of a dash of Emersonian self-reliance. That this translation was important to the devotees of success suggests not only the emotional intensity of their dedication to the ideal of the powerful, success-winning personality, but their need to identify the secular pursuit of material goods with some more transcendent end. This process of identification reached its climax in 1924 when Bruce Barton, the successful advertising executive, published his striking and highly popular reinterpretation of the life of Christ, *The Man Nobody Knows.* In his preface, "How it Came to Be Written," Barton explains how as a little boy he found it hard to admire the "sissified" and narrow portrayal of the founder of Christianity given in Sunday School. He determined to discover the real Jesus by reading "what the men who knew Jesus personally said about him." When he did so, he was "amazed." The Sunday School Jesus was a physical weakling. "Where did they get that idea?" A kill-joy. "He was the most popular dinner guest in Jerusalem!" Most important, the Sunday School presented Jesus as a worldly failure. On the contrary, "he picked up twelve humble men and created an organization that won the world." Barton continued, "when the man had finished his reading, he exclaimed, 'This is a man nobody knows!' " [36]

The true Jesus which Bruce Barton discovered was none other than the ideal hero of energy, service, and philanthropy. Barton's chapter headings summarize the primary characteristics and significance of the Jesus of this new New Testament: The Executive; The Outdoor Man; The Sociable Man; His Method; His Advertisements; The Founder of Modern Business; The Master.[37] Barton's argument is simple and effective. The real Jesus was a dynamic leader with a revolutionary idea and the personal magnetism which enabled him to build an organization which conquered the world. He is to be admired not as the meek lamb of God but for his idea and for his personal achievement. With one great push, Barton sweeps away the theology of centuries and makes his hero the pre-eminent expositor and example of the gospel of success.

197

What was Jesus' revolutionary idea? None other than the ideal of service which the philosophy of success so earnestly set forth. "Presidents of railroads and steamship companies; the heads of banks and investment houses—*all* of them tell the same story. They call it the 'spirit of modern business'; they suppose, most of them, that it is something very new. Jesus preached it more than nineteen hundred years ago." [38] The "main points of His philosophy" were three: "1. Whoever will be great must render great service. 2. Whoever will find himself at the top must be willing to lose himself at the bottom. 3. The rewards come to those who travel the second, undemanded mile." [39] In other words, the message of Jesus is "service," "starting at the bottom," and "the will to success."

As Barton tells it, the story of Jesus' life is the supreme parable of success. Like the hero of "The Magic Story," Jesus, "somehow, somewhere," had awakened to "the inner consciousness of power . . . . Somewhere, at some unforgettable hour, the daring filled His heart. He knew that He was bigger than Nazareth." [40] Illuminated by this conversion to success-potency, Jesus reveals the major success-winning qualities: "the personal magnetism which begets loyalty and commands respect"; the "powerful gift of picking men and recognizing hidden capacities in them" ; "His vast unending patience." [41] Summing up his argument, Barton exhorts his readers:

Let us forget all creed for the time being, and take the story just as the simple narratives give it—a poor boy, growing up in a peasant family, working in a carpenter shop; gradually feeling His powers expanding, beginning to have an influence over his neighbors, recruiting a few followers, suffering disappointments, reverses and finally death. Yet building so solidly and well that death was only the beginning of His influence! Stripped of all dogma, this is the grandest achievement story of all! [42]

It is not hard to understand why many Americans responded favorably to the basic ethical and social ideas of the philosophy of success. But it is far more difficult to explain these quasi-religious aspects of the veneration of success, for that requires us to recapture an emotional mood long past. When *The Man Nobody Knows* was republished in a paperback edition in 1962, the original chapter headings were changed in such a way that the identity between the example and ideals of Jesus and those of business were strongly de-emphasized; "The Executive" became simply "The Leader," "His Advertisements" became "His work and Words"; most important, "The Founder of Modern Business" became the completely neutral "His Way in Our World." Although the gospel remains the same, it is apparent that either author or publishers had become a little embarrassed about preaching it, at least in its pristine form.

CHAPTER VII

DREAM OR RAT RACE: Success in the Twentieth Century

> Yet aware as we are that today's necessities for the many were only yesterday the luxuries of the favored few, we find no peace. When everybody is somebody, nobody is anybody. What we have and we know it, is only access. But *access* is not the bitch-goddess herself, *success*.
>
> Mark Hanan, *The Pacifiers*

> So the rat race is run desperately by bright fellows who do not believe in it, because they are afraid to stop.
>
> Paul Goodman, *Growing Up Absurd*

In the booming twenties, criticism of success was drowned out by the paeans of the success-philosophers. It was not, for that reason, negligible. Such books as Fitzgerald's *The Great Gatsby,* Dreiser's *An American Tragedy,* and a sociological classic, Sorokin's *Social Mobility* (1927), were evidence that many Americans had rejected the frenetic exuberance of the Babsons and the Bartons. But Fitzgerald and Dreiser, if widely read, hardly set the dominant tone of the period. For this we must look to the ponderous assurance of the business community and the enthusiastic hymns of its popular prophets.

Forty years later, even the comic strips were launching somewhat wavery darts at the bitch-goddess. Rex Morgan, M.D., himself an example of the new professional hero who was rapidly replacing the old self-made

201

man, spent much of his time treating the heart attacks and ulcers of his success-seeking patients. Dr. Morgan's attempts to cure the ills of the self-made man were backed up by the health columns and, frequently, by the editorials of the daily newspapers of the 1960's. Series of articles exposed the relationship between the struggle for success and heart disease, alcoholism, divorce, and other individual and social ills. A new kind of popular self-improvement literature stressing "release from nervous tension" rather than fame and fortune and psychological well-being rather than the will to win increasingly competed with more traditional success guides for the attention of Americans. Few areas of American culture failed to show some sign of this new mood which, if not explicitly critical of the idea of business success, placed primary emphasis on a different range of values: health, leisure, fun, family life.

This new mood led many contemporary social critics to infer that the American character had changed significantly since the late nineteenth century. David Riesman's other-directed character type, Whyte's "organization man," Packard's "status-seeker," and Mills's "new middle class" offered in common the observation that Americans no longer danced to the tune of individualistic achievement. According to these critics, contemporary Americans, instead of seeking success, were more strongly motivated by the need for adjustment to the groups or to the organizations to which they belonged. The new American, they said, was sensitive to the opinions of others rather than to an inner drive for achievement. He was concerned with the attainment of status rather than success. He preferred fitting in to standing out.

Some saw this new mood as a failure of nerve. They lamented the loss of the traditional faith in the individual and complained that Americans had exchanged the dream of rising in the world for a mindless search for security. Other thinkers were heartened by the new mood and expressed hope that Americans had turned away from the narrow pursuit of business success toward a broader and more meaningful ideal of human life.

If American faith in the dream of success had declined, the basic pattern of life remained much the same. Even in the cool 1960's, Americans still flocked to buy books showing how to make millions in real estate and on the stock market. Self-improvement courses, including the Dale Carnegie program, continued to flourish. Politicians, businessmen, and journalists still paused to give homage to the self-made man, whenever he could be found. No popular ideal had yet emerged to take the place once held by the philosophy of success. Instead, it seemed that the ideal of the self-made man had gradually eroded without generating a new standard for the determination of individual and social goals. Seemingly, Americans were to be left to pursue individual success without much interest or faith in the outcome of their quests.

Success and the Pattern of Contemporary Life

The apostles of the self-made man had always insisted that any American should be able to better his condition, but late nineteenth-century critics pointed out with increasing force that there were all too many reasons why the majority of Americans were doomed to failure. As Richard T. Ely put it, "if you tell a single . . . working man . . . that he may yet be the president of the company, it is not demonstrable that you have told him what is not true, although it is within bounds to say that he is far more likely to be killed by a stroke of lightning." [1] The response to this criticism was political action. Expanding equality of opportunity through social and political reform was one of the leading themes of twentieth-century American politics.

Woodrow Wilson attacked the growth of trusts and monopolies which seemed to have limited the opportunities of the average middle-class American. He called for a New Freedom to clear the path to individual success. Later, Franklin Roosevelt criticized the economic royalists whose industrial dictatorship crushed individual enterprise in the cogs of a great machine and urged that "if the average citizen is guaranteed equal opportunity in the polling place, he must have equal opportunity in the market place." [2] Wilsonian and Rooseveltian social legislation was frequently based on the principle of self-help. The New Deal's early attempt at a planned economy, the NRA system of industrial organizations and production codes, failed to establish itself in American life. Instead, Americans preferred more indirect forms of social legislation, fearing that politically centered planning would restrict and discourage individual achievement. A graduated income tax, social security, minimum wages and hours, and aid to education were most in line with American attitudes. This type of social legislation tried to free the individual from abject poverty and illiteracy, giving him the possibility of competing with those who had the economic and cultural advantages of higher status. The design of such acts was to encourage self-help rather than to make the most efficient use of social resources for the general welfare.

Although the New Freedom and the New Deal sought to increase individual opportunities, there was a paradox in the result. Twentieth-century social legislation spread the productive abundance of America more widely without equalizing opportunity or making individual success more meaningful. By raising the wages

and status of organized labor and by giving political ex-
pression and greater economic security to farmers and
minority groups, the New Deal extended middle-class
standards of consumption to a major portion of the pop-
ulation without depressing the living standard of exist-
ing middle- and upper-class groups. Success, in the sense
of a higher level of income and consumption, was indeed
broadened. But this kind of success was more a function
of group mobility than of individual achievement. The
result was an increasing ambiguity about individual
success. In the mobility of the group, individual accom-
plishment was muted and lost its moral and psychologi-
cal significance. As success became the norm, it lost
much of its power to give the individual a sense of ac-
complishment and satisfaction. Making everyone suc-
cessful could only render meaningless the idea of suc-
cess.

Still another paradox emerged from the American at-
tempt to create a society of equal opportunity. Twen-
tieth-century reformers had hoped to increase the flow
of mobility. As it turned out, the New Deal did rela-
tively little to change the situation of either the estab-
lished upper classes or the most depressed elements of
the population. Far from equalizing opportunity by giv-
ing all Americans a chance to grasp the instruments of
wealth and power, twentieth-century reforms probably
helped to stabilize the top and bottom groups of the
American hierarchy. The graduated income tax oper-
ated against the accumulation of new personal fortunes
except in areas where there were large loopholes. While
few of the large fortunes of the later nineteenth and
early twentieth centuries were broken up, it became
more difficult for new men to accumulate great wealth.
Although social security, the political recognition of or-
ganized labor, farm price supports, wage and hour legis-
lation, and other New Deal measures raised the living

205

standards of many lower and lower-middle-class groups and made it easier to rise from blue-collar to white-collar occupations, this kind of mobility meant far less than it had in the nineteenth century. Moreover, these measures accomplished little for Negroes, unskilled laborers, migrant workers, and other groups who were barred from the same opportunity by prejudice, cultural deprivation, regional backwardness, or mental and physical handicaps. In spite of a half-century of reform, many Americans were becoming aware that a large number of citizens—estimates ranged as high as thirty million—had little chance to better their position. The traditional images of work and win and acres of diamonds were beginning to seem a little tarnished.

There was little indication in the early 1960's that new patterns of behavior were evolving in American life. Public attention had shifted from questions of economic organization and policy to the issue of civil rights, but the terms in which reformers articulated their goals were not greatly different. Where the 1930's had found a ready villain in the monopolists and economic royalists who had restricted the opportunity of the little man, the 1960's attacked those who refused equal opportunity to the Negro. Whether equal opportunity ultimately meant anything more than the chance to join the pursuit of a higher standard of living which white Americans were carrying on with so many ulcers and so little enthusiasm was not an easy question. Did human dignity require something more than a chance to compete for a second car, a house in the suburbs, and a secure niche in the bureaucracy of a large corporation? The popular concern with nervous tension, status-seeking, and suburbia suggested that this question had wide echoes.

Social and economic reforms failed to resolve the contemporary ambivalence toward success. Neither did changes in educational organization and content. The increasingly technical and specialized character of modern work made formal education a much more essential part of the normal career line. Both the apprenticeship system and individual entrepreneurship, major success strategies of the nineteenth century, had been largely superseded by formal education. Today's self-made man does not rise from the ranks; he is hired as an executive trainee on the basis of a college degree in business administration, engineering, or economics. The office boy of Horatio Alger's day might have had some hope of rising to a partnership, although he was probably mistaken if he thought that diligence and punctuality in filing correspondence would help him to do so. Today's office boy knows that a year at Harvard Business School will do more for his career than a lifetime of industry, economy, temperance, and piety.

Yet, greater emphasis on education probably did not mean a greater equalization of opportunity. The quality and type of education available to different classes and the effect of different social environments on learning made it hard to say whether education had increased or decreased the opportunities available to the average person. On the one hand, the number of students and the average age at which they left school continually rose; on the other, the poor schools available to lower-class children and the increasingly prevalent practice of ability grouping tended to divide children along existing class lines and to reinforce the existing social structure more strongly than increased educational facilities promoted upward mobility. Whatever the effect of the expansion of formal education in America might ultimately be, and one hoped it would be great, it had not yet created the dramatic change in social patterns which some of its proponents expected so optimistically.

Nor was there any very convincing evidence that increased education had made American culture more humanistic. Apart from the reforms associated with the name of John Dewey, American education remained predominantly utilitarian, oriented toward the work or profession which its students were expected to perform when they finished their schooling. With the exception of a relatively small number of liberal arts colleges and universities which insisted on some form of a general education, American schools were, in the main, training grounds for economic success.

If the form of American education in the 1960's exemplified the pattern of success, the content sometimes suggested quite another range of values. Dewey's ideas had not penetrated into the heart of the curriculum, but they had had a considerable impact. If one compares the values and ideas of life reflected in selected children's books from the mid-nineteenth and mid-twentieth centuries, one finds striking differences. The Rollo series by Jacob Abbott, Goodrich's Peter Parley Books, the McGuffey readers, and other nineteenth-century children's books emphasized the hard moral discipline of self-improvement. The virtues and habits of industry, economy, temperance, and piety were understood to be not only the road to personal achievement, but primary ends in themselves. The child learned these virtues from his parents and teachers. Contemporary school texts, such as the popular Dick and Jane series, put greater stress on play, on creative activity, on "getting along" with friends and neighbors. The young hero is the one who is inventive and sensitive to the needs and wishes of others. Sibling or peer group takes over the role occupied by the authoritative adult in earlier books. Sharing rather than achieving or acquiring is perhaps the central moral theme of the Dick and Jane series.

In education as in other areas of American life one

finds a deep ambivalence toward success. Mobility through individual economic achievement remains the primary career pattern for which young Americans are educated. Yet, the major values and goals of the mobile life are no longer taught as the center of moral value. A similar ambivalence is reflected in the most successful and widely read works of moral and social instruction for adults: the contemporary analogues to the self-improvement handbooks of the past.

The Failure of Positive Thinking

To a considerable extent, books like Norman Vincent Peale's *The Power of Positive Thinking* (1952), Dale Carnegie's *How to Win Friends and Influence People* (1936), and Napoleon Hill's *Think and Grow Rich* (1937) are lineal descendants of nineteenth-century success books. They stress the same central themes: success is within the grasp of every individual; it is the result of inner qualities of character and will irrespective of environment or heredity; these qualities can be developed by any person; finally, all this is possible because America is a land of uniquely unlimited opportunity and freedom. Contemporary popular self-improvement books still repeat these platitudes of the philosophy of success, but they also emphasize a number of themes which suggest that their commitment to the traditional ideal of rising from rags to riches is by no means as wholehearted as it seems on the surface.

Popular thinking about mobility in the nineteenth century—as exemplified in such guides to self-improvement as those by T. S. Arthur and Henry Ward Beecher—found one of its central themes in the individual's ability to change the external world. By hard work and constant saving, the individual could achieve economic security and social status which would place him

209

beyond the power of external necessity. Mid-twentieth-century counselors of positive thinking also sing paeans to the miraculous capacity of the individual will. However, their primary emphasis is not on the will's impact on reality. For them, the changing of the individual's mental outlook, the transformation of "negative" into "positive" thinking, has become more important than the control of external reality. As Norman Vincent Peale explains, "how you think about a fact may defeat you before you ever do anything about it. You may permit a fact to overwhelm you mentally before you start to deal with it. On the other hand, *a confident and optimistic thought pattern can modify or overcome the fact altogether.*" [3]

With mental transformation their primary aim, it is not surprising that Hill, Carnegie, and Peale reject certain of the more physically strenuous aspects of the traditional gospel of self-improvement. For them, the idea that the road to success requires long and tireless industry is no longer valid. "Riches begin with a state of mind, with definiteness of purpose, with little or no hard work," insists Napoleon Hill.[4] So, also, with the Alger drama of the shoeshine boy slowly rising up the ladder from rags to riches. "This idea of starting at the bottom and working one's way up may appear to be sound, but the major objection to it is this—too many of those who begin at the bottom never manage to lift their heads high enough to be seen by opportunity, so they remain at the bottom." [5] Dale Carnegie also insists that hard work and diligence are much overrated. "The chairman of the board of directors of one of the largest rubber companies in the United States told me that, according to his observations, a man rarely succeeds at anything unless he has fun doing it. This industrial leader doesn't put much faith in the old adage that hard work alone is the magic key that will unlock the door to our desires." [6]

Insisting on the primacy of mental transformation, Peale, Carnegie, and Hill still hold out material success as the most important goal. Positive thinking, according to Peale, teaches the individual how to cultivate peace of mind, "not as an escape from life into protected quiescence, but as a power center out of which comes driving energy for constructive personal and social living." [7] Throughout *The Power of Positive Thinking*, Peale's primary examples of successful converts are salesmen and executives who have found greater efficiency and power over others in positive thinking. Dale Carnegie, in explaining the importance of a cheerful disposition to the successful man of affairs, cites approvingly one of his student's remarks: "I find that smiles are bringing me dollars, many dollars every day." [8] In the very title of his major opus, *Think and Grow Rich*, Napoleon Hill sums up the equation between positive thinking and material wealth.

In their frank approbation of the pursuit of wealth, contemporary positive thinkers go beyond their nineteenth-century predecessors. Mid-nineteenth-century popular philosophers of self-improvement like Henry Ward Beecher and T. S. Arthur rarely presented wealth as a sole or primary end. More important were the social and religious goals of middle-class respectability in this life and salvation in the next, which the moral and physical disciplines associated with industry and economy insured. Peale, Hill, and Carnegie, however, frankly sanction the desire for hard cash and assume that material wealth is an ultimate human motive. "You may as well know, right here," Napoleon Hill assures his readers, "that you can never have riches in great quantities unless you can work yourself into a white heat of *desire* for money." [9] He recommends that his followers begin their efforts by fixing in their minds "the *exact* amount of money" they wish to gain and by re-

211

peating this amount to themselves "once just before retiring at night and once after arising in the morning." [10] This total insistence on the precise material result of the quest for success is the major theme of another popular type of success manual, books which give detailed and specific instructions on how to make money in specialized areas of business like real estate and stocks. One such book, William Nickerson's *How I Turned $1000 into a Million in Real Estate in My Spare Time,* was on the *New York Times* best-seller list for several months. The hundreds of similar "How-to" books listed in *Books in Print* suggest a widespread popular acceptance of a frankly materialistic attitude toward human affairs.

Yet, the curious thing is that, for all their open acceptance of money as the goal, the positive thinkers ultimately reject the very materialism they so frankly espouse. Napoleon Hill concludes his book by indicating the final treachery of the material world:

You have absolute control over but one thing, and that is your thoughts. . . . If you must be careless with your possessions, let it be in connection with material things. *Your mind is your spiritual estate!* Protect and use it with the care to which divine royalty is entitled.[11]

Similarly, Norman Vincent Peale teaches the method of positive thinking "not as a means to fame, riches or power, but as the practical application of faith to overcome defeat and accomplish worthwhile creative values in life." [12] Dale Carnegie sums up the positive thinker's ambivalent desire for material success and inner happiness when he points to one of his prize pupils and shows how he "now has more profit, more leisure, and—what is infinitely more important—he finds far more happiness in his business and in his home." [13] Thus, Peale, Carnegie, and Hill justify the techniques they teach with references to material values, but ultimately they seem more concerned with inner certitude and serenity than with the conquest of the external world, more with personal joy than with upward mobility. At the same time, they seem unable to envision peace of mind without the sanction of material success. This is not the only ambivalence in positive thinking. Peale, Carnegie, and Hill also vacillate between other values. To develop the individual's power over others as a means to wealth is certainly the explicit theme of positive thinking. Peale teaches "prayer power" as a technique of individual accomplishment. Hill's "think and grow rich" is ostensibly a procedure to bring the power of mind and spirit to bear on the problem of acquiring a certain amount of cold cash. Yet, it often seems that the establishment of a close relationship with other individuals or with God is really more important than using others for self-aggrandizement. Dale Carnegie captures this ambivalence nicely in the catchy title of his *chef-d'oeuvre*. Clearly it is not enough simply to "influence people"; one must also "win friends." In *The Power of Positive Thinking*, it is never entirely clear whether one enlists God as an ally in the struggle for power or as a loving friend. Even Napoleon Hill's concern for the aggrandizement of the individual involves the obliteration of the individual self and its re-emergence as a part of the "Infinite Intelligence." In one revealing passage, Hill tells how he tried to remodel his life by holding, each night, an imaginary meeting with a group of great men —Emerson, Paine, Edison, Darwin, Lincoln, Burbank, Napoleon, Ford, and Carnegie—after whom he was trying to pattern his life. The way in which he describes this meeting is indicative of its quasi-mystical character:

My purpose was to rebuild my own character so it would represent a composite of the characters of my imaginary counselors.

213

Realizing, as I did, early in life, that I had to overcome the handicap of birth in an environment of ignorance and superstition, I deliberately assigned myself the task of voluntary rebirth through the method I have described above.[14]

With its strange reference to rebirth, this passage suggests an ambivalence about method as well as a confusion about goals. Indeed, Peale, Carnegie, and Hill move between a quasi-mystical and a quasi-scientific description of the process of self-improvement. On the one hand, they insist on a rational, mechanistic approach to the training of the mind, a gradual, piecemeal discipline which will result in complete control of both conscious mind and unconscious impulses. On the other hand, they promise that their method will have the impact and immediacy of instant mystical illumination. Positive thinking, says Peale, "teaches a hard, disciplinary way of life, but one which offers great joy to the person who achieves victory over himself and the difficult circumstances of the world." [15]

The rational, "scientific" aspect of positive thinking results both in the continual formulation of lists of rules—a characteristic of success literature from its earliest days—and in a peculiar use of twentieth-century psychology. Peale gives his readers such lists as "ten simple, workable rules for overcoming inadequacy attitudes and learning to practice faith," "ten rules for getting effective results from prayer," and "the simple formula for solving . . . problems and over-coming . . . difficulties, to wit, (1) PRAYERIZE, (2) PICTURIZE, (3) ACTUALIZE." [16] Napoleon Hill contributes such infallible formulas as "six ways to turn desires into gold," "the self-confidence formula," "six steps to stimulate your subconscious mind," "the ten major causes of failure in leadership," "the thirty-one major causes of failure," "fifty-five famous alibis by old man IF," and innumerable others.[17]

214

In addition to the reduction of success to a series of simple, mechanical steps, Peale, Carnegie, and Hill make use of an oversimplified form of psychology. Peale, for example, attributes much human failure and misery to "the malady popularly called the inferiority complex," [18] and recommends psychological counseling in addition to the power of faith. Both Peale and Hill suggest that, by making use of the power latent in the unconscious, the individual may greatly increase his success. According to Hill, the unconscious mind is like "a fertile garden-spot, in which weeds will grow in abundance, if the seeds of more desirable crops are not sown therein." [19] And Peale shows how "if you drop a prayer into the subconscious at the moment of its greatest relaxation, the prayer has a powerful effect." [20]

The psychoanalytic gospel of the positive thinkers, if examined with a critical eye, turns out to have more in common with Emerson's conception of the Oversoul than with the ideas of Freud or Jung. Hill's explanation of the power of Eros transforms the sex drive into a vapid mystical force which can help the individual to arrive at a more positive mental outlook.

The emotions of faith, love and sex are the most powerful of all the major positive emotions. When the three are blended, they have the effect of "coloring" thought in such a way that it instantly reaches the subconscious mind, where it is changed into its spiritual equivalent, the only form that induces a response from Infinite Intelligence.[21]

The quasi-mystical jargon which so frequently creeps into the prose of Peale, Hill, and Carnegie is one indication that, for all their emphasis on scientific discipline, the positive thinkers are equally attracted to a completely unworldly state of mystical illumination. A number of the procedures suggested by Peale are simplified forms of the disciplines traditionally used by mystics as a means to transcendent experience. His sugges-

tion that the reader continually repeat and meditate
upon such biblical sayings as "if God be for us, who can
be against us" resembles the discipline of meditation on
a saying by a famous Zen master. The disciple is taught
to contemplate the saying until its meaning comes to
him in a flash of enlightenment. Like Peale, Napoleon
Hill and Dale Carnegie emphasize the miraculous spir-
itual transformation which a conscientious use of their
techniques will produce. A typical description of the ex-
perience of conversion to positive thinking clearly illus-
trates this emphasis:

> I sought for guidance and found myself, quite to my surprise,
> standing beside him and placing my hand upon his head. I
> prayed, asking God to heal the man. I suddenly became aware
> of what seemed to be the passing of power through my hand
> which rested upon his head. I hasten to add that there is no
> healing power in my hand, but now and then a human being
> is used as a channel, and it was evidently so in this instance, for
> presently the man looked up with an expression of the utmost
> happiness and peace and he said simply, "He was here. He
> touched me. I feel entirely different."
> From this time on his improvement was pronounced, and at
> the present time he is practically his old self again, except for
> the fact that he now possesses a quiet and serene confidence
> which was not present previously. Apparently the clogged chan-
> nel in his personality through which the passage of power had
> been impeded was opened by an act of faith and the free flow
> of energy was renewed.[22]

Not surprisingly, the positive thinkers' ambivalence
is reflected in their treatment of the business world—
the primary theater of success. In one sense, the world
of business is evidently all in all for them. Peale, Carne-
gie, and Hill rarely mention any forms of human activ-
ity not associated with the making and selling of goods.
Nor is there anything resembling criticism of the struc-
ture or practices of enterprise in America, something

216

which even such earlier proponents of success like Orison Marden and Roger Babson indulged in occasionally. The positive thinkers seem to accept the American business world wholeheartedly. If it has flaws, they are the result of some failure to assume a positive attitude.

In spite of the absence of explicit criticism, or any suggestion of alternative ways of life, the world of business frequently reveals itself in the works of Carnegie, Peale, and Hill as an unhappy and unsatisfactory place, a world of tension, anxiety, neurosis, and overwork. The broken, distraught salesmen and executives who parade through the pages of *The Power of Positive Thinking* and *How to Win Friends and Influence People* were certainly planted there to show the need for positive teaching, but they are also eloquent testimony to the failure of the business world to fulfil human needs.

On the whole, positive thinking is less a new expression of the traditional ideal of rising in the world than a revelation of the failure of the dream. Without the social and religious sanctions of the eighteenth and nineteenth centuries, the dream of success is no longer a magical idea for Americans. Once success had been the road to religious salvation and middle-class respectability. When these goals lost their force, success, too, lost much of its savor. There is no particular satisfaction in being able to purchase more of the same goods which an ever-more-efficient technology produces in ever-increasing amounts, and it is not easy to see what else success, without its social and religious sanctions, can offer. Sensing this vacuum, the exponents of positive thinking try to fill it by establishing a relation between material success and an inner serenity and sense of security, showing that happiness is the true way to success. Where its nineteenth-century proponents had proclaimed that the quest for success would lead to those moral and religious ends which alone create true happiness, the positive thinkers seem to be affirming the contrary, that success itself is contingent upon the individual achieving a happy and serene mental outlook. But such a reversal suggests that mid-twentieth-century prophets of success are no longer very sure of the value of what they preach. If, in order to become successful, one must first become confident, serene, and happy, what then is the point of going on to become successful?

Social Science Studies Mobility

> Our data allow us, therefore, to question the validity of the doctrine that the successful businessman had proved himself to be the fittest in the struggle for survival. This doctrine, an amalgamation of classic economic liberalism with a popularized Darwinism, drew its strength from the folklore of the American frontier and the thriving business civilization of the late nineteenth century, and was bolstered by selected examples of the "rags to riches" story, liberally embellished by wishful thinking.
>
> Bendix and Lipset, *Social Mobility in Industrial Society*

The ambivalence of popular success literature is a pale mirror of the profoundly critical attitude toward mobility of many twentieth-century American intellectuals. In the 1960's, while the Peales, the Carnegies, and conservative politicians like Senator Goldwater continue to preach their ambiguous versions of the philosophy of success, American social scientists have demonstrated convincingly that many traditional beliefs about success in America simply have no basis in fact.

Even in the late nineteenth century, social scientists had begun to question the received view of mobility. One of the first serious sociological treatments of the subject, Frank Lester Ward's essay "Broadening the Way to Success" (1886), adumbrates several of the themes which later sociologists would stress. Ward's major thesis is that, in their admiration for successful men, Americans had failed to realize that the social environment in which an individual grows up is as important a factor in his eventual success or failure as his character or will. "Success in all cases is the product of two forces—the force from within and the force from without." [23] Ward goes on to ridicule such conventional notions as the belief that a society led by self-made men is more democratic than one ruled by an aristocracy of blood, or the idea that it is "hard knocks" that lead an individual to success. On the contrary, Ward argues, "everyone who has accomplished anything against adverse circumstances, would have accomplished proportionately more had such circumstances been removed." [24]

Ward's attack centers on the narrowness of the prevailing definition of success and the failure of society to provide sufficient opportunities for the majority of individuals. Like the philosophers of success, Ward dreamt of a society in which everyone would be successful. "The central truth which I have sought to enforce is that, like plants and animals, men possess latent capacities which, for their development simply require opportunity." However, unlike the Conwells and the Babsons, Ward does not believe that this happy state can be realized without a drastic reform of the narrowly competitive American social system in the direction of more opportunities and a broader definition of accomplishment. "I look upon existing humanity as I look upon pristine vegetation. The whole struggling mass is held by the relentless laws of competition in a condition far below its possibilities." [25]

Ward's way of thinking about the problem of "broadening the way to success" had a considerable currency in twentieth-century reform movements. By the end of the nineteenth century, some social scientists had gone beyond Ward's criticism of the conventional idea of success to a broader question: what, in fact, is the social function of mobility? In 1899, Charles Horton Cooley, a sociologist at the University of Michigan and an early follower of John Dewey, prepared a monograph on *Personal Competition; Its Place in the Social Order and Effect upon Individuals; with Some Considerations on Success.* Cooley looked at success in its relationship to the social order as a whole. By doing so, he brought to the center of the discussion a problem which the popular philosophers of self-improvement and success had largely ignored but which had been central to the thinking of Jefferson: the way in which the dominant social institutions control and shape the process of mobility.

According to Cooley, individual competition for wealth, power, and position is not unique to America. It is a principle of social organization which operates more or less in all societies and its function is to assign to each individual a place in the social system:

If "all the world's a stage," this is a process that distributes the parts among the players. It may do it well or ill, but, after some fashion, it does it. Some may be cast in parts unsuited to them; good actors may be discharged altogether and worse ones retained; but nevertheless the thing is arranged in some way and the play goes on.[26]

The only alternative way in which this vital social function can be accomplished is through the principle of status, "some fixed, mechanical rule, usually a rule of inheritance, which decides the function of the individual without reference to his personal traits, and thus dispenses with any process of comparison." [27]

Throughout history, these alternative principles of social organization have operated, and most societies have used both. Neither principle is inherently more efficient or moral than the other; rather, each has different advantages and results in the intensification of certain social values at the expense of others. Status leads to order and continuity, but its chief disadvantage is "that of suppressing personal development, and so of causing social enfeeblement, rigidity and ultimate decay." [28] Competition, on the other hand, "develops the individual and gives flexibility and animation to the social order," but it has the disadvantage of tending toward social disintegration and disorder. [29]

Both competition and status have taken many different forms, and different societies have applied them in varying ways. To think of competition solely as hostile contention is to mistake a particular form of competition for the general method of assigning each individual a social role in accordance with some aspect of his personal character. Often the competing individual is not even aware of the process through which he is selected for a particular place in society. Nor is competition inimical to collective or associative activities.

The two . . . are supplementary and each has its proper sphere. One is achievement, the other process. Competition is an organizing force, and its relation to association is . . . one of inferior rank but prior necessity. [30]

Co-operation arises when men see that they have a common interest and possess enough intelligence and self-control to pursue it. The place of competition lies in areas where interests are divergent or undetermined. Thus, the members of a large organization co-operate toward the attainment of the organization's goals but compete with each other either for their places or roles within the organization. Or, to take another case, a society which chooses its leaders through a highly selective educational process may be completely competitive in the placement of individuals and completely collective in the attainment of its general goals.

The character of competition within a social group is determined by the standards and goals of that group as articulated in its definition of success. Once they have provided for their animal necessities, men seek respect,

221

honor, power, and love, "the production of some desired
effect upon the minds of other persons." They tend to do
this through the pursuit of what society has defined as
valuable and desirable. Consequently, success "is what-
ever men think it is." [31] Therefore, within a social
group, success is a sign of high virtue, since it demon-
strates that the individual has played his social role
effectively. From a more objective point of view, how-
ever, success *per se* is amoral, since it indicates only
that the individual has been able to meet the standards
set by the group. The real problem lies in the nature of
the standards set by the dominant social institutions.
These can be either narrow and stultifying or broad and
humane. The businessman can be a loyal and affection-
ate husband and father and a totally unscrupulous spec-
ulator without any real inconsistency. In both cases, he
is merely seeking to live up to the standards his society
has established for him.

Cooley concludes that the question of success is not
whether individualistic competition is the most desir-
able principle of social organization or whether the pur-
suit of success is a worthwhile end. Such a formulation
only confuses the issue. Every society, unless it is
rigidly bound by the principle of status, has some form
of competition between individuals and groups. The real
need is to create forms of competition and standards of
success which will support the values most desirable for
both society and the individual citizen. If men wish to
improve society, it is useless to attack the problem by
exhorting individuals to self-improvement. More indi-
vidual success will result only in a further solidification
of the existing situation. If current values are inade-
quate, a greater number of self-made men will only
make the situation worse. Nor is it possible to create a
Utopia in which competition is eliminated. The only

way to eliminate competition is by the establishment of a rigid status system.

According to Cooley, the only possible course is the gradual redefinition of standards of success in accordance with a broader, more rational, and more humane view of the possibilities of human life.

We must, then, conclude that the standard of success which our age presses most strongly upon our attention is a narrow and, in some sense, a low one. It needs to be raised and diversified. The standard of success should be the symmetrical reflection of all the needs of human nature, not the exaggerated image of a few of them. Without expecting that wealth will cease to be an object of pretty general esteem and endeavor, we may hope and strive to break down the ascendency which it exercises over a class of persons who would serve the world better and find more happiness for themselves if they could devote their energies to the discovery of truth, the creation of beauty, or some other of the more imaginative aims. It may be asked, what is to hinder? The answer however, is not difficult: to undertake careers of this sort in the face of the indifference to them which for the most part prevails, requires a self-confidence and vigor of initiative which is rare; the special education necessary is often unattainable; the chance of making a living is not encouraging; and, most fatal of all by far, the state of public sentiment denies to the follower of art, for example, that appreciative sympathy which is essential to the unfolding of talent. The present age acts upon a large class of minds of the finer order as an uncongenial climate acts upon a plant: it chills them and stunts their growth: they feel home-sick. And aside from these, people in general would be much the better for the broader and richer life which a widening of the field of endeavor would bring with it.[32]

The work of Cooley and Ward, perceptive as it is, was largely speculative. The empirical investigations of the twentieth century accumulated the statistical and historical facts to bear them out. These investigations, though not absolutely conclusive, established beyond reasonable doubt that mobility is not a unique trait of American democracy but a process which has existed in one form or another in all human societies. Moreover, these studies tended to throw into question the nineteenth-century assumption that there is a direct connection between a high rate of mobility and a democratic polity.

Just three decades after Cooley's monograph appeared, Pitirim A. Sorokin was able to assemble a vast amount of historical and statistical data on mobility in different countries and at different historical periods in his classic study *Social Mobility* (1927). The data which Sorokin brought together made it clear that America is not unique as the land of opportunity. "The records show that climbing from a farmer to a king or a president is as old as human history." [33] Sorokin argues, with innumerable instances to prove his point, "there has scarcely been any society whose strata were absolutely closed, in which vertical mobility was not present." [34] Americans have eliminated such barriers to mobility as a legally established hereditary aristocracy, but this does not mean that they have created a freely mobile society. "One obstacle gone, another has taken its place. In theory, in the United States of America, every citizen may become the President of the United States. In fact, 99.9 per cent of the citizens have as little chance of doing it as 99.9 per cent of the subjects of a monarchy have of becoming a monarch." [35]

Not only is America far from unique in its social openness, but, according to Sorokin, democracy and mobility are not invariably correlated. Democratic societies are frequently characterized by a more intensive vertical mobility, but this is not always true. "In some of the non-democratic groups, mobility has been greater than in the democracies," through other channels than the political ones—the church, for example. Moreover, Sorokin argues that intensive mobility is not incompatible with a highly stratified social order and that democracies are no less divided into classes than monarchies in spite of a popular belief to the contrary. "Such a belief is a kind of mental aberration." [36]

Sorokin also questions the traditional ideal of success when he considers the effects of mobility. Many of these effects are, as Sorokin sketches them, desirable. Mobility facilitates economic growth and social progress. It leads to an increase in inventions and discoveries and to a more rapid development of the intellectual life. But, Sorokin emphasizes, mobility may have very deleterious effects both on the individuals involved and on the social order. By weakening the individual's ties to his family and his class, intensive mobility can threaten both the social order and the individual's sense of security within it. The result is an increase in mental disease and neurosis, in alienation, psychological isolation, and loneliness, which in turn may lead to anarchy and revolution. Sorokin indicates his own preference for a highly mobile society, in spite of its anxieties and tensions, but he warns that the strains of mobility will lead to attempts to re-establish "the lost paradise" of an immobile society, and to make the individual again only "a finger of the hand of a social body."

More recent studies of mobility have concentrated on careful empirical research and on the creation of more accurate measures of the extent and intensity of mobility. Bendix and Lipset, in *Social Mobility in Industrial Society* (1959), emphasize the relationship between industrial economies and mobility, bringing forth evidence that the mobility rates in major European countries and in America have been essentially the same since the rise of industry. Furthermore, in a study of the American business elite, Bendix and Lipset throw doubt on the belief that there has ever been a period in American history when the "rags to riches" myth resembled reality. The work of Bendix and Lipset and other recent studies shows that mobility rates have been fairly constant in America since the late eighteenth century, though the routes have changed with the greater contemporary emphasis on education; that America has never approached the ideal of equality of opportunity; and that the upper or upper-middle-class child is far more likely to be successful than the lower or lower-middle-class offspring.

The publication in English of Max Weber's classic *The Protestant Ethic and the Spirit of Capitalism* (1930) also contributed to a more critical attitude toward success. Weber's study influenced American historians to study the development of popular success ideologies and their relationship to the development of American society. A. Whitney Griswold's pioneering monograph on the "American cult of success" showed the continuity between the social ethic of the American puritans and later success philosophies. More recently, Kenneth Lynn studied the impact of the success philosophy on late nineteenth-century American writers and concluded that many of their weaknesses resulted from their inability to escape its influence. In addition, Irvin Wyllie published his excellent study, *The Self-Made Man in America,* anatomizing the common themes to be found in nineteenth-century success books. Their approach to the subject of success is essentially critical, and they show clearly that for the twentieth-century historian and social scientist the ideal of success has become a popular myth, interesting because of its wide currency, but lacking any significant value as a description of human ends.

226

The Failure of Success

While social scientists and historians shattered many of the assumptions which cluster around the ideal of success, twentieth-century novelists also dealt with the theme of success in an increasingly critical way. A few Cameron Hawleys still try to throw a mantle of romance and adventure around the self-made businessman, but they are decidedly in the minority. The central emphasis in twentieth-century American fiction is on the woes of success.

The novels of Theodore Dreiser, whose writing career spanned a considerable portion of the first half of the twentieth century, show how one writer, who began as a devotee of success, became increasingly critical of the dream. As Kenneth Lynn has convincingly demonstrated in *The Dream of Success,* Dreiser's early novels are marked by a considerable ambivalence about the ideal of success. On one hand, he was a great admirer of successful men and an ardent exponent of the success philosophy promulgated by Orison Swett Marden. On the other, as a reader of Spencer and a convinced, if somewhat naïve, social and biological determinist, Dreiser thought that extreme voluntarism and its emphasis on morality were nonsense. In his early novels— *Sister Carrie* (1900), *The Financier* (1912), *The Titan* (1914), and others—Dreiser attacks these moralistic assumptions. Yet, at the same time, his portraits of successful men and women like Frank Cowperwood and Carrie Meeber show more than a little admiration for their prowess and their ability to gain wealth and power in a jungle world. Sister Carrie enters the world of modern urban America as a sweet, chaste, innocent girl, but her virtues only make it impossible for her to cope effectively with her new environment. It is after her loss of

227

moral innocence that Carrie begins to be successful. So, too, the career of Frank Cowperwood, hero of *The Financier* and *The Titan,* makes it clear that it is not the virtuous man but the amoral and unscrupulous man who is likely to achieve fame and fortune. Cowperwood learns early that success is won by force and fraud. His lack of scruples, the force of his personality, and his mental superiority—described by Dreiser in the language of Orison Marden and the philosophers of personal magnetism—make Cowperwood more than a match for the other denizens of the urban jungle. Although Dreiser obviously admires Cowperwood's prowess, he also stresses the emptiness of this kind of amoral success. Cowperwood's victories bring him no satisfaction or happiness. Each financial or amatory coup only leads to another. One world conquered, the restless and unhappy Cowperwood can only turn about and look for another.

Cowperwood makes the discovery that success is meaningless. Yet, at the same time, he finds it impossible to imagine any other direction for his formidable energies and abilities. Lynn suggests, probably with reason, that Cowperwood's dilemma reflects Dreiser's own ambiguity toward the ideal of success. By the time he wrote *An American Tragedy* (1925), Dreiser had lost whatever remained of his faith in the philosophy of success. Here he offers the anatomy of failure. His verdict is that neither the individual's virtues nor his will can account for success or failure. Cowperwood's instinctual force drives him on to defy conventional opinion and to become rich and desperate. The ordinary American is simply victimized by society's delusions and his own. Clyde Griffiths, the protagonist of Dreiser's tragedy, has most of the qualities of an Alger hero. He is an intelligent, eager, pleasant boy with poor but honest parents who have given him an intense but narrow religious education. Clyde's story is the long and profusely detailed account of why such a youth is as likely to end up in the electric chair as at a desk as a junior partner. Whatever success may mean, it cannot, in the world of *An American Tragedy,* be attributed to the diligence, virtue, or will of the individual.

America itself, in Dreiser's novel, is hardly a land of opportunity. Its society falls into three main classes: the rich and powerful, who are complacently content with their superior position, their luxuries and frivolities, and their indifference to the mass of their fellows; the poor, working classes, apathetic, brutalized, largely immersed in the daily grind from which they emerge only to lose themselves in drink and sex; and the desperate ones, like Clyde Griffiths, who scramble to rise from one class to another. This group's lot is the worst. Deluded by the irrelevant ideals of popular religion, unprepared by their environment to compete with family wealth and power, their fate is to struggle hopelessly, or, like Clyde, to be driven into crime. What happens to Clyde is in no way proportionate to his own actions. He does not have the will to carry out his murder plan; his victim is drowned by accident. On trial for his life, Clyde becomes the pawn of other men's ambitions. That he is convicted and executed has less to do with his own guilt than with the political aspirations of the prosecuting attorney.

For Dreiser, like other novelists of his generation— David Graham Phillips, Jack London, Robert Herrick— disillusion with the traditional ideal of success meant despair and disillusion with America, and to an extent, with human society itself. For these writers the metaphysics of mid-nineteenth-century scientific naturalism was a port in a storm. Dreiser in particular used a rigid simplistic form of determinism as a means of pointing up the gap between the moral romance of the success ideal and what he felt to be the reality of an amoral world. But the very intensity of his insistence on the gap between ideal and reality reflected his own anguished loss of faith. A later generation of writers had fewer ambivalences. In their work the theme of mobility is transformed from Dreiser's essentially satirical assault on the inadequacy of the middle-class Protestant ethic to a complex exploration of the problem of success and its effect on the individual's quest for moral identity and happiness. The archetypal self-made man of the mid-twentieth century is neither Dreiser's pathetic Clyde Griffiths nor Sinclair Lewis's confused and dreary Babbitt, but the strong, tragic heroes of Fitzgerald's *The Great Gatsby*, Faulkner's *Absalom, Absalom,* and Robert Penn Warren's *All the King's Men.* These heroes are neither hopeless failures nor exponents of chicanery and fraud. On the contrary, they are men of daring and courage, of pride and honor, of imagination and vision, through whose quest for happiness their authors are able to portray in depth the moral ambiguities of ambition. Jay Gatsby, Thomas Sutpen, and Willie Stark are bound together by the meteoric rhythm of their rise and fall. Each is a self-made man; each rises rapidly from poverty and obscurity to the highest pinnacles of wealth and power. Then each falls, hopelessly lost in the illusions he has attempted to force upon an unyielding reality and is destroyed by an agency which he himself has brought into being.

For Gatsby the pursuit of success is a quest for his lost love. When Daisy, after her moment of romance with Gatsby, returns to the world of wealth from which she has come, Gatsby sets out to win her back. He dreams that, with success once won, he can turn time back and recapture the lovely girl who had loved him. The closer he comes to the realization of his dream, the more illusory it becomes. Not only is Daisy no longer the romantic young girl he had loved, but Gatsby himself has changed. His feelings have been encrusted with the demands of his expanded ego until love is no longer enough. Ultimately, Gatsby has to destroy the past by making Daisy admit that she has never loved her husband. As long as Tom Buchanan controls even a small portion of Daisy's history, Gatsby's triumph is incomplete. "He wanted nothing less of Daisy than that she should go to Tom and say, 'I never loved you.' After she had obliterated four years with that sentence they could decide upon the more practical measures to be taken." [37] Thus, success leads Gatsby to demand that reality be changed to authenticate his triumphant rise from obscurity to wealth. But no man can escape the limitations of time and history. Having failed to gain Daisy's total love, Gatsby attempts to take on himself her guilt in the killing of Tom's mistress. Thus, Tom becomes the agent of Gatsby's death when he tells George Wilson that Gatsby is responsible for the death of his wife. Wilson's murder of Gatsby is the physical analogue of the moral and spiritual death that has already occurred. When Gatsby realizes that his dream is unattainable, that Daisy loves Tom and is afraid of what Gatsby has become, the whole basis of his life is destroyed. The pursuit of success has led Gatsby to the point where he seeks to escape from the limitations of time and history, only to discover that such an escape is impossible.

Like Gatsby, Thomas Sutpen, the protagonist of Faulkner's *Absalom, Absalom,* tries to rise beyond the human condition. Sutpen's career is a tragic inversion of the Alger story. Born in the poverty and ignorance of the southern mountains, the young Sutpen conceives his grand design, the intention to raise himself from poverty and to found a great house. The quest soon leads to acts of inhumanity. In Haiti, Sutpen marries the daughter of a wealthy planter and sires a son. When he discovers both wife and son may have Negro blood, he casts them off. The nearer he comes to his goal, the more he feels the need for the total security of unquestionable status. Sutpen goes to Yoknaptawpha County to begin his life again. Rapidly, he becomes one of the leading planters in Mississippi. Again, he marries and sires a family. Again, his design seems near completion. But Sutpen's determination to both wipe out the past and insure himself a place in the future leads to his destruction. Sutpen's refusal to recognize his first son results in the destruction of both families. Sutpen himself, ruined by the Civil War, desperately tries to father still another son on the slatternly granddaughter of one of his hangers-on. The girl produces a daughter. When Sutpen callously casts her off, he is murdered by the girl's grandfather. As in the case of Gatsby, Sutpen's physical death is only the corroboration of the moral emptiness left by the increasing inhumanity of his design.

Robert Penn Warren's narrative of the career of Willie Stark is a commentary on the myth of "log cabin to White House." In *All The King's Men,* Willie Stark, a country lawyer, begins his rise to power and fame when he rebels against the corruption and social injustice of the established political machine. Like Huey Long, whose career provided Warren with his model, Willie learns quickly how to arouse and manipulate the passionate resentments and prejudices of the redneck farmers who are the source of his power. His rise is meteoric, and Willie becomes governor. But something has happened in the process. The more successful Willie is, the more ambiguous and complicated his motives. Soon, it becomes difficult for him to distinguish the public good from the personal will of Willie Stark, and as this happens his life becomes increasingly confused and unhappy. He has alienated his wife; his son goes to the bad and is seriously injured in an accident. Willie's own increasing confusion and corruption are echoed in a compulsion to demonstrate the corruption of others. Willie brooks no opposition; he has to destroy everyone who stands in his way. At this point, Willie begins an affair with Anne Stanton, whose family belongs to the entrenched aristocracy—Willie's mortal enemies. For Willie, Anne's love is another political victory—another way of suborning and corrupting those who oppose him. His will to impose such degradation on others leads to Willie's own death. Anne's brother, outraged at the affair, murders Willie. Like Sutpen and Gatsby, Willie dies knowing that something has gone wrong, but too far gone in the world of illusion to know what.

The moral and human sacrifices demanded by success preoccupied Fitzgerald, Faulkner, and Warren. Where William Dean Howells' Silas Lapham retained enough personal autonomy to throw off the moral confusion into which success had thrust him, Gatsby, Sutpen, and Willie Stark are captives of their illusions. Greater achievement brings with it only greater unhappiness. As seen by twentieth-century writers, the self-made man is caught up in a fundamental confusion of means and ends. Beginning as a means to happiness or love, the pursuit of success becomes an all-encompassing end which further separates the individual from his initial goals. As he becomes more ambitious, it is harder and harder for the individual to retain a coherent moral identity. His original motives and ideals are confused and distorted, and he is no longer able to accept and relate what he has been to what he is becoming. In the end there is nothing left for him but the emptiness of constant movement toward a goal which becomes more and more impossible to reach. Desperately attempting to reestablish a lost identity, Gatsby, Sutpen, and Willie

233

Stark try to recreate the past or to dominate the future. Only by such a transcendence of the limits of mortality can they reconstruct their lost selves.

The first major expression of this theme of lost identity was the work of a late nineteenth-century immigrant to America. Abraham Cahan's novel *The Rise of David Levinsky,* although modeled on Howell's *The Rise of Silas Lapham,* is quite different in its treatment of the theme of success. At the end of the novel, David Levinsky feels an increasing hopelessness and emptiness in spite of his great accomplishments. The root of his problem is the impassable gulf between the young Talmudic scholar who left the old country and the millionaire garment king who has made such a success in America. Unable to bridge the gulf between his past and present selves, Levinsky fails to find any meaning or satisfaction in his life. The same difficulty afflicts Gatsby when he feels compelled to make up stories about his past. As he explains pathetically to Nick, "I didn't want you to think I was just some nobody." But his attempts to create a new identity ring hollow. As Nick points out, Gatsby's words "evoked no image except that of a turbaned 'character' leaking sawdust at every pore as he pursued a tiger through the Bois de Boulogne." [38] Thomas Sutpen struggles desperately to discover at what point his grand design failed, but he can never bridge the gulf between the young mountain boy turned away from the big house and the rich and powerful Colonel Sutpen who finds neither satisfaction nor peace in a house fit for royalty. Willie Stark, too, loses the capacity to put the pieces of his life together. In the end, he can only dream that his life could have had the moral meaning it lost somewhere between the poor farmhouse and the governor's mansion.

While late nineteenth-century novels of success attacked American society's failure to live up to its ideal

of equal opportunity and free mobility, twentieth-
century novelists reflect increasing doubts about the
ideal itself. Some, like Dreiser, point up the gap between
a world of irresistible social and biological forces and
the sentimental moralism and voluntarism of the philoso-
phy of success. More profoundly, novelists like Faulkner,
Fitzgerald, and Warren express a later generation's
quest for a more complex sense of human possibil-
ities and limitations than that available in the tradi-
tional ideal of individual success. Like many twentieth-
century social scientists, the major American novelists
seriously question the assumption that mobility is an
unqualified good.

Yet, despite their attack on the dream of success,
twentieth-century novelists do not think to reform or
reconstruct the social order. They are as wary of visions
of a non-competitive utopia as they are of the ideal of
individual achievement. Indeed, their treatment of the
grand designs of characters like Sutpen and Willie
Stark suggests that there is a kinship between the com-
pulsive self-made man driven to impose his ego on real-
ity and the social reformer who wants to make humanity
over in terms of his own personal model of rational-
ity and justice. As Faulkner, Warren, and Fitzgerald
present it, the tragedy of success is more a spiritual
than a social failure. The problem is not a false princi-
ple of social organization. It is, instead, a collective fail-
ure of the moral imagination which has resulted in an
over-emphasis on the need for individual economic ac-
complishment at the expense of the rich diversity and
complexity of human capacities and motives. Gatsby,
Sutpen, and Willie Stark are destroyed because their
lives are reduced to a single drive for dominance, because
they have become sterile automatons doomed to push in
hopeless frustration against the inescapable limits of the
human condition. In the work of Faulkner, Fitzgerald,

and Warren the ideal of success is the reflection of the larger delusion that the individual can exercise complete control over his destiny. Insofar as this delusion causes men to neglect the values of tradition and community and the virtues of self-knowledge and acceptance, it has become a dangerous and destructive delusion. After a century of dedication to the dream of individual advancement and social progress, it is time, these writers seem to say, to reopen the question of man's nature, to rediscover its limits, and to learn once more how to live within those limits.

CHAPTER VIII

INDIVIDUAL SUCCESS AND THE COMMUNITY: John Dewey's Philosophy of Success

> To gain an integrated individuality, each of us needs to cultivate his own garden. But there is no fence about this garden: it is no sharply marked-off enclosure. Our garden is the world, in the angle at which it touches our own manner of being. By accepting the corporate and industrial world in which we live, and by thus fulfilling the precondition for interaction with it, we, who are also parts of the moving present, create ourselves as we create an unknown future.
> John Dewey, *Individualism Old and New*

To re-evaluate the relationship between individual success and democracy in an age of large industrial organizations is a central concern of twentieth-century American thought. John Dewey was one of the major figures to undertake the task. Unlike some earlier critics of success, Dewey did not reject individualism. Emerson's concept of individual self-culture and Jefferson's dream of the integral democratic community were both central sources of his philosophy. Dewey redefined and reasserted the concept of individual achievement. Yet, at the same time, by emphasizing the inextricable relationship between the individual and the community and by insisting that a failure of community meant a breakdown of individuality, Dewey went far beyond the traditional ideal of rising in society to mark out an important new direction for democratic thought.

No idea is more central to Dewey's philosophy than

239

the belief that individual fulfilment is the major end of democracy and that freedom is essential to this goal. "The foundation of democracy is faith in the capacities of human nature," he insists.[1] In diagnosing the problems of contemporary society, Dewey argues that the primary task is to "find out how all the constituents of our existing culture are operating and then see to it that whenever and wherever needed they be modified in order that their workings may release and fulfill the possibilities of human nature."[2] Moreover, Dewey emphasizes the idea that the individual is continually in the process of creating himself. "Freedom or individuality . . . is not an original possession or gift. It is something to be achieved, to be wrought out."[3] Dewey's insistence on learning by doing and on the need for continual experimentation and discovery of new values are also an outgrowth of his concept of life as a continual and open process of individual development.

In spite of his concern with individual fulfilment, Dewey could not accept the received idea of individualism. He felt that, as Americans had conceived it, individualism was too narrowly related to the pursuit of economic success. "Individualism has been identified with ideas of initiative and invention that are bound up with private and exclusive economic gain."[4] Historically, this economic individualism had had an important creative function in freeing human energies from the overly static society of an earlier epoch:

It sought to release from legal restrictions man's wants and his efforts to satisfy those wants. It believed that such emancipation would stimulate latent energy into action, would automatically assign individual ability to the work for which it was suited, would cause it to perform that work under stimulus of the advantage to be gained, and would secure for capacity and enterprise the reward and position to which they were entitled.[5]

But, by the middle of the nineteenth century the rise of

corporate industry had changed the social conditions on which this economic individualism had had a creative effect. In the twentieth century, the ideal of individual success had become a rationalization for the status quo, a narrow and mechanical ideal which kept men from facing up to the real problems of an urban industrial society.

The uncontrolled development of industrial society revealed all too clearly the inadequacies of the earlier concept of economic individualism. In the modern world, mass action and the operation of complex, seemingly impersonal forces overshadowed the economic individual. "The situation has been transformed since the day when the problem of freedom and democracy presented itself as essentially a *personal* problem capable of being decided by strictly personal action and choice." [6] In a society where "an indefinite number of immediately ramifying conditions" intervened between "what a person does and the consequences of his actions, including even the consequences which return upon him," the individual had lost his sense of the coherence of his life and his own power to control it.[7] "The theory of the self-actuated and self-governing individual receives a rude shock when massed activity has a potency which individual effort can no longer claim." [8]

So long as individualism is defined in terms of private economic gain, Dewey doubts that the individual will be able to re-establish a sense of significance. "A stable recovery of individuality waits upon an elimination of the older economic and political individualism, an elimination which will liberate imagination and endeavor for the task of making corporate society contribute to the free culture of its members." [9] Furthermore, the traditional idea of the individual assumes a total distinction between the individual and society which simply does not exist:

Whether complete identification of human nature with individuality would be desirable or undesirable if it existed is an idle academic question. For it does not exist. Some cultural conditions develop the psychological constituents that lead toward differentiation; others stimulate those that lead in the direction of the solidarity of the beehive or anthill. The human problem is that of securing the development of each constituent so that it serves to release and mature the other.[10]

According to Dewey, when the philosophy of success assumes that the general welfare is best served by encouraging complete freedom of individual economic activity, it is mistaken. Freedom of this kind is as likely to lead to demands for conformity as to individual development, for the few beneficiaries of the regime of individual economic success fear freedom of thought and new social ideas as a threat to their own position. Consequently, the successful individual tends to demand and enforce a conformity of thought and action which prevents any serious attempts to change or improve the status quo. On the other hand, the existence of a strong, integral community does not necessarily mean the elimination of individuality. "If we want individuals to be free," Dewey insists, "we must see to it that suitable conditions exist." [11] The conditions of freedom cannot come about without the existence of a community determined to create and preserve them. Moreover, it is in the give and take of his relationships with other human beings that the individual develops a truly distinctive and meaningful identity:

To learn to be human is to develop through the give-and-take of communication an effective sense of being an individually distinctive member of a community; one who understands and appreciates its beliefs, desires and methods, and who contributes to a further conversion of organic powers into human resources and values.[12]

Politically, Dewey thought of himself as a Jeffersonian. In his view, Jefferson "was the first modern to

state in human terms the principles of democracy." [13]
But unlike most nineteenth-century followers of Jefferson, Dewey reasserts that side of his philosophy which
had been generally ignored: Jefferson's emphasis on the
need for strong social institutions to encourage individual freedom and responsible self-government. Although
he does not deny the importance of the Jefferson of limited government and inalienable individual rights,
Dewey calls to the attention of the twentieth century
the Jefferson who had insisted on the democratic community as the creator and guarantor of individual opportunities. Dewey argues that since Jefferson had been
unable to foresee the way in which the country would
change from an agrarian to an urban industrial culture,
his philosophy needs reinterpretation to fit the present
day:

The real source of the weakness that has developed later in the
position of our democratic progenitors is not that they isolated
the problem of freedom from the positive conditions that would
nourish it, but that they did not—and in their time could not—
carry their analysis far enough. . . . They did not foresee the
non-political causes that might restrict freedom, nor the economic
factor that would put a heavy premium on centralization.[14]

Dewey's critique of the idea of success centers around
his concept of community. For Dewey, the existence of a
community is a prerequisite for meaningful individual
development. He distinguishes between what he calls an
association—an organization of persons without common values and meaningful communication about their
individual needs and aspirations—and a community
which is the result of shared goals and endeavor.
"Human associations," he writes "may be ever so organic in origin and firm in operation, but they develop
into societies in a human sense only as their consequences, being known, are esteemed and sought for." [15]
Communities came into existence when men recognized
that they faced common problems and saw the need for

co-operation in resolving these problems. It was the re-
sultant communication and co-operative action which,
in Dewey's view, make the difference between a mean-
ingless pursuit of individual impulse and a truly articu-
late individual life. Communities of communication and
action not only make for the improvement of human
life, but they are essential for the growth of humanly
understood meaning. "Events cannot be passed from one
[person] to another, but meanings may be shared by
means of signs. Wants and impulses are then attached
to common meanings. They are thereby transformed
into desires and purposes, which, since they implicate a
common or mutually understood meaning, present new
ties, converting a conjoint activity into a community of
interest and endeavor." [16]

Though such mutual communication and co-operation
are an important part of any social order, they are es-
sential to democracy. Above all else, democracy de-
mands that each individual have the chance to govern
his own life and make his own choices. In an age of
large organizations and impersonal forces, however,
such control can only be exercized in participation with
other men. Thus,

the keynote of democracy as a way of life may be expressed . . .
as the necessity for the participation of every mature human
being in formation of the values that regulate the living of men
together: which is necessary from the standpoint of both the
general social welfare and the full development of human beings
as individuals.[17]

By distinguishing between association and commu-
nity, Dewey shows how the economic concept of success
cannot achieve its goal of individual fulfilment and hap-
piness. The philosophy of success assumes that individu-
als will be freer and the general welfare best served if
society is more like an association than a community.
But an association can never produce the conditions of

true individuality, because associations lack the communication and shared endeavor necessary to the creation of meaningful individual identities. Therefore, the more society assumes the form of a loose grouping of economic individuals, the less able these individuals will be to achieve meaningful and satisfying lives.

Dewey's conception of the democratic community was also strongly influenced by his interest in science. As Jefferson looked to the independent self-governing agrarian community for his social ideal, Dewey looks to science, not simply as a major cultural force, but also as the model modern community. Science, as Dewey understands it, is a fundamentally important social phenomenon since it involves the organization of human intelligence in an inquiry into the nature of things. It is to the development of the scientific attitude of free inquiry and discussion and to the growth of the organized scientific community that Dewey attributes the great social changes of the modern era. In his view, the proponents of individual mobility incorrectly understand these changes as the result of the freeing of individuals from traditional social and political restrictions, failing to see that

the great expansion which was occurring was in fact due to the release of *physical* energies; that as far as human action and human freedom [*were*] concerned, a problem not a solution was thereby instituted: the problem, namely, of management and direction of the new physical energies so they would contribute to realization of human potentialities.[18]

In their concern for "securing and protecting the freedom of individuals" the philosophers of success fail to recognize that "the true and final source of change has been and now is the corporate intelligence embodied in science." Since science has become the major cultural force of the contemporary era, democracy cannot afford to ignore its power to investigate and improve the conditions of human existence. The great need of the present is to extend "from its present limited field to the larger field of human relations the control of organized intelligence, operating through the release of individual powers and capacities." [19]

There is a further reason for the close relationship between science and democracy. Science can become the tool of authoritarian governments and a source of power for anti-democratic ends, but when freed to pursue knowledge in terms of its own methods and ideals, the scientific community embodies many of the most important values of democracy. Thus, science can serve not only as a means for releasing human energies and improving material conditions, but it can also be a source of democratic values:

Freedom of inquiry, toleration of diverse views, freedom of communication, the distribution of what is found out to every individual as the ultimate intellectual consumer are involved in the democratic as in the scientific method. When democracy openly recognizes the existence of *problems* and the need for probing them *as* problems as its glory, it will relegate political groups that pride themselves upon refusing to admit incompatible opinions to the obscurity which already is the fate of similar groups in science.[20]

Dewey contributes an important new direction to the American philosophy of individual freedom by emphasizing the crucial role of free intelligence in the democratic community. To the traditional American ideal of individual economic and social success Dewey adds a concept of intellectual mobility.

The democratic idea of freedom is not the right of each individual to *do* as he pleases, even if it be qualified by adding "provided he does not interfere with this same freedom on the part of others." While the idea is not always, not often enough expressed in words, the basic freedom is that of freedom of *mind,* and of whatever degree of freedom of action and experience is necessary to produce freedom of intelligence.[21]

The Future of Success

There are signs in the 1960's that a concern for the place of community and the development of intelligence in democratic culture is spreading from philosophers and intellectuals to the public at large. Politicians, particularly of a conservative persuasion, continue to sing the praises of success, but those who think of themselves as liberals generally reject the principles of economic individualism and the philosophy of success. Confronting the problems of mid-twentieth-century American life, liberal critics often insist that the American emphasis on *individual* success makes it difficult for society to confront basic *public* problems. As Professor David Truman puts it, "whether the question at issue is one of education, urban renewal, or national security, a concern for the relative poverty of the public sector of the economy is a common element in a developing debate." [22] John Kenneth Galbraith, whose *The Affluent Society* and *The Liberal Hour* are widely influential books, leads the debate over the allocation of American resources between what he calls the private and public sectors of the economy. Galbraith calls it disastrous that Americans insist on funneling their great productivity into private hands rather than spending some significant proportion on common concerns like education, the improvement of urban living conditions, better transportation, and other public services. As long as Americans insist that their increasing wealth be awarded to individuals rather than collectively spent for the general good, Galbraith fears that the nation will be faced with increasing urban squalor, inescapable poverty, and insecurity in the world at large. Like Dewey, however, Galbraith is critical of utopian reforms and simple, general solutions. For him, as for many other contemporary thinkers, the problem is how

American society can retain its openness without impoverishing the collective life. A hundred years of overemphasis on economic and social mobility has created a society of individual affluence and community degredation. It is .time, these thinkers insist, to redress the balance.

The philosophy of success is threatened as well from another direction. Many thinkers of the 1960's share Dewey's concern for the place of intelligence in American culture. The increasing affluence of American society adds urgency to their pleas. The historian John M. Blum sums up their point of view when he points out that the development of production in the twentieth century has made obsolete the old gospel of "work and win." On the contrary, Americans now need a transformation of the gospel of work which will elucidate "the best meaning of success." Only if Americans rise to the new challenge of abundance and leisure by opening "for exploration the boundless life of the mind" can they "demonstrate that a system productive of wealth could also produce satisfying individuality.

"Only such men," Blum insists, "are finally successful, for only they are satisfied. Only such men, in the last analysis, are free." [23]

NOTES

I. NATURAL ARISTOCRACY AND THE NEW REPUBLIC

1. Carl Van Doren, *Benjamin Franklin.* (New York: Viking Press, 1938), p. 272.
2. John Bigelow (ed.) *The Works of Benjamin Franklin,* 10 vols. (New York: G. P. Putnam's Sons, 1887), I, 335.
3. Max Farrand (ed.) *Benjamin Franklin's Memoirs.* (Berkeley, California: University of California Press, 1949), p. 238.
4. *Ibid.,* p. 238.
5. *Ibid.,* p. 242.
6. *Ibid.,* p. 242.
7. *Ibid.,* p. 8.
8. *Ibid.,* pp. 23–24.
9. *Ibid.,* p. 20.
10. *Ibid.,* p. 48.
11. *Ibid.,* p. 42.
12. *Ibid.,* p. 86.
13. *Ibid.,* p. 210.
14. *Ibid.,* p. 230.
15. Saul K. Padover (ed.) *The Complete Jefferson.* (New York: Duell, Sloan and Pearce, 1943), p. 283.
16. *Ibid.,* p. 283.
17. *Ibid.,* p. 283.
18. *Ibid.,* pp. 289–90.
19. *Ibid.,* p. 386.

Notes

20. Enos Hitchcock, D.D., *The Farmers Friend* . . . (Boston: I. Thomas and E. T. Andrews, 1793), pp. 116–17. In this connection Hitchcock approvingly quotes Jefferson's dictum, "Those who labor in the earth are the chosen people of God."

21. *Ibid.*, p. 40.

22. *Ibid.*, p. 16.

23. H. H. Brackenridge, *Adventures of Captain Farrago*. 2 vols. (Philadelphia: T. B. Peterson, 1856), I, 28–29.

24. *Ibid.*, p. 30. Italics mine.

25. *Ibid.*, pp. 32–33.

26. *Ibid.*, II, 148–49.

II. THE AGE OF THE SELF-MADE MAN

1. Quoted in Irvin G. Wyllie, *The Self-Made Man in America* (New Brunswick, N. J.: Rutgers University Press, 1954).

2. Margaret E. White (ed.) *A Sketch of Chester Harding, Artist* (Boston: Houghton Mifflin, 1890), p. 64.

3. Quoted in Monica Kiefer, *American Children Through Their Books* (Philadelphia: University of Pennsylvania Press, 1948), pp. 52–53.

4. Calvin Colton (ed.) *The Works of Henry Clay* (New York: A. S. Barnes and Burr, 1857), V, 464.

5. Marvin Meyers, *The Jacksonian Persuasion* (New York: Vintage Books, 1960), p. 12.

6. Alexis de Tocqueville, *Democracy in America* (New York: Vintage Books, 1957), II, 144–45.

7. T. S. Arthur, *Advice to Young Men on Their Duties and Conduct in Life* (Boston: N. C. Barton, 1849), p. 178.

8. Sylvester Judd, *Richard Edney and the Governor's Family* (Boston: Phillips Sampson, 1850), p. 457.

9. Harriet Martineau, *Society in America*. Edited by S. M. Lipset (Garden City, New York: Anchor Books, 1962), p. 164.

10. Hannah F. Lee, *The Log Cabin: or, The World Before You* (Philadelphia: George F. Appleton, 1844), p. 173.

11. Freeman Hunt, *Worth and Wealth, A Collection of Maxims, Morals and Miscellanies for Merchants and Men of Business* (New York: Stringer and Townsend, 1856), p. 63.

12. *Ibid.*, p. 45.

13. Asa Greene, *The Perils of Pearl Street, Including a Taste of the Dangers of Wall Street* (New York: Betts and Anstice, and Peter Hill, 1834), p. 90.

14. *Ibid.*, pp. 7–8.

15. Judd, *op. cit.*, p. 10.

16. Hunt, *op. cit.*, p. 60.

17. Arthur, *op. cit.*, p. 16.

18. Henry Ward Beecher, *Twelve Lectures to Young Men on Various Important Subjects* (New York: D. Appleton and Co., 1890), pp. 256–57.

19. *Ibid.*, p. 259.

20. John Frost, *The Young Merchant* (New York: W. H. Graham, 1848), p. 11.

21. Alexander Lovell Stimson, *Easy Nat; or, The Three Apprentices* (New York: J. C. Derby, 1854), p. 449.

22. T. S. Arthur, *Sparing to Spend* (New York: Charles Scribner, 1853), pp. 331–32.

23. Mrs. Susan A. L. Sedgwick, *Allen Prescott; or, The Fortunes of a New-England Boy.* 2 vols. (New York: Harper, 1834), I, 128.

24. Timothy Flint, *George Mason, The Young Backwoodsman* (Boston: Hilliard, Gray and Wilkins, 1829), pp. 4–5.

25. Thomas H. Shreve, *Drayton: A Story of American Life* (New York: Harper, 1851), p. 36.

26. *Ibid.,* p. 13.

27. *Ibid.,* p. 23.

28. George Bancroft, *Literary and Historical Miscellanies* (New York: Harper, 1855), pp. 462–63

29. Flint, *op. cit.,* p. 138.

30. Arthur, *Sparing to Spend,* pp. 5–6.

31. Judd, *op. cit.,* pp. 159–60.

32. T. S. Arthur, *The Way to Prosper and Other Tales* (Philadelphia: J. W. Bradley, 1851), p. 201.

33. Charles F. Briggs, *The Adventures of Harry Franco, A Tale of the Great Panic.* 2 vols. (New York: F. Saunders, 1839), I, 3.

34. *Ibid.,* p. 6.

35. *Ibid.,* p. 6.

36. *Ibid.,* p. 11.

37. *Ibid.,* p. 31.

38. *Ibid.,* II, 236–37.

39. Seba Smith, *My Thirty Years Out of the Senate by Major Jack Downing* (New York: Oaksmith, 1859), p. 25.

40. *Ibid.,* p. 25.

41. *Ibid.,* p. 29.

42. *Ibid.,* p. 33.

43. *The Life and Adventures of Col. David Crockett of West Tennessee* (Cincinnati, 1833), p. 19.

44. Thomas C. Haliburton, *The Clockmaker; or, the Sayings and Doings of Samuel Slick of Slickville* (Philadelphia: Lea and Blanchard, 1839), p. 112.

45. *Ibid.,* p. 114.

46. Johnson J. Hooper, *Simon Suggs' Adventures* (Americus, Ga.: American Book Co., 1928), p. 13.

47. *Ibid.,* pp. 59–60.

48. Rchard B. Kimball, *Henry Powers (Banker), How He Achieved a Fortune and Married* (New York: G. W. Carleton, 1869), p. 329.

III. SELF-IMPROVEMENT AND SELF-CULTURE

1. Wilbur Schramm (ed.), *Francis Parkman: Representative Selections* (New York: American Book Co., 1938), pp. 175–76.

2. James Fenimore Cooper, *The American Democrat* (New York: Knopf, 1956), p. 89.

3. *Ibid.,* p. 89.

4. Schramm, *op. cit.,* p. 52.

5. Walt Whitman, *Leaves of Grass and Selected Prose* (New York: The Modern Library, 1950), p. 479.

6. *Ibid.*, pp. 501–2.

7. *Ibid.*, p. 485.

8. *Ibid.*, p. 489.

9. William E. Channing, *Self-Culture* (Boston: Dutton and Wentworth, 1838), p. 54.

10. *Ibid.*, p. 55.

11. *Ibid.*, pp. 28–29.

12. *Ibid.*, p. 34.

13. *Ibid.*, p. 14.

14. Edward W. Emerson (ed.), *The Complete Works of Ralph Waldo Emerson.* 12 vols. (Boston, Houghton Mifflin, 1904), II, 78.

15. *Ibid.*, p. 289.

16. *Ibid.*, I, 76.

17. *Ibid.*, II, 76.

18. *Ibid.*, III, 59.

19. *Ibid.*, p. 205.

20. *Ibid.*, VI, 101.

21. *Ibid.*, p. 54.

22. *Ibid.*, p. 100.

23. *Ibid.*, p. 73.

24. *Ibid.*, p. 71.

25. *Ibid.*, I, 37.

26. *Ibid.*, VI, 261.

27. *Ibid.*, p. 72.

28. *Ibid.*, IV, 239.

29. *Ibid.*, p. 224.

30. *Ibid.*, p. 253.

31. *Ibid.*, pp. 253–56.

32. *Ibid.*, p. 256.

33. *Ibid.*, p. 258.

34. *Ibid.*, I, 72.

35. *Ibid.*, VII, 308.

36. *Ibid.*, I, 261.

37. *Ibid.*, I, 386.

38. *Ibid.*, III, 146.

39. *Ibid.*, p. 128.

40. *Ibid.*, I, 232.

41. *Ibid.*, III, 210.

42. *Ibid.*, XI, 537–38.

43. Quoted in A. Whitney Griswold, "New Thought: A Cult of Success," *The American Journal of Sociology.* Vol. XL, No. 3 (November, 1934), p. 316.

44. Roger W. Babson, *What is Success?* (New York: Fleming H. Revell, 1923), p. 49.

IV. FROM RAGS TO RESPECTABILITY

1. Quoted from "this 'n' that," a handout of the La Salle National Bank, Chicago, May, 1958, p. 3.

2. "Cynical Youngest Generation," *Nation*, CXXXIV (February 17, 1932), p. 186.

3. *The New York Times* for January 13, 1947, quoted in R. Richard Wohl, "The 'Rags to Riches' Story," Bendix and Lipset (eds.), *Class, Status and Power* (Glencoe, Illinois: Free Press, 1953), n. 4.

4. Mrs. Louisa C. Tuthill, *I will be a Gentleman* (Boston: Crosby and Nichols, 1845), pp. 66–67.

5. J. H. Ingraham, *Jemmy Daily; or, The Little News Vender* (New York: M. Y. Beach, Sun Office, 1843), p. 13.

6. Elizabeth O. Smith, *The Newsboy* (New York: J. C. Derby, 1854). Mrs. Smith's treatment of the newsboy as a sentimental curiosity is indicated by her description of him in these terms (p. 9): "I learned to await the coming of the Newsboy with solemn expectancy, and the shuffling of his weary feet grew to have a majesty about them; his ragged habiliments were right royal robes over his great heart, and the brimless hat became him like a regal crown, for Bob had that innate dignity of soul which neither crown nor sceptre could augment."

7. Joseph C. Neal, *Peter Ploddy* (Philadelphia: T. B. Peterson and Brothers, 1856), p. 64.

8. Kenneth S. Lynn, *The Dream of Success* (Boston: Little, Brown, 1955), p. 7.

9. Alger, *Mark, the Match Boy* (Philadelphia: Porter and Coates, n.d.), p. 38.

10. *Mark, the Match Boy*, p. 141. Cf. also Ben Gibson in the same book and Peter Groot in *Strive and Succeed* (New York: New York Book Co., 1910).

11. Alger, *Phil, the Fiddler* (Philadelphia, n.d.), pp. 145–46.

12. Crouse (ed.) *Struggling Upward and Other Works* (New York: Crown Publishers, 1945), p. 135.

13. *Ibid.*, p. 148.

V. THE SELF-MADE MAN AND INDUSTRIAL AMERICA

1. Mrs. E. D. E. N. Southworth, *Ishmael; or, In the Depths* (New York: Grosset and Dunlap, n.d.), p. 10.

2. *Ibid.*, p. 10.

3. E. P. Roe, *Barriers Burned Away* (New York: Dodd, Mead and Co., 1872), p. 148.

4. *Ibid.*, p. 22.

5. Ella Wheeler Wilcox, *An Ambitious Man* (Chicago: E. A. Weeks, 1896), pp. 7–9.

6. Cf. chap. ii.

7. T. S. Denison, *An Iron Crown; or, The Modern Mammon . . .* (Chicago: T. S. Denison, 1885), p. 10.

8. *Ibid.*, p. 10.

9. *Ibid.*, p. 11.

10. *Ibid.*, p. 22.

11. *Ibid.*, p. 153.

12. *Ibid.*, pp. 479–80.

13. *Ibid.*, p. 34.

14. *Ibid.*, p. 57.

15. Woodrow Wilson, *The New Freedom* (New York: Doubleday, Page, 1913), p. 17.

16. Quoted in Philip S. Foner, *Mark Twain: Social Critic* (New York: International Publishers, 1957), pp. 68–69.

17. Samuel L. Clemens, *The Writings of Mark Twain* (Author's National Edition), 25 vols. (New York: Harper and Brothers, 1903), XIX, 61–62.

18. *Ibid.*, p. 67.

19. *Ibid.*, pp. 211–12.

20. *Ibid.*, p. 215.

21. Samuel L. Clemens, *Mark Twain's Speeches* (New York: Harper and Brothers, 1910), pp. 371–72.

22. Clemens, *Writings*, X, v–vi.

23. *Ibid.*, XI, 17–18.

24. I have found Paul Baender's unpublished doctoral dissertation, "Mark Twain's Transcendent Figure," University of California, 1956, especially helpful in the analysis of Twain's later novels.

25. Clemens, *Writings*, XVI, 25.

26. *Ibid.*, p. 63.

27. *Ibid.*, p. 65.

28. *Ibid.*, p. 144.

29. Quoted in Bernard De Voto (ed.), *The Portable Mark Twain* (New York: Viking Press, 1946), p. 569.

30. William Dean Howells, *A Hazard of New Fortunes* (New York: E. P. Dutton, 1952), p. 551.

31. *Ibid.*, p. 537.

32. Henry James, *The American Scene* (New York: Charles Scribner's Sons, 1946), p. 237.

33. *Ibid.*, pp. 345–46.

34. *Ibid.*, p. 164.

35. *Ibid.*, pp. 12–13.

36. *Ibid.*, p. 156.

37. *Ibid.*, p. 103.

38. *Ibid.*, p. 104.

39. *Ibid.*, pp. 237–38.

40. Jane Addams, *Democracy and Social Ethics* (New York: Macmillan, 1905), pp. 3–4.

41. *Ibid.*, p. 153.

VI. PHILOSOPHERS OF SUCCESS

1. Andrew Carnegie, *The Empire of Business* (New York, Doubleday, Page and Co., 1902), p. 5.

2. James Warren Prothro, *Dollar Decade* (Baton Rouge, La.: Louisiana State University Press, 1954), p. 68.

3. Edward Wortley (ed.), *Impulses to Success* (New York: Park Row Publishing House, 1957), pp. 32–33.

4. *Ibid.*, p. 51.

5. *Ibid.*, p. 50.

6. Russell Conwell, *The New Day* (Philadelphia: Griffith and Rowland, 1904), p. 9.

7. Wortley, *op. cit.*, p. 31.

8. *Ibid.*, pp. 8, 12.

9. George H. Lorimer, *Letters from a Self-Made Merchant to His Son.* (Boston: Small, Maynard, 1902), pp. 141–43.

10. Wortley, *op. cit.*, p. 52.

11. *Ibid.*, p. 55.

12. *Success Magazine*, IV (November, 1901), 1161.

13. *Ibid.*, p. 1192.

14. Roger Babson, *What is Success?* (New York: Fleming H. Revell, 1923), p. 76.

15. William Matthews, *Getting on in the World* (Chicago: S. C. Griggs, 1877), p. 280.

16. Wortley, *op. cit.*, p. 52.

17. *Ibid.*, pp. 50, 57–58.

18. *Ibid.*, p. 32.

19. Quoted in Edward C. Kirkland, *Industry Comes of Age* (New York: Rinehart, 1961), p. 407.

20. Matthews, *op. cit.*, p. 284.

21. *Success Magazine*, X (November, 1907), 754.

22. Quoted in Edward C. Kirkland, *Dream and Thought in the Business Community* (Ithaca, N. Y.: Cornell University Press, 1956), pp. 156–57.

23. *Success Magazine*, IV (November, 1901), 1161.

24. *Ibid.*, X (December, 1907), 841.

25. Andrew Carnegie, *The Gospel of Wealth* (Garden City, N. Y.: Doubleday, 1933), pp. 5–6.

26. Wortley, *op. cit.*, p. 32.

27. *Ibid.*, p. 79.

28. Carnegie, *The Gospel of Wealth*, p. 11.

29. *Ibid.*, p. 85.

30. *Success Magazine*, V (November, 1902), 645.

31. Wortley, *op. cit.*, p. 68.

32. *Success Magazine*, V (November, 1902), 643.

33. Wortley, *op. cit.*, pp. 108–9.

34. *Ibid.*, p. 109.

35. *Ibid.*, p. 111.

36. Barton, *The Man Nobody Knows* (Indianapolis: Charter Books, 1962), pp. 11–13.

37. Cf. the original edition of *The Man Nobody Knows* (Indianapolis, Ind.: Bobbs-Merrill Co., 1925).

38. Barton, *op. cit.*, p. 104.

39. *Ibid.*, p. 109.

40. *Ibid.*, pp. 20–21.

41. *Ibid.*, pp. 24, 26, 29.

42. *Ibid.*, p. 19.

VII. DREAM OR RAT RACE

1. Quoted in Henry F. May, *Protestant Churches and Industrial America* (New York: Harper and Brothers, 1949), p. 141.

2. "Address of Acceptance of the Nomination for a Second Term," Philadelphia, June 27, 1936, quoted in Basil Rauch (ed.) *Franklin D.*

Roosevelt: Selected Speeches, Messages, Press Conferences, and Letters (New York: Rinehart, 1957), pp. 150–51.

3. Norman Vincent Peale, *The Power of Positive Thinking* (New York: Crest Books, 1963), p. 22. Italics mine

4. Napoleon Hill, *Think and Grow Rich* (New York: Crest Books, 1963), p. 27.

5. *Ibid.*, p. 85.

6. Dale Carnegie, *How to Win Friends and Influence People.* (New York: Pocket Books, 1940), p. 71.

7. Peale, *op. cit.*, p. viii.

8. Carnegie, *op. cit.*, p. 72.

9. Hill, *op. cit.*, p. 37. Italics mine.

10. *Ibid.*, p. 36. Italics Hill's.

11. *Ibid.*, p. 248. Italics Hill's.

12. Peale, *op. cit.*, p. viii.

13. Carnegie, *op. cit.*, p. 16.

14. Hill. *op. cit.*, p. 215.

15. Peale, *op. cit.*, p. viii.

16. *Ibid.*, pp. 24, 65, 66.

17. Hill, *op. cit.*, *passim.*

18. Peale, *op. cit.*, p. 13.

19. Hill, *op. cit.*, p. 68.

20. Peale, *op. cit.*, p. 61.

21. Hill, *op. cit.*, p. 49.

22. Peale, *op. cit.*, p. 47.

23. Frank Lester Ward, "Broadening the Way to Success," *Forum*, II (September, 1886–February, 1887), 342.

24. *Ibid.*, p. 346.

25. *Ibid.*, p. 349.

26. Charles Horton Cooley, *Personal Competition: Its Place in the Social Order and Effect upon Individuals: With Some Considerations on Success. Economic Studies.* IV (April, 1889), 78.

27. *Ibid.*, p. 80.

28. *Ibid.*, p. 83.

29. *Ibid.*, p. 83.

30. *Ibid.*, p. 95.

31. *Ibid.*, p. 167.

32. *Ibid.*, p. 172.

33. Pitirim A. Sorokin, *Social and Cultural Mobility.* (Glencoe, Ill.: Free Press, 1959), p. 146.

34. *Ibid.*, p. 139.

35. *Ibid.*, p. 154.

36. *Ibid.*, p. 138.

37. F. Scott Fitzgerald, *The Great Gatsby.* (New York: Charles Schribner's Sons, 1953), p. 111.

38. *Ibid.*, pp. 66–67.

VIII. INDIVIDUAL SUCCESS AND THE COMMUNITY

1. Joseph Ratner (ed.), *Intelligence in the Modern World: John Dewey's Philosophy* (New York: Modern Library, 1939), p. 402.

2. John Dewey, *Culture and Freedom* (New York: G. P. Putnam's Sons), p. 126.

3. *Ibid.*, p. 627.

4. John Dewey, *Individualism Old and New* (New York: Minton, Balch and Co., 1930), p. 71.

5. *Ibid.*, pp. 76–77

6. Dewey, *Culture and Freedom*, p. 56.

7. *Ibid.*, p. 58.

8. *Ibid.*, p. 63.

9. Dewey, *Individualism Old and New*, pp. 71–72.

10. Dewey, *Culture and Freedom*, pp. 22–23.

11. *Ibid.*, p. 34.

12. Ratner, *op. cit.*, p. 389.

13. Dewey, *Culture and Freedom*, p. 155.

14. *Ibid.*, pp. 40–41.

15. Ratner, *op. cit.*, p. 307.

16. *Ibid.*, p. 388.

17. *Ibid.*, p. 400.

18. Dewey, *Culture and Freedom*, p. 168.

19. Ratner, *op. cit.*, p. 361.

20. Dewey, *Culture and Freedom*, p. 102.

21. Ratner, *op. cit.*, p. 404.

22. Clarence Morris (ed.), *Trends in Modern American Life* (Philadelphia: University of Pennsylvania Press, 1962), p. 117.

23. *Ibid.*, pp. 35–36.

BIBLIOGRAPHICAL NOTES

GENERAL

The most complete and authoritative study of the ideal of the self-made man is Irvin G. Wyllie's *The Self-Made Man in America* (New Brunswick, N. J.: Rutgers University Press, 1954). Wyllie based his work primarily on an exhaustive examination of self-help handbooks, and his discussion of the basic ideological pattern of these handbooks should be definitive for some time. Wyllie's book also contains an excellent annotated bibliography of success handbooks and related materials.

The pioneering study of the idea of success in America was A. Whitney Griswold's Yale dissertation, "The American Cult of Success," portions of which were published in 1934 in the *American Journal of Sociology* and the *New England Quarterly*. Another early work in the general field of American attitudes toward success was Donald McConnell's, *Economic Virtues in the United States* (New York: n.p., 1930). I have also found the following which touch on the idea of success at various points most helpful: Ralph H. Gabriel, *The Course of American Democratic Thought* (New York: Ronald Press, 1940), and Merle Curti, *The Growth of American Thought* (New York: Harper, 1951), two general intellectual histories with important sections on the idea of success; Alexis de Tocqueville, *Democracy in America*, and James Bryce, *The American Commonwealth*, are two classic commentaries on nineteenth-century American society; Joseph Dorfman, *The Economic Mind in American Civilization* (New

259

York: Viking, 1949), is filled with comments on the role of success in economic thought. Walter F. Taylor, *The Economic Novel in America* (Chapel Hill, N. C.: University of North Carolina Press, 1942), touches frequently on the theme of success in literature. Kenneth Lynn, *The Dream of Success* (Boston: Little, Brown, 1955), explores the dominance of the ideology of success in late nineteenth and early twentieth-century novels, while Leo Lowenthal in his classic "Biographies in Popular Magazines," in Lazarsfeld and Stanton (eds.), *Radio Research, 1942–43* (New York: Duell, Sloan and Pearce, 1943), traces important shifts in attitude toward success reflected in the changing character of twentieth-century magazine biographies. Other studies of topics related to the ideal of the self-made man include: David M. Potter, *People of Plenty* (Chicago: University of Chicago Press, 1954), Robert G. McCloskey, *American Conservatism in the Age of Enterprise* (Cambridge, Mass.: Harvard University Press, 1951), Sigmund Diamond, *The Reputation of the American Businessman* (Cambridge, Mass.: Harvard University Press, 1955), Edwin H. Cady, *The Gentleman in America* (Syracuse, N. Y.: Syracuse University Press, 1949), Dixon Wecter, *The Hero in America* (New York: Charles Scribner's Sons, 1941), Richard D. Mosier, *Making the American Mind* (New York: King's Crown Press, 1947), and Arthur M. Schlesinger, *Learning How to Behave. A Historical Study of American Etiquette Books* (New York: Macmillan, 1946).

The following references are particularly helpful in understanding the development of popular literature in America and for suggestions about its use as a historical source: James D. Hart, *The Popular Book* (New York: Oxford University Press, 1950), Frank L. Mott, *Golden Multitudes* (New York: Macmillan, 1947), and Van R. Halsey, "Fiction and the Businessman: Society through all its Literature," *American Quarterly*, XI, No. 3 (Fall, 1959), 391–402.

The European background of the idea of success is a complex one. The classic in the field is, of course, Max Weber, *The Protestant Ethic and the Spirit of Capitalism*, Rev. ed. (New York: Charles Scribner's Sons, 1958). Other important works in this area are: Richard H. Tawney, *Religion and the Rise of Capitalism* (New York: New American Library, 1948), Hector M. Robertson, *Aspects of the Rise of Economic Individualism* (Cambridge, England: Cambridge University Press, 1935), Ernst Troelstch, *Protestantism and Progress* (Boston: Beacon Press, 1958), Louis B. Wright, *Middle-Class Culture in Elizabethan England* (Chapel Hill, N. C.: University of North Carolina Press, 1935), Charles F. Palm, *The Middle Classes: Then and Now* (New York: Macmillan, 1936), and Alan Simpson, *Puritanism in Old and New England* (Chicago: University of Chicago Press, 1955).

The scope of sociological study of the problem of mobility is indicated in the bibliography edited by Raymond Mack, Linton Freeman, and Seymour Yellin, *Social Mobility: Thirty Years of Research and Theory* (Syracuse, N. Y.: Syracuse University Press, 1957). Pitirim Sorokin's *Social and Cultural Mobility* (Glencoe, Ill.: Free Press, 1959), though three decades old, remains the broadest and most philosophical study of the topic. Some of the more important recent work in the study of mobility can be found in Reinhard Bendix and Seymour Lipset, *Social Mobility in Industrial Society*

(Berkeley, Calif.: University of California Press, 1959), and in the same authors' anthology, *Class, Status and Power* (Glencoe, Ill.: Free Press, 1953.) For the situation in America see also W. Lloyd Warner *et. al., Social Class in America* (Chicago: Science Research Associates, 1949), and W. Lloyd Warner and James Abegglen, *Big Business Leaders in America* (New York: Harper and Brothers, 1955). C. Wright Mills and William Miller have published important articles on the mobility of businessmen in the *Journal of Economic History* and *The Quarterly Journal of Economics*. Two other recent works in the field of social psychology are particularly interesting on the topic of success: David McClelland, *The Achieving Society* (Princeton, N. J.: D. Van Nostrand Co., 1961), and C. Addison Hickman and Manford Kuhn, *Individuals, Groups, and Economic Behavior* (New York: The Dryden Press, 1956).

Finally, I have made much use of Henrietta M. Larson, *Guide to Business History* (Cambridge, Mass.: Harvard University Press, 1948), a first-rate annotated bibliography.

I. NATURAL ARISTOCRACY AND THE NEW REPUBLIC

My primary sources for the first part of this chapter were the works of Benjamin Franklin and Thomas Jefferson and some of the vast secondary literature which clusters around these major figures. For the Puritan tradition of self-improvement, so influential in the case of Franklin, the most accessible text is the one mentioned by Franklin in his *Memoirs*, Cotton Mather's *Essays to Do Good* (Boston: Lincoln and Edmonds, 1808). The eighteenth-century image of the natural man, important for both Franklin and Jefferson, is surveyed in Hoxie N. Fairchild, *The Noble Savage* (New York: Columbia University Press, 1928).

The self-made man appeared early in the American novel. In addition to the works by Brackenridge and Hitchcock discussed in the text, that curious literary figure Charles Brockden Brown created a fascinating version of the self-made man in his novel *Arthur Mervyn*. For a general survey of trends in the late eighteenth and early nineteenth-century American novel see Lillie D. Loshe, *The Early American Novel* (New York: Columbia University Press, 1907).

II. THE AGE OF THE SELF-MADE MAN

Secondary studies which deal with various aspects of the place of the self-made man in American culture up to the Civil War include Carl R. Fish, *The Rise of the Common Man* (New York: Macmillan, 1927), a general social history of the period 1830–50; Arthur M. Schlesinger, Jr., *The Age of Jackson* (Boston: Little, Brown, 1945); Joseph L. Blau (ed.), *Social Theories of Jacksonian Democracy* (New York: Hafner Publishing Co., 1947); John W. Ward, *Andrew Jackson: Symbol for an Age* (New York: Oxford University Press, 1955), which includes an excellent discussion of Jackson as self-made hero; Clement Eaton, *Henry Clay and the Art of American Politics* (Boston: Little, Brown, 1957), together with Richard Chambers (ed.), *Speeches of the Hon. Henry Clay* (Cincinnati: Shepard and Stearns,

261

1842), give insight into the thought of the man who may have coined the term "self-made man"; Robert Riegel, *Young America, 1830–40* (Norman, Okla.: University of Oklahoma Press, 1949), Marvin Meyers, *The Jacksonian Persuasion* (Stanford, Calif.: Stanford University Press, 1957), brilliantly discuss the element of self-improvement in Jacksonian thought; Robert G. Gunderson, *The Log-Cabin Campaign* (Lexington: University of Kentucky Press), an insightful and thoroughly delightful history of the campaign of 1840, shows the role played by the rhetoric of self-made manhood in the election of Harrison; James A. Shackford, *David Crockett, The Man and the Legend* (Chapel Hill, N. C.: University of North Carolina Press, 1956), discusses fact and fiction in the self-made legend of Davy Crockett, while Roy P. Basler, *The Lincoln Legend: A Study in Changing Conceptions* (Boston: Houghton Mifflin, 1935), is an excellent guide to the theme of the self-made man in the popular veneration for Lincoln.

George Bancroft, *Literary and Historical Miscellanies* (New York: Harper and Brothers, 1855), includes a eulogy of Jackson which sums up the symbolism of the Jacksonian version of the self-made man. Merle Curti, *The Learned Blacksmith* (New York: Wilson-Erickson, 1937), presents the remarkable Jacksonian figure of Elihu Burritt, the self-made classical scholar and reformer. Margaret E. White, *A Sketch of Chester Harding, Artist* (Boston: Houghton Mifflin, 1890), is a brief life of the self-taught painter whose reputation so perplexed and infuriated Mrs. Trollope.

Lyle H. Wright, *American Fiction, 1774–1850* (San Marino, Calif.: Huntington Library, 1939), and *American Fiction, 1850–1875* (San Marino, Calif.: Huntington Library, 1957), are indispensable bibliographies. The didactic novel of sentiment and uplift is incisively surveyed in Herbert R. Brown, *The Sentimental Novel in America, 1789–1860* (Durham, N. C.: Duke University Press, 1940). Brief discussions of the theme of the go-getter in humor can be found in Walter Blair, *Native American Humor* (New York: American Book Co., 1937), and Constance Rourke, *American Humor* (Garden City, N. Y.: Doubleday and Co., 1953).

Wyllie's *The Self-Made Man in America* is the best secondary guide to the self-help books of the pre-Civil War period and contains a large list of these manuals. Carl Bode, *The Anatomy of American Popular Culture, 1840–1861* (Berkeley, Calif.: University of California Press, 1959), also contains a discussion of the theme of self-improvement in popular didactic literature. I have used these works and done a substantial sampling of the primary sources, examples of which include: William Arnot, *The Race for Riches* (Philadelphia: Lippincott, Grambo and Co., 1853); T. S. Arthur, *Advice to Young Men on their Duties and Conduct in Life* (Boston: N. C. Barton, 1849); Henry Ward Beecher, *Twelve Lectures to Young Men on Various Important Subjects* (New York: D. Appleton and Co., 1890; originally published 1844); Abner Forbes, *The Rich Men of Massachusetts* (Boston: Hotchkiss and Co., Fetridge and Co., and W. Spencer, 1852); Edwin T. Freedley, *Common Sense in Business* (Philadelphia: Claxton, Remsen and Haffelfinger, 1879); John Frost, *The Young Merchant* (Philadelphia: R. W. Pomeroy, 1839); Asa Greene, *The Perils of Pearl Street, Including a Taste of the Dangers of Wall*

Street (New York: Betts and Anstice, and Peter Hill, 1834) ; Freeman Hunt, *Worth and Wealth* (New York: Stringer and Townsend, 1856) ; Charles C. B. Seymour, *Self-Made Men* (New York: Harper and Brothers, 1858) ; William H. Van Doren, *Mercantile Morals; or, Thoughts for Young Men entering Mercantile Life* (New York, Charles Scribner, 1852) ; and S. N. Winslow, *Biographies of Successful Philadelphia Merchants* (Philadelphia, James K. Simon, 1864).

T. S. Arthur was the most prolific author of moral tales intended to show the way to self-improvement. Examples of his works are *Sparing to Spend; or, The Loftons and Pinkertons* (New York, Charles Scribner, 1853) ; *The Two Merchants; or, Solvent and Insolvent* (Philadelphia, Burgess and Zieber, 1843) ; *The Way to Prosper; or, In Union There is Strength and Other Tales* (Philadelphia, J. W. Bradley, 1851) ; *Riches Have Wings; or, A Tale for the Rich and Poor* (New York: Baker and Scribner, 1847) ; *Rising in the World; or, A Tale for the Rich and Poor* (New York: Baker and Scribner, 1848) ; and *Making Haste to be Rich; or, The Temptation and Fall* (New York: Baker and Scribner, 1848). Other samples of the self-made man genre are: Charles F. Briggs, *The Adventures of Harry Franco, A Tale of the Great Panic* (2 vols.; New York: F. Saunders, 1839) ; Timothy Flint, *George Mason, The Young Backwoodsman* (Boston: Hilliard, Gray, and Wilkins, 1829) ; Mrs. Emily Judson, *Allen Lucas, The Self-Made Man* (New York: L. Colby and Co., 1848) ; Sylvester Judd, *Richard Edney and the Governor's Family* (Boston: Phillips, Sampson and Co., 1850) ; Charles Burdett, *Three Per Cent. a month; or, The Perils of Fast Living* (New York: D. W. Evans and Co., 1860) ; Mrs. Hannah F. Lee, *The Log Cabin; or, The World Before You* (Philadelphia: George S. Appleton, 1844) ; J. N. Smith, *The Way of the World; or, Honesty the Best Policy* (Dedham, Mass.: Cox and Hutchins, 1854) ; Mrs. Susan A. L. Sedgwick, *Allen Prescott; or, The Fortunes of a New-England Boy* (2 vols.; New York: Harper and Brothers, 1834) ; Thomas H. Shreve, *Drayton: A Story of American Life* (New York: Harper and Brothers, 1851) ; Alexander Lovett Stimson, *Easy Nat; or, The Three Apprentices* (New York: J. C. Derby, 1854) ; and Bayard Taylor, *John Godfrey's Fortunes* (New York: G. P. Putnam; Hurd and Houghton, 1865).

The career of Major Jack Downing can be found in Seba Smith, *My Thirty Years Out of the Senate by Major Jack Downing* (New York: Oaksmith and Co., 1859). The first biography of Davy Crockett was James S. French, *The Life and Adventures of Colonel David Crockett of West Tennessee* (Cincinnati: James S. French, 1833), while Davy's own narrative can be consulted in Hamlin Garland (ed.) *The Autobiography of David Crockett* (New York: Charles Scribner's Sons, 1923). The Crockett persona also appeared in numerous magazine sketches and almanacs. Sam Slick appeared in Thomas C. Haliburton, *The Clockmaker; or, The Sayings and Doings of Samuel Slick of Slickville* (Philadelphia, Lea and Blanchard, 1839). Other humorous and satirical books in which the self-made man as go-getter appeared are Johnson J. Hooper, *Simon Suggs Adventures* (Americus, Ga.: American Book Co., 1928) ; John B. Jones, *The Western Merchant* (Philadelphia: Grigg, Elliot and Co., 1849) and *Life and Adventures of a Country Merchant* (Philadelphia: Lippin-

cott, Grambo and Co., 1854) ; Mrs. Ann S. Stephens (Jonathan Slick),
High Life in New York (2 vols.; London: Jeremiah How, 1844) ; and
Joseph G. Baldwin, *The Flush Times of Alabama and Mississippi*
(New York: Sagamore Press, 1957).

III. SELF-IMPROVEMENT AND SELF-CULTURE

Though primarily known as a historian, Francis Parkman published
some pungent social criticism in the *Nation* and other journals. Ex-
amples can be found in Wilbur Schram (ed.), *Francis Parkman:
Representative Selections* (New York: American Book Co., 1938).
James Fenimore Cooper was an eager critic of his contemporaries,
both in essay and novelistic form. His major books of essays were
Notions of the Americans (2 vols.; London: Henry Colburn, 1828)
and *The American Democrat* (New York: Knopf, 1956). Cooper's
novels attacking the self-made man are *Home as Found* (New York:
G. P. Putnam's Sons, 1896) and *Homeward Bound* (New York: G. P.
Putnam's Sons, 1896). For a contemporary rejoinder to Cooper's at-
tack see Frederick Jackson, *The Effinghams; or, Home As I Found It*
(2 vols.; New York: Samuel Colman, 1841). See also Marvin Meyers'
brilliant chapter on Cooper in *The Jacksonian Persuasion*.

The self-culture movement in all its ramifications awaits its defin-
itive historian, although there are a number of good studies of ly-
ceums, Chautauquas, and other particular institutions. Carl Bode,
The American Lyceum: Town Meeting of the Mind (New York: Ox-
ford University Press, 1956), is an excellent survey of its subject.
Merle Curti, in *The Growth of American Thought*, treats broadly of
"the popularization of knowledge." Joseph Gould, *The Chautauqua
Movement* (New York: State University of .New York, 1961), treats
interestingly but briefly of the inception and development of the Chau-
tauqua movement, while Harry P. Harrison, *Culture Under Canvas*
(New York: Hastings House, 1958), is the reminiscences of a Chau-
tauqua manager early in the twentieth century.

In addition to these secondary works, there are a large number
of handbooks of self-culture which stress the individual's moral and
intellectual development rather than his rise to status and wealth.
Among these are William Ellery Channing, *Self-Culture* (Boston:
Dutton and Wentworth, 1838) ; O. S. Fowler, *Self-Culture and Per-
fection of Character* (New York: Fowler and Wells, 1851) ; James
Freeman Clarke, *Self-Culture* (Boston: James R. Osgood and Co.,
1880) ; and Edwin P. Whipple, *Success and its Conditions* (Boston:
Houghton, Mifflin, 1888).

Walt Whitman's concept of self-culture and the future of American
democracy is implicit in much of his poetry but was developed most
systematically in his essay "Democratic Vistas" (1871). For a general
survey of Whitman's social and philosophical beliefs and a bibliog-
raphy of secondary sources consult Gay Wilson Allen, *Walt Whitman
Handbook* (New York: Packard and Co., 1946).

My discussion of Emerson's philosophy of self-culture is derived
from an examination of his essays which can be found in Edward W.
Emerson (ed.), *The Complete Works of Ralph Waldo Emerson.* (12
vols.; Boston: Houghton Mifflin, 1904). John C. Gerber's unpublished

Ph.D. dissertation, "Emerson's Economics," University of Chicago, 1941, was a particularly helpful guide through the intricacies of Emerson's thinking on economics. See also Alexander C. Kern, "Emerson and Economics," *New England Quarterly*. XIII (December, 1940), 678–96, and Sherman Paul, *Emerson's Angle of Vision* (Cambridge, Mass.: Harvard University Press, 1952).

IV. FROM RAGS TO RESPECTABILITY

Children's books are one of the great, largely untapped sources for the history of popular attitudes. A good general introduction to the subject is May Arbuthnot, *Children and Books* (Chicago: Scott, Foresman, and Co., 1957). For nineteenth-century American children's books see Alice M. Jordon, *From Rollo to Tom Sawyer* (Boston: The Horn Book, 1948). Two very interesting attempts to use children's books for the insight they shed on social history are Monica Kiefer, *Amercan Children Through Their Books* (Philadelphia: University of Pennsylvania Press, 1948), and F. J. Harvey Darton, *Children's Books in England, Five Centuries of Social Life* (London: Cambridge University Press, 1932). See also Richard D. Mosier, *Making the American Mind* (New York: King's Crown Press, 1947), a study of the McGuffey readers.

Examples of some of Horatio Alger's predecessors in the writing of children's books are Jacob Abbott, *The Young Christian; or, A Familiar Illustration of the Principles of Christian Duty* (Boston: Pierce and Parker, 1832), *Caleb in the Country* (New York: Clark and Maynard, 1863), *Caleb in Town* (New York: Clark and Maynard, 1863), *Rollo at Work* (Boston: Phillips, Sampson and Co., 1855) and *Franklin, the Apprentice Boy* (New York: Harper and Brothers, 1855); John S. C. Abbott, *The School-boy; or, A Guide for Youth to Truth and Duty* (Boston: Crocker and Brewster, 1839); Charles Francis Barnard, *The Life of Collin Reynolds, the Orphan Boy and Young Merchant* (Boston: Samuel G. Simpkins, 1835); Louisa C. Tuthill, *I Will be a Gentleman: A Book for Boys* (Boston: William Crosby and H. P. Nichols, 1845) and *Onward! Right Onward!* (Boston: Crosby, Nichols and Co., 1844).

Earlier versions of the urban street boy can be found in Joseph H. Ingraham, *Jemmy Daily; or, The Little News Vendor* (New York: M. Y. Beach, Sun Office, 1843); Alexander Stimson, *Easy Nat; or The Three Apprentices* (New York: J. C. Derby, 1854); Elizabeth Oakes Smith, *The Newsboy* (New York: J. C. Derby, 1854); and Joseph C. Neal, *Peter Ploddy* (Philadelphia: T. B. Peterson and Brothers, 1856).

With a few exceptions, secondary studies of Horatio Alger are extremely feeble. Herbert R. Mayes, *Alger: A Biography without a Hero* (New York: Macy-Masius, 1928), illustrates the genre of fictionalized biography at its worst. Ralph D. Gardner, *Horatio Alger; or, The American Hero Era* (Mendota, Ill.: Wayside Press, 1964), and John W. Tebbel, *From Rags to Riches; Horatio Alger, Jr. and the American Dream* (New York: Macmillan, 1963) show that Alger is still largely the preserve of the book collector and free-enterprise enthusiast. Frank Gruber, *Horatio Alger, Jr.: A Biography and Bib-*

liography (West Los Angeles: Grover Jones Press, 1961), is the most satisfactory and straghtforward account of what is known about Alger's life and contains a good bibliography of his novels. The best of the analytical articles on Alger is R. Richard Wohl, "Alger: An Episode in Secular Idealism," included in Bendix and Lipset (eds.), *Class, Status and Power* (Glencoe, Ill.: Free Press, 1953).

Alger's own works number over one hundred. I have sampled them liberally for this study. A few are *Abraham Lincoln, The Backwoods Boy; or, How a Young Rail-Splitter Became President* (New York: John R. Anderson and Henry S. Allen, 1883); *Adrift in New York* (Chicago: The Saalfield Publishing Co., n.d.); *Bob Burton; or, The Young Ranchman of the Missouri* (Philadelphia, Porter and Coates, 1888); *Bound to Rise; or, Up the Ladder* (New York: Consolidated Retail Booksellers, n.d.); *The Erie Train Boy* (New York: Hurst and Co., 1900); *Frank Hunter's Peril* (Philadelphia: Henry T. Coates and Co., 1896); *From Canal Boy to President; or, The Boyhood and Manhood of James A. Garfield* (New York: John R. Anderson and Co., 1891); *Julius, the Street Boy; or, Out West* (Rahway, N. H.: Mershon Co., n.d.); *Mark the Match Boy; or, Richard Hunter's Ward* (Philadelphia, Porter and Coates, n.d.); *Phil, The Fiddler; or, The Story of a Young Street Musician* (Philadelphia: Porter and Coates, n.d.); *Rufus and Rose; or, The Fortunes of Rough and Ready* (Philadelphia: Porter and Coates, n.d.); *Slow and Sure; or, From the Street to the Shop* (Chicago: M. A. Donohue and Co., n.d.); *The Store Boy; or, The Fortunes of Ben Barclay* (Philadelphia: Porter and Coates, 1887); *Strive and Succeed; or, The Progress of Walter Conrad* (New York: New York Book Co., 1910); *Struggling Upward and Other Works*, edited by Russel Crouse (New York: Crown Publishers, 1945); *The Young Outlaw; or, Adrift in the Streets* (Boston: Loring, 1875); and *The Young Salesman* (New York: Hurst and Co., n.d.).

Many of Alger's contemporaries wrote books using a similar formula, although none were as successful in winning the affection of the young: William T. Adams (Oliver Optic), *Desk and Debit; or, The Catastrophies of a Clerk* (Boston: Lee and Shepard, 1873); Mary A. Atkins, *Little Pea-nut Merchant; or, Harvard's Aspirations* (Boston: Henry A. Young and Co., 1869); Harry Castlemon, *No Moss; or, The Career of a Rolling Stone* (Philadelphia: John C. Winston, 1896); Mrs. Madeline Leslie, *Tim, The Scissors Grinder; or, Loving Christ and Serving Him* (Boston: Henry Hoyt, 1861); Frank A. Munsey, *The Boy Broker; or, Among the Kings of Wall Street* (New York: F. A. Munsey, 1888); F. Ratchford Starr, M. A., *Didley Dumps; or, John Ellard The Newsboy* (Philadelphia: American Sunday-School Union, 1884); and Louise M. Thurston, *How Charley Roberts Became a Man* (Boston: Lee and Shepard, 1871).

V. THE SELF-MADE MAN AND INDUSTRIAL AMERICA

The major sources for this chapter were novels and other works by Mrs. Southworth, E. P. Roe, Ella Wheeler Wilcox, T. S. Denison, Mark Twain, William Dean Howells, and Henry James. Many of these are referred to in the text. A great many other novels dealing with self-made men or with the problem of success were published in the period. Some of those which I consulted were Richard B. Kimball, *Henry Powers (Banker), How He Achieved a Fortune and Married* (New York: G. W. Carleton and Co., 1869); Henry Adams, *Democracy* (New York: Farrar, Straus and Young, 1952); Edward Bellamy, *Looking Backward: 2000–1887* (Boston: Houghton Mifflin, 1926); Hjalmar H. Boyesen, *The Mammon of Unrighteousness* (New York: John W. Lovell Co., 1891); Edgar Fawcett, *A Gentleman of Leisure* (Boston: Houghton Mifflin, 1881); Charles Gayler, *Out of the Streets; A Story of New York Life* (New York: Robert M. DeWitt, 1869); Albion W. Tourgee, *Murvale Eastman, Christian Socialist* (New York: Fords, Howard and Hulbert, 1890); Octave Thanet, *The Heart of Toil* (New York: Charles Scribner's Sons, 1898); Will Payne, *The Money Captain* (Chicago: Herbert S. Stone and Co., 1898); E. W. Howe, *The Story of a Country Town* (New York: Albert and Charles Boni, 1926); Robert Herrick, *The Memoirs of an American Citizen* (New York: Macmillan, 1905); Edward Everett Hale, *Ups and Downs* (Boston: Roberts Brothers, 1873); and Robert Grant, *An Average Man* (Boston: James R. Osgood and Co., 1884).

Some of the secondary works which have been particularly helpful to me in understanding the cultural impact of industralism are: Nelson M. Blake, *A Short History of American Life* (New York: McGraw-Hill, 1954); Kenneth Boulding, *The Organizational Revolution, a Study in the Ethics of Economic Organization* (New York: Harper and Brothers, 1953); Thomas C. Cochran and William Miller, *The Age of Enterprise: A Social History of Industrial America* (New York: Macmillan, 1949); Thomas C. Cochran, *Basic History of American Business* (Princeton, N. J.: D. Van Nostrand, 1959) and *Railroad Leaders, 1854–1890: The Business Mind in Action* (Cambridge, Mass.: Harvard University Press, 1953); Merle Curti, *The Social Ideas of American Educators* (New York: Charles Scribner's Sons, 1935); Bernard De Voto, *Mark Twain's America* (Boston: Little, Brown, 1932); Joseph Dorfman, *The Economic Mind in American Civilization*, Vol. 3 (New York: Viking, 1949); Eric F. Goldman, *Rendezvous with Destiny* (New York: Knopf, 1952); Samuel P. Hays, *The Response to Industrialism, 1885–1914* (Chicago: University of Chicago Press, 1957); Robert Heilbroner, *The Quest for Wealth* (New York: Simon and Schuster, 1956); Richard Hofstadter, *The Age of Reform* (New York: Knopf, 1955); Stewart Holbrook, *The Age of the Moguls* (Garden City, N. Y.: Doubleday, 1953); Henry F. May, *Protestant Churches and Industrial America* (New York: Harper, 1949); and Allan Nevins, *The Emergence of Modern America* (New York: Macmillan, 1935).

I have also made use of a number of sources dealing specifically with the fiction of the period under consideration. Among these I would particularly mention Paul E. Baender, "Mark Twain's Transcendent Figure," Unpublished Ph.D. dissertation, University of California, 1956; H. H. Boyesen, *Literary and Social Silhouettes* (New York: Harper and Brothers, 1894); Quentin Anderson, *The American Henry James* (New Brunswick, N. J.: Rutgers University Press, 1957); Regis L. Boyle, *Mrs. E. D. E. N. Southworth, Novelist* (Washington: Catholic University of America Press, 1939); Edwin H. Cady, *The Road to Realism* (Syracuse, N. Y.: Syracuse University Press,

1956) and *The Realist at War* (Syracuse, N. Y.: Syracuse University Press, 1958); Everett Carter, *Howells and the Age of Realism* (Philadelphia: J. B. Lippincott, 1954); F. W. Dupee, *Henry James* (Garden City, N. Y.: Anchor Books, 1956); Philip S. Foner, *Mark Twain: Social Critic* (New York: International Publishers, 1957); Kenneth S. Lynn, *The Dream of Success* (Boston: Little, Brown, 1955); Walter F. Taylor, *The Economic Novel in America* (Chapel Hill, N. C.: University of North Carolina Press, 1942); and Charles C. Walcutt, *American Literary Naturalism: A Divided Stream* (Minneapolis: University of Minnesota Press, 1956).

VI. PHILOSOPHERS OF SUCCESS

Rare indeed is the social historian or observer of American life who has not had his say on the American worship of success. But it is surprising that systematic analyses of the literature of success are relatively few. Wyllie's study, *The Self-Made Man in America*, is the best, although he does not emphasize, as I do, the differences between the late nineteenth- and early twentieth-century philosophy of success and the earlier gospel of self-improvement. The late R. Richard Wohl was working on the subject of ideologies of success at the time of his death, but his study had apparently not reached the point of publication. For other secondary studies bearing on the topic see the first section of this bibliography.

My analysis is largely based on success manuals and related materials (magazines, books by business leaders on the subject of success, and other books oriented toward the subject of success). A sample of these materials follows: Roger W. Babson, *What is Success* (New York: Fleming H. Revell Co., 1923) and *Religion and Business* (New York: Macmillan, 1927); Andrew Carnegie, *Triumphant Democracy* (New York: Charles Scribner's Sons, 1886), *The Gospel of Wealth and Other Timely Essays* (New York: The Century Co., 1900), *The Empire of Business* (New York: Doubleday, Page and Co., 1902), and *Autobiography* (Boston: Houghton Mifflin, 1924); Burton J. Hendrick (ed.), *Miscellaneous Writings of Andrew Carnegie.* (2 vols.; Garden City, N. Y.: Doubleday, Doran & Co., 1933); Russell H. Conwell, *The New Day* (Philadelphia: Griffith and Rowland Press, 1904) and *Acres of Diamonds* (New York: Harper and Brothers, 1915); John T. Dale, *The Way to Win* (Chicago: Hammond Publishing Co., 1891); Harlow N. Higinbotham, *The Making of a Merchant* (Chicago: Forbes and Co., 1915); James J. Hill, *Highways of Progress* (New York: Doubleday, Page and Co., 1910); Elbert Hubbard, *Health and Wealth* (East Aurora, N. Y.: Roycrofters Press, 1908); George H. Knox, *Ready Money* (Des Moines, Iowa: Personal Help Publishing Co., 1905); George H. Lorimer, *Letters from a Self-Made Merchant to His Son* (Boston: Small, Maynard, 1902) and its sequel *Old Gorgon Graham* (New York: Doubleday, Page and Co., 1904); James D. McCabe Jr., *Great Fortunes and How they were Made; or, the Struggles and Triumphs of our Self-Made Men* (New York: Maclean, 1871); Orison S. Marden, *Talks with Great Workers* (New York: Thomas Y. Crowell, 1901) and *The Progressive Business Man* (New York: Thomas Y. Crowell, 1913); William Matthews, *Getting on in the World; or, Hints on Success in Life* (Chicago: S. C. Griggs and Co., 1877) ; G. B. Moore, *Practical and Scientific Self-Culture* (Chicago and London: Self-Culture Society, 1901) ; H. L. Reade, *Money, and How to Make it* (New York: John P. Jewett, 1872) ; John D. Rockefeller, *Random Reminiscences of Men and Events* (Garden City, N. Y.: Doubleday, Doran and Co., 1933) ; and Matthew H. Smith, *Successful Folks* (New York: G. W. Carleton and Co., 1878).

Lorimer's *Letters from a Self-Made Merchant to His Son* produced a rash of imitations and rejoinders among which were Charles E. Merriman, *Letters from a Son to his Self-Made Father* (Boston: Robinson, Luce Co., 1903) ; Maurice Switzer, *Letters of a Self-Made Failure* (Boston: Small, Maynard, 1914), and the delightful *Letters of a Self-Made Diplomat to His President* by Will Rogers (New York: Albert and Charles Boni, 1926).

The English also had their cult of success, and its most popular prophet was Samuel Smiles, whose works had a wide following in this country as well. A recent edition of Smiles's *Self-Help* (London: John Murray, 1958) has an excellent introduction by Asa Briggs describing the English version of the philosophy of success.

Edward Wortley (ed.), *Impulses to Success* (New York: Park Row Publishing House, 1957), collects four of the most popular success pieces, including Elbert Hubbard's "A Message to Garcia."

Several books about American business and businessmen gave me important insight into business attitudes toward the philosophy of success: Henry Clews, *Fifty Years in Wall Street* (New York: Irving Publishing Co., 1908) ; Thomas C. Cochran, *Basic History of American Business* (Princeton, N. J.: D. Van Nostrand, 1959) and *Railroad Leaders, 1854–1890: The Business Mind in Action* (Cambridge, Mass.: Harvard University Press, 1953) ; Edward C. Kirkland, *Business in the Gilded Age; The Conservative's Balance Sheet* (Madison, Wis.: University of Wisconsin Press, 1952), *Dream and Thought in the Business Community, 1860–1900* (Ithaca, N. Y.: Cornell University Press, 1956), and *Industry Comes of Age* (New York: Rinehart, 1961) ; Burton J. Hendrick, *The Life of Andrew Carnegie* (2 vols.; Garden City, N. Y.: Doubleday, Doran and Co., 1932) ; Stewart Holbrook, *The Age of the Moguls* (Garden City, N. Y.: Doubleday and Co., 1953) ; Joseph Dorfman, *Thorstein Veblen and His America* (New York: Viking Press, 1934) ; Richard Hofstadter, *Social Darwinism in American Thought* (Boston: Beacon Press, 1955) ; Matthew Josephson, *The Robber Barons* (New York: Harcourt, Brace and Co., 1934) ; Gail Kennedy (ed.), *Democracy and the Gospel of Wealth* (Boston: D. C. Heath and Co., 1949) ; Rupert C. Lodge, *Philosophy of Business* (Chicago: University of Chicago Press, 1945) ; William Miller (ed.), *Men in Business* (Cambridge, Mass.: Harvard University Press, 1952) ; National Association of Manufacturers, Economic Principles Commission, *The American Individual Enterprise System, Its Nature and Future* (2 vols.; New York: McGraw-Hill, 1946) ; James Warren Prothro, *Dollar Decade; Business Ideas in the 1920s* (Baton Rouge, La.: Louisiana State University Press, 1954) ; and Francis X. Sutton *et al.*, *The American Business Creed* (Cambridge, Mass.: Harvard University Press, 1956).

The new slick magazines which emerged at the turn of the century were important forums for the expression of the success philosophy. As a basis for my analysis I examined with care the files of *The Saturday Evening Post* from 1899 to 1920 and *Success Magazine* from 1900 to 1908.

VII. DREAM OR RAT RACE

On changing attitudes toward individualism and success in the twentieth century the following are particularly illuminating: Howard R. Bowen, *Social Responsibilities of the Businessman* (New York: Harper and Brothers, 1953); Marquis W. Childs and Douglas Cater, *Ethics in a Business Society* (New York: Harper and Brothers, 1954); Thurman Arnold, *et al. The Future of Democratic Capitalism* (Philadelphia; University of Pennsylvania Press, 1950); Robert S. and Helen M. Lynd, *Middletown* (New York: Harcourt, Brace and Co., 1929) and *Middletown in Transition* (New York: Harcourt, Brace and Co., 1937); Frederick L. Allen, *The Big Change* (New York: Harper and Brothers, 1952) and *Since Yesterday* (New York: Harper and Brothers, 1940); C. Wright Mills, *White Collar* (New York: Oxford University Press, 1951); David Riesman, *Individualism Reconsidered* (Garden City, N. Y.: Doubleday and Co., 1955) and *The Lonely Crowd* (Garden City, N. Y.: Doubleday and Co., 1955).

On income distribution and poverty see C. Wright Mills, *The Power Elite* (New York: Oxford University Press, 1956) and Michael Harrington, *The Other America; Poverty in the United States* (New York: Macmillan, 1962).

On sociological studies of the problem of mobility see the first section of this bibliography and the discussion of the subject in Chapter seven.

The criticism of the success ideology in the twentieth century has been many-faceted and various. The novels discussed in the text sum up many of the criticisms made, but for those who might like to consult non-fictional criticism of success the following list is a sample of the material available: Thorstein Veblen, *The Theory of Business Enterprise* (New York: Charles Scribner's Sons, 1904); Harry F. Ward, *Our Economic Morality and the Ethic of Jesus* (New York: Macmillan, 1929); James Truslow Adams, *Our Business Civilization* (New York: Albert and Charles Boni, 1929); Bouck White, *The Book of Daniel Drew* (Garden City, N. Y.: Doubleday and Co., 1936); Thurman Arnold, *The Folklore of Capitalism* (New Haven, Conn.: Yale University Press, 1941); Elijah Jordan, *Business Be Damned* (New York: Henry Schuman, 1952); William H. Whyte Jr., *Is Anybody Listening* (New York: Simon and Schuster, 1952), and *The Organization Man* (New York: Simon and Schuster, 1956); David E. Lilienthal, *Big Business: A New Era* (New York: Harper and Brothers, 1953); Peter Viereck, *The Unadjusted Man: A New Hero for Americans* (Boston: Beacon Press, 1956); Vance Packard, *The Status Seekers* (New York: D. McKay Co., 1959); and Mark Hanan, *The Pacifiers* (Boston; Little, Brown, 1960).

Contemporary success literature runs to three different types. The first is the quasi-mystical "positive thinking" approach exemplified in the works of Dale Carnegie, Norman Vincent Peale, and Napoleon Hill, discussed in the text. Their followers are legion and for examples the reader need only consult the *Subject Guide to Books in Print* under the the heading "Success." The second type of current self-help literature is very specific and deals with the particular stratagems and devices necessary to making money in specific fields. Three samples are William Nickerson, *How I Turned $100 into a Million in Real Estate in My Spare Time* (New York: Simon and Schuster, 1959) ; E. Joseph Cossman, *How I Made $1,000,000 in Mail Order* (New York: Prentice-Hall, 1963) ; and Karl Bach, *How I Sell $12,000,000 of Life Insurance Year after Year* (Palo Alto, Calif.: Pacific Books, n.d.). For over a hundred other examples consult *Books in Print* under the word "How."

The third type of success literature is less popular but equally indicative. These books take a thoroughly satirical approach to the subject. Examples are Shepherd Mead, *How to Succeed in Business Without Really Trying* (New York; Ballantine Books, n.d.) ; Mark Caine, *The S-Man* (Boston: Houghton Mifflin, 1961) ; and William J. Reilly, *How to Make your Living in Four Hours a Day: Without Feeling Guilty About It* (New York: Harper and Brothers, 1955).

Most major contemporary novelists have dealt in one way or another with the problem of the mobile individual. Aside from those mentioned in the text, the following contemporary writers have created notable fictional portraits embodying the problems of success and mobility: Thomas Wolfe, John Dos Passos, John P. Marquand, Arthur Miller, James T. Farrell, Ralph Ellison, Budd Schulberg, Norman Mailer, and Saul Bellow. For the most part, the work of these novelists treats the theme of success in much the same way as Fitzgerald, Faulkner, and Warren to whom I have devoted intensive discussion.

The problem of identity as viewed by contemporary psychologists is discussed in a variety of ways in Maurice Stein, Arthur Vidich and David M. White (eds.), *Identity and Anxiety: Survival of the Person in Mass Society* (Glencoe, Ill.: Free Press, 1960).

VIII. INDIVIDUAL SUCCESS AND THE COMMUNITY

Chapter eight is based largely on the following works by John Dewey: *Democracy and Education* (New York: Macmillan, 1916) ; *The Public and its Problems* (New York: Henry Holt and Co., 1927) ; *Individualism Old and New* (New York: Minton, Balch and Co., 1930) ; *Art as Experience* (Minton, Balch and Co., 1935) ; *Intelligence in the Modern World: John Dewey's Philosophy*, edited by Joseph Ratner (New York: Modern Library, 1939) ; and *Culture and Freedom* (New York: G. P. Putnam's Sons, 1939).

INDEX

Abbott, Jacob (author of "Rollo" books), 103–4, 208

Addams, Jane, 162–63

Alger, Horatio: 96; and common man, 110; current misconceptions concerning, 108–9; decline in popularity of, 103; and early Alger-type stories, 106–7; first Alger story, 30; Freudian interpretation of, 123; and hero's virtues, 117–20; Horatio Alger Award, 101; and humanitarianism, 117; and ideal of respectability, 110; and immigrants, 113; and importance of gentility, 105–6; and industrialism, 120–23; and luck, 115–16; and plot formula, 115; and portrayal of mothers, 114; and relation to didactic novels, 111; and religion, 117; and snobs, 112; sources of popularity of, 121–23; two heroes of, 111; and wealth, 109–10; as traditionalist, 121

— Compared with: Franklin, 119; Jacob Abbott, 103–4; J. H. Ingraham, 107; Louisa M. Tuthill, 105–6; Emerson, 119–20

American character: changes in, 202

American society: in didactic fiction, 56–57, 61–62; nineteenth-century changes in, 168–72; in nineteenth and twentieth-century novels, compared, 234–35; in twentieth century, 204–6

— Portrayed by: Franklin, 15; Alger, 116; James, 159–62; Twain, 145–46; Emerson, 94; Russell Conwell, 178–79; Dreiser, 229; T. S. Denison, 135–36; Howells, 154–55, 157–58; Channing, 84–85

Balzac, Honoré de (*La Grandeur et Décadence de César Birotteau*), 155–56

Index

Barton, Bruce (*The Man Nobody Knows*), 197–99
Brackenridge, H. H. (*Modern Chivalry*), 32–35
Briggs, Charles F. (*The Adventures of Harry Franco*), 63–66
Burritt, Elihu, 41
Business enterprise: in novels of Alger, 121–22; and ideal of service, 187; in positive thinking, 216–17; and self-made man, 45; in self-improvement handbooks, 51; and success philosophy, 172, 184–85, 192–93

Cahan, Abraham (*The Rise of David Levinsky*), 234
Campaign of 1840: and self-made man, 40
Carnegie, Andrew, 96, 144, 167, 170, 187–88, 189, 192–93
Carnegie, Dale, 209–18
Chautauquas, 174–75
Children's books: changes in, in twentieth century, 208
Cities: attacked by E. P. Roe, 132–33; criticized by T. S. Denison, 138
Clay, Henry: coins term "self-made man," 43; compared with Franklin and Jefferson, 44; and concept of success, 43–46; identifies self-made man with business, 45; as self-made man, 40
Competition: and co-operation, 221; opposed to status, 220–21; and success, 221–23. *See also* Success
Conwell, Russell: answers critics of success, 178–79
Cooley, Charles Horton (*Personal Competition*), 220–23
Cooper, James Fenimore (*The American Democrat*), 78–80
Crockett, David (*Life*), 68–69

Denison, T. S.: attacks Gilded Age, 135–36; and cities, 138; and didactic novel, 135; criti-cizes pursuit of wealth, 136–37; *The Modern Mammon*, 134–38; reasserts traditional ideals, 135–36
Dewey, John: 208; and concept of intellectual mobility, 246; influenced by Jefferson and Emerson, 239; as Jeffersonian, 242–43; and re-evaluation of success, 239; rejects economic success, 242; on success and community, 243–44; on success and individual fulfillment, 244–45; on traditional idea of individualism, 241–42
"Dick and Jane" books, 208
Didactic fiction (1830–60): burlesqued by C. F. Briggs, 63–65; and character of hero, 55–56; and conception of society, 56–57, 59, 61–62; and gentility, 58; and luck or providence, 62–63; and natural aristocracy, 59; and Protestant ethic, 60–61; and self-improvement handbooks, 55–57; compared with didactic hero, 67–68; compared with Twain's Connecticut Yankee, 147–48
Downing, Major Jack: as self-made man, 66
Dreiser, Theodore: and Algerism, 228; *An American Tragedy*, 228–30; and determinism, 229–30; *The Financier*, 227–28; *Sister Carrie*, 201, 227–28; *The Titan*, 227–28
Drew, Daniel, 73

Edison, Thomas A., 187–88
Emerson, Ralph Waldo: compared with Alger, 119–20; compared with Jefferson, 93–94; and concept of natural aristocracy, 92–93; and concept of success, 87–90; and criticism of success, 90–92; and New Thought, 97–98; and politics 94–95; and relation to popular thought, 98;

and "school of hard knocks," 89; and self-made man, 87

Failure: Dreiser's anatomy of, 228–29
Faulkner, William (*Absalom, Absalom!*), 231–32
Fitzgerald, F. Scott (*The Great Gatsby*), 201, 230–31
Franklin, Benjamin: and analysis of American society, 15; as archetypal self-made man, 9–11; "Art of Virtue," 20–23; and business activities, 19; compared with Alger, 119; compared with Jefferson, 24; compared with success philosophers, 191–92; compared with Washington, 9–11; criticized by Twain, 141–42; and early satires, 13; and idea of natural goodness, 13; and ideal of self-improvement, 23; *Memoirs*, 16–23, 119; and Poor Richard, 15–16; and Protestant ethic, 21–22; as public figure, 11; on self-education, 20; and self-improvement handbooks, 50; on self-made man, 14–15; and self-made man and public responsibility, 16–19; and social process, 23–24; and voluntary associations, 14; "The Way to Wealth," 16; "The Way to Wealth" and *Memoirs* compared, 16; and weakness in social thought, 14–15

Galbraith, John Kenneth (*The Affluent Society*), 247–48
Gentility: in didactic fiction, 58; in writings of Parkman, 80; in writings of Lorimer, 182; in writings of Alger, 105–6; in writings of Cooper, 80; in writings of Howells, 155–56
George, Henry, 178
Gould, Jay, 187–88

Harding, Chester, 41
Harrison, William Henry, 40
Hawley, Cameron, 227
Hill, Napoleon, 209–18
Hitchcock, Enos (*The Farmer's Friend*), 30–32
Hooper, J. J. (*Simon Suggs' Adventures*), 70–71
Howells, William Dean: on class distinctions, 155–56; and concern with social order, 154–55; criticizes mobility, 157–58; criticizes self-improvement, 153; and early Algerism, 153; *A Hazard of New Fortunes*, 157–58; on influence of institutions, 157; *The Minister's Charge*, 156–57; *A Modern Instance*, 153–54; on pursuit of success, 154; *The Rise of Silas Lapham*, 154–57

Immigrants: attacked by Wilcox, 134; attacked by later nineteenth-century novelists, 131; portrayed by E. P. Roe, 132; portrayed by Alger, 110, 113; and self-made man, 35; and success philosophy, 183, 234
Industrialism: in writings of Alger, 120–23; in writings of Dewey, 241; and mobility, 225–26; in self-improvement handbooks, 51–52; and success philosophy, 169, 191; in writings of Jefferson, 27–28
Ingraham, Joseph H., 106

Jackson, Andrew, 40–41
James, Henry: on American pursuit of wealth, 159; on success and the individual, 160–162
James, William, 167, 195
Jefferson, Thomas: and Charles H. Cooley, 220; compared with Franklin, 24; compared with Emerson, 93; compared with success philosophers.

Jefferson, Thomas (*continued*) 191–92; and democratic community, 26–27; and Federal government, 28–29; and industrialism, 27–28; and Dewey, 242–43; and mobility and political leadership, 24; and natural aristocracy, 24–25; and program for America, 25–27; and reasons for failure of ideal, 27–29
Jesus Christ: as parable of success, 198

Lincoln, Abraham, 40, 95–96, 153
Lorimer, George H.: 176; "Letters from a Self-Made Merchant to his Son," 181–82
Luck: in didactic fiction, 62–63; in writings of Alger, 115–16
Lynn, Kenneth, 226, 227, 228

Marden, Orison S., 175, 176, 227
McGuffey readers, 208
Mills, C. Wright, 202
Mobility: and business elite, 226; criticized by Howells, 157–58; current estimates of, 2; and economic opportunity, 44; in Europe and America, 225–26; and industrialism, 2, 225–26; in other societies, 224–25; and political leadership, 24; questioned by twentieth-century novelists, 234–35; and self-culture, 85; social function of, 219–22; in twentieth century, 205–6. *See also* Self-made man; Success
Morgan, J. P., 187

Napoleon Bonaparte, 89–90
Natural aristocracy: and democratic community, 26–27; in didactic fiction, 59; and ideal of gentleman, 34–35; in writings of Twain, 150–51; in writings of Emerson, 92–93; in success philosophy, 192; and natural genius, 59–60

New Deal, 204–6
New Freedom, 204
New Thought: 183–84; and Emerson, 97–98

Opportunity: America as land of, 46; and civil rights, 206; equality of, and education, 207; equality of, in twentieth century, 204–6; in success philosophy, 178–79. *See also* Mobility; Self-made man; Success
Organized labor: criticized by popular novelists, 131

Packard, Vance, 202
Parkman, Francis: as critic of self-made man, 77–78; and Cooper, 78
Peale, Norman Vincent, 5, 92, 209–18. *See also* Positive thinking
Personal magnetism: as key to success, 183
Politics: in success philosophy, 192–93
Positive thinking: and Algerism, 210; and dream of success, 217–18; and portrayal of business world, 216–17; and Protestant ethic, 210; quasi-mystical character of, 213–16; quasi-scientific character of, 214–15; and success philosophy, 209–10; and wealth, 211–13. *See also* New Thought; Peale, Norman Vincent
Protestant ethic: and Franklin, 21–22; in early American fiction, 30–31, 60–61; and positive thinking, 210; in self-improvement handbooks, 49–50; and success, 4–5, 74; transformed by success philosophers, 168

Riesman, David, 202

Roe, E. P.: *Barriers Burned Away*, 131–133; and cities, 132–33; criticizes immigrants, 132; identifies enemies of self-made man, 133

Roosevelt, Franklin D., 204

Self-culture: compared to self-improvement handbooks, 84–85; expounded by Whitman, 81–82; expounded by Channing, 84–85; fundamental weakness of, 93–95; and Lyceums, 83; as popular movement, 83–84; reflected in writings of Alger, 118; and success, 174–75

Self-help: and twentieth-century reforms, 204

Self-improvement: *See* Success

Self-improvement handbooks (1830–60): basic paradox of, 54; and Franklin, 50; and business, 51; compared to humor and satire, 71–72; compared to self-culture, 84–85; and confusion of success and moral merit, 52–53; and emigration, 48–49; and industrialism, 51–52; and keys to success, 49–50; minatory character of, 50–51; and persistence of ideas, 55; and Protestant ethic, 49–50; and reasons for moralism, 53–54; and speculation, 49; and wealth, 47

Self-made man: American and European attitudes compared, 2–3; Americans as proponents of, 1–3; and Protestant ethic, 4–5; and varying cultural attitudes, 2

— To 1830: Franklin as archetype, 9–11; Franklin's conception of, 14–15, 23; and democratic community, 26–27; in early American fiction, 30–36; failure of Jefferson's ideal, 27–29; and immigrants, 35; and natural aristocracy, 24–25; reasons

for popularity, 2–3; as upstart, 32

— 1830–70: burlesqued by C. F. Briggs, 63–65; criticized by Parkman, 77–78; criticized by Cooper, 78–80; and economic power, 44; first use of term, 43; identified with business, 45; and Major Jack Downing, 65–67; Napoleon Bonaparte as, 90; in nineteenth-century humor, 66; in nineteenth-century politics, 40; portrayed in didactic fiction, 55–56; and self-culture, 81; and self-educated intellectual, 41; as symbol for Emerson, 87; enemies identified by Roe, 133; in late nineteenth-century novel, 126–27; and Mark Twain, 143, 144–46, 147, 152; and Mrs. E. D. E. N. Southworth, 127–29; portrayed by Lorimer, 181–82

— 1929 to present: confusion of means and ends, 233–34; and education in twentieth century, 207; erosion of ideal, 203; twentieth-century archetypes, 230. *See also* Mobility; Success

Service, ideal of: 186–88; and Christianity, 198

Slick, Sam, 69–70

Smith, Seba ("Sketch of My Early Life by Major Jack Downing"), 66–67

Social Darwinism: and success, 172–74

Socialism: rejected by success philosophy, 191

Sorokin, Pitirim A. (*Social Mobility*), 201, 224–25

Southworth, Mrs. E. D. E. N.: compared with earlier novelists, 128–29; *Ishmael*, 127–31; and nostalgia, 129–30; reflects traditional ideals, 127–29

Speculation: in self-improvement handbooks, 49

Success: definitions summarized,

Success (*continued*)
4–6; as getting ahead, 5; as individual fulfillment, 5–6; and Protestant ethic, 4–5
— To 1830: ambiguity in idea of, 23–24; Franklin's conception of, 23; in eighteenth-century fiction, 30–36; and Franklin and Jefferson compared, 24; and natural aristocracy, 24–25
— 1830–70: conflict with traditional ideals, 26–47; conflicting strands of, 72; criticized by Emerson, 90–92; Clay's conception of, 43–46; ideas of Emerson, 87–90; and luck in didactic fiction, 62–63; and opportunity, 45–46; overshadows natural aristocracy, 43; and Protestant ethic, 74; and wealth, 45–46
— 1870–1929: ambiguous definition of, 185; and aristocracy, 193–94; and business enterprise, 192–93; changing spokesmen of, 175; comparison of philosophies of, 168–72; and competition, 171–73, 221–23; criticized by Denison, 136–37; criticized by Howells, 153–54; emergence of new philosophy of, 168; in writings of Alger, 110, 117–20; and ideal of service, 186–88; and industrialism, 169; influence of Social Darwinism, 172–74; and Jesus, 197–98; as narrow ideal, 160–61, 223; and natural aristocracy, 192; and opportunity, 178–79; and personal magnetism, 183; and politics, 192–93; in relation to social order, 220–22; rejected by humanitarians, 162–63; as school of character, 188; and self-culture, 174–75; and social environment, 218–19; and socialism, 191; and status, 220–21; and trusts, 193; and wealth, 185–86; and "will to win," 182

— 1929 to the present: ambivalence toward, in twentieth century, 208–9; and community in writings of Dewey, 243–44; as delusion, 236; and determinism, 229–30; and education in twentieth century, 207–8; and human condition, 230–32; and individual fulfillment, 244–45; and life of the mind, 246, 248; mood of 1960's, 201–2; as popular myth, 226; in positive thinking, 217–18; in social science, 218–26; as tragedy, 235–36; and twentieth-century reforms, 204–5; twentieth-century re-evaluation of, 239. *See also* Mobility; Opportunity; Self-made man; Wealth
Success Magazine: 176–77; criticizes false business practices, 188–89; and Progressive reforms, 190
Suggs, Simon, 70–71

Twain, Mark: and ambivalence toward self-made man, 146–47; and ambivalence toward wealth, 144; on Franklin, 141–42; *A Connecticut Yankee in King Arthur's Court*, 147–52; defends self-made man, 143; and natural aristocracy, 150–51; portrays American society, 145–46; ridicules Algerism, 141; satirizes self-made man, 144–46
Twain, Mark, and Charles Dudley Warner (*The Gilded Age*), 144–47

Ward, Frank Lester ("Broadening the Way to Success"), 218–19
Warren, Robert Penn (*All the King's Men*), 232–33
Wealth: changing attitudes toward, 170; Henry James criticizes pursuit of, 159;

honest and dishonest, 137; in writings of Alger, 109–110; Twain's ambivalence toward, 144; and positive thinking, 211–13; in success philosophy, 185–86. *See also* Success

Weber, Max, 226

Webster, Daniel, 40
Whitman, Walt (*Democratic Vistas*), 81–82
Whyte, William H., 202
Wilson, Woodrow, 204
Wyllie, Irvin (*The Self-Made Man in America*), 226